SOCIOLOGICAL REVIEW MONOGRAPH

D1462409

The Sociology of Literature:
Theoretical Approaches

Issue Editors: Jane Routh and Janet Wolff

64355

Managing Editors: W. M. Williams and Ronald Frankenberg
University of Keele
August 1977

The Sociology of Literature: Theoretical Approaches

The Sociology of Literature: Theoretical Approaches
Monograph 25
Editors Jane Routh and Janet Wolff
Contents

University of Keele, Keele, Staffordshire.

Notes on Contributors

Stephen Bann MA, PhD
Senior Lecturer, Department of History, University of Kent at Canterbury

Ian H. Birchall MA, BLitt
Senior Lecturer, Faculty of Humanities, Middlesex Polytechnic

David Coward BA, PhD
Lecturer, Department of French Language and Literature, University of
Leeds

Terry Eagleton MA, PhD
Fellow, Wadham College, Oxford

Jim McGuigan BSc, MPhil
Sometime Research Student, Department of Sociology, University of Leeds

John Orr BSocSc, PhD
Lecturer, Department of Sociology, University of Edinburgh

Joan Rockwell BA
Lecturer, Department of Sociology, University of Reading

Jane Routh BA
Director, School of Independent Studies, University of Lancaster

John Rutherford MA, DPhil
Fellow in Spanish, The Queen's College, Oxford

Alan Swingewood BSc, PhD
Lecturer, Department of Sociology, London School of Economics and
Political Science

Philip Thody MA
Professor, Department of French Language and Literature, University of
Leeds

Janet Wolff BSocSci, PhD
Lecturer, Department of Sociology, University of Leeds

Cover Design by Cal Swann FSIAD

Note

ISBN 0904425 04 5

Printed and bound in Great Britain
by Wood Mitchell & Co. Limited, Hanley, Stoke-on-Trent, Staffs.

Introduction

Jane Routh and Janet Wolff

At the beginning of the 1970s, courses on the Sociology of Literature or the Sociology of Culture taught in British universities and polytechnics were still very few. Since then, the number of scholars and students working in the field has grown so rapidly that the theme of the BSA Annual Conference in 1978 is the Sociology of Culture.

This expansion of interest has not taken place solely within departments of sociology. Many English and Comparative Literature courses are now concerned to situate literature within its social context, and 'cultural studies' is a term which is beginning to be granted disciplinary status, particularly in polytechnics and colleges of further education. Although the sociologist of literature may be concerned to clarify, for example, a Marxist theory of the novel, while the English scholar considers the use of language in the novels of the 1920s, their work is beginning to converge. They now often share an interest in the same texts, and face similar problems of methodology and theoretical perspective. With their disparate purposes, and from their different starting points, they refer to the same body of material, and pay homage to (or perhaps rail against) the same writers. It is a growing body of material, steadily being increased by translations of the work of French and German writers.

The rather late development of interest in the sociology of literature in this country is not easily explained, but an understanding of the history of the academic context suggests that the reasons lie in the traditions of both English literature and sociology. The strength of the tradition of British literary criticism, whose major figures have often been social as much as literary critics, may have meant that there has been little room for sociologists to move into an already well-occupied and jealously defended territory. The empiricist emphasis of much British sociology, which has traditionally been less theoretical, and perhaps less humanistic and philosophical, than some of its European counterparts, has meant that the work done in the field has fewer affinities with literature than it has on the Continent: indeed, all the significant figures discussed in this monograph are European. British academics are often unwilling and perhaps unable to bridge the two disciplines, and it is still rare to find practitioners of the one discipline who are simultaneously well versed in the language and tools of the other. Yet a certain convergence is apparent and a number of recent conferences (such as those at the universities of Essex, Liverpool and

East Anglia) attest to the increasing collaboration of literature specialists, sociologists, media students and others. The present volume itself demonstrates the true inter-disciplinary nature of the area called 'the sociology of literature', with contributions from a variety of disciplines.

Early in the development of any new area of sociological investigation, one can often find a host of different dicta, defining its concepts, tracing its pre-history, delimiting its field, and describing its methods. We have had a number of these in the sociology of literature[1], and while some contain useful ideas it would be a mistake to hope that any could be definitive. There are still unsolved problems and debates about the meaning of 'culture', and the relationship of literature and culture to social structure. Nevertheless, there is some kind of consensus as to what are the most profitable paths to be explored. We have therefore chosen, in compiling this volume, not to immerse ourselves in these definitional debates, and discussions about the 'real' area of the sociology of literature, the relationship of 'highbrow' and popular art, and so on, but to strike out in the most useful direction.

We have mentioned already the vast amount of literature now becoming available in translation from the French and German. Major theoretical schools lay claim to showing the way forward, yet critical evaluation of these theories – where it exists – is often obscure and difficult to find and to assess. For the increasing number of students studying the sociology of literature, as well as for non-specialists who need to assess how useful for them might be scholarship in the field, there are still surprisingly few guidelines. This monograph brings together articles on the main theoretical approaches in the field, showing the conflicting evaluations as well as the agreed status of major thinkers. Although as editors we feel that ideally the focus of our work should be 'culture', rather than the narrower area of literature, realistically we have to acknowledge that most of the significant writers to be discussed have concentrated on literature. The sociology of literature is far more advanced than the sociological study of the other arts. To have included discussions of painting , music, dance and so on, would not only have led to an unevenly balanced level of theory represented in the papers, but would also have rendered comparison more difficult. Critical evaluation of theoretical work on the sociology of literature is, then, the gap which we have chosen to fill here. Another issue of the *Sociological Review Monographs*, to be published subsequently and edited by Diana Laurenson, addresses itself to the gap in empirical work.

Introduction

Each paper in this collection has been specially written to evaluate a major theoretical position and, where appropriate, to make comparisons with other writers. We have tried to avoid the formula of one-theorist/one-paper, so that something of the range of critical interpretation can be shown. We are well aware, however, that the collection is by no means exhaustive of the field. For example, we have not included a paper specifically on Formalism, although this is discussed in the paper by Bann, nor one on semiotics in general although Thody's paper on Barthes raises general questions about this approach. Similarly the writings of Lévi-Strauss, Walter Benjamin, Raymond Williams or Bertolt Brecht have a significance for the sociology of literature which merits a special essay to discuss their work. We do not wish to attempt to justify omissions, but rather to make some introductory comments on the logic of the way in which we have organised the papers which follow. This is perhaps best done in the context of a brief, but more general, discussion of the present nature and state of the sociology of literature.

Many different types of work lay claim to the title 'sociology of literature'. Some have in common only the fact that they can be said to be 'about' the relationship of literature and society. This relationship is conceived in many different ways. It might be helpful to look at the various approaches according to the following five broad conceptions.

1. We can be offered a *sociologically aware* study of literature. Sociological problems or the development of theory are not at issue in such work: the focus of the study is literature. Here we have in mind the type of literary criticism which is informed by, and makes reference to, the social co-ordinates and conditions of the literature. The findings and concepts of sociology may be abridged as a tool for criticism: 'alienation' is one of the concepts which most readily lends itself to use by literary critics. Raymond Williams's *The country and the city* (1975) and Malcolm Bradbury's *The social context of modern English literature* (1971) are examples of some of the best work of this kind. As well as practical criticism, the theoretical work of literary scholars may also be informed by, or at least compatible with, a social-historical perspective on the work. In the following collection of papers the hermeneutic tradition is seen as an example of such an approach.

(2) Literature has been used by some writers *as a kind of sociology*. It is seen as a source of data, often data of a type which would not otherwise be accessible to a sociologist, and as a carrier of crystallised values and attitudes, as well as information about institutions. Lewis Coser's collection of excerpts from novels in *Sociology through literature* (1963)

3

illustrates how aspects of social life studied by sociologists with the aid of concepts like role, anomie, bureaucracy and deviance, are often well described and precisely captured in works of literature. More recently, sociologists have compared sociology with literature, and recommended that it takes some hints from the latter, in order to understand and depict its subject matter adequately.[2] The idea that literature tells us about social life raises a number of questions – apart from predictable arguments about 'objectivity'[3]. The fact that we are likely to confirm the validity of literary evidence by reference to sociological and historical 'facts' suggests a disparity between the two types of social commentary. It may be a legitimate exercise for a sociologist to take literary texts as a source of data, but this must be justified by advancing at the level of theory an explanation of how a generalised reality can be transformed into a specific expression. Joan Rockwell has indicated in her *Fact in fiction* (1974) that language is the important mechanism of transformation, but we still require an account of the nature of an individual's participation in a general world-view.

(3) Probably the bulk of work in the field takes as its central problem the *social genesis of literature*, the question, that is, of how literature arises in society. The social forces affecting literary production are studied, whether in empirical investigations, as in the work of Escarpit[4], or at a theoretical level, as in the work of many of the writers discussed in this monograph. Here we would include theories which see literature as social facts or contradictions (including structuralism, and some versions of historical materialism), displaced on to another plane or as the symbolic transformation of social reality (semiotics). One of the most common criticisms of this type of sociology of literature is that it cannot acknowledge the unique and imaginative qualities of a writer's work, and leaves no room for individual creativity. As David Caute has said of Lucien Goldmann, the author becomes merely a 'midwife' at the birth of a work of literature.[5] The dangers of sociological reductionism are discussed in the paper by McGuigan.

(4) For other critics such as Terry Eagleton[6], literature is understood as both *social product and social force*, affecting society and continually involved in the process of social development. On the micro-social level of the writer and the reader, the work of Walter Benjamin has emphasised the nature of writing as production, which is both socially and historically situated and limited, and at the same time capable of political education and social transformation.[7] Sartre, too, has recognised the dual reality of the writer, as both determined and determining.[8] In a different way, the work of Raymond Williams has

4

made important advances in the comprehension, on the macro-level, of the dialectical relationship of ideas and social structure in historical development.[9]

(5) The final approach focusses on the ways in which *literature may affect society*, and effect social change. This power can be perceived as a social problem: here it leads to studies like the Presidential *Report on obscenity and pornography*[10], and to censorship. Brecht, on the other hand, sees it as a positive feature of literature, which committed socialists must use to advantage.

This categorisation of approaches to the study of literature in society may be seen as beginning with a notion of the two as separate but related, through a conception of literature as produced by society, to the obverse of this – the idea that society is in some ways produced by literary activity. Clearly, the most comprehensive account would be of the fourth type, which is not restricted to one side of the equation, and which, at its best, will retain both a literary awareness and appreciation, and a grasp of the complexities of social reality. But the particular contribution of writers in the other areas has also been crucial, for we need to know how literary products may be traced back to their social origins, as well as how a novel or an epic poem can itself be understood and analysed.[11]

The papers presented below illustrate this logic. After Coward's paper, which we have placed as a kind of cautionary preface, questioning the possibilities for a sociological understanding of literature, we move from a concern with the study of literature itself, in Wolff's discussion of hermeneutics, through the papers of Rockwell, Rutherford, Thody and Bann, which are concerned with literature as an expression of social facts, to the studies of writers more prepared to state or suppose some determining connection between literature and society, with, for example, the papers by Birchall, Eagleton, Swingewood and Routh. This group of papers offers discussion of theories which posit a simple connection (social-structure-determines-literature) as well as theories which suggest a more complex, reciprocal and mediated relationship between literature and society. The final paper, by McGuigan, examines Sartre's consideration of literature as social product, and raises the possibility, seen by Sartre, for committed, effective literature.

We have also thought it appropriate to conclude with a paper on Sartre because of our belief, argued in Wolff's paper, that a fully sociological account of literature will not only interpret it and consider its social co-ordinates, but will also explain the written work as social

Jane Routh and Janet Wolff

and individual creation. We must examine the dynamics of society which produce not just literature, but particularly literary products. The articles presented here also move in this direction, but only in Sartre's work do we encounter an explanation of literature as individual creativity as well as social event.

Where a group of papers illustrates different interpretations of an approach (structuralism, Marxism, etc.), we have placed them according to this logic of increasing concern with the autonomy of literature as itself determinant; we have also tried to put those papers which provide an overall introduction to the area before others which take some knowledge for granted.

We hope that the value of the papers will not only be that they map the movement in theory which we have outlined above, but that they offer to students a readily available entry into the pivotal points of discussion of a burgeoning theoretical field of sociology.

University of Lancaster
University of Leeds

NOTES

1 Examples of outlines of the field can be found in Lowenthal (1967), Watt (1964), Leenhardt (1967), Laurenson and Swingewood (1972).

2 For example, Dawe (1973) and Craib (1974). See also Hoggart (1973).

3 On this, we would argue that literature and sociology are not as far apart as one might think. As Nisbet says (1968: 143-62), sociology too is a kind of 'art form'; and the creativity and selectivity involved in the very formulation of research, recognised to some extent by Weber, is now fairly generally accepted, particularly since Kuhn's work in the sociology of science (Kuhn: 1962)

4 *Sociologie de la litterature*, Paris 1958.
 See also M. Albrecht et al (eds): *The sociology of art and literature*, Duckworth 1970.

5 'A portrait of the artist as midwife: Lucien Goldmann and the "transindividual subject"' in *Collisions*, London, Quartet, 1974.

6 See his recent *Criticism and ideology*, London, New Left Books, 1976.

7 'The work of art in the age of mechanical reproduction' in *Illuminations*, London, Fontana 1973 and 'The author as producer' in *Understanding Brecht*, London, New Left Books 1973.

8 *What is literature?*, London, Methuen 1967, and *Politics and Literature*, London, Calder & Boyars, 1973.

9 'Literature and sociology', *New Left Review* 67, 1971 and 'Base and superstructure in Marxist cultural theory', *New Left Review* 82, 1973.
 See also 'Developments in the sociology of culture', *Sociology*, Vol. 10 No. 3 1976.

10 Report of the Commission on Obscenity and Pornography, U.S. Government, 1970.

11 Here the work of some of the Russian and Czech Formalists, which is not discussed in these pages, has been of great importance. See Fredric Jameson's *The prisonhouse of language* (Princeton, New Jersey 1972) for a discussion of this work.

6

Introduction

BIBLIOGRAPHY

Albrecht, M. et al (eds) (1970), *The sociology of art and literature*, Duckworth, London.

Benjamin, Walter (1973a), 'The work of art in the age of mechanical reproduction', In *Illuminations*, Fontana, London.

Benjamin, Walter (1973b), 'The author as producer', in *Understanding Brecht*, New Left Books, London.

Bradbury, Malcolm (1971), *The social context of modern English literature*, Blackwell, Oxford.

Caute, David (1974), 'A portrait of the artist as midwife: Lucien Goldmann and the "transindividual subject"' in *Collisions*, Quartet, London.

Coser, Lewis (1963), *Sociology through literature*, Prentice-Hall, New Jersey.

Craib, Ian (1974), 'Sociological literature and literary sociology: some notes on *G* by John Berger', *Sociological Review*, 22, 3.

Dawe, Alan (1973), 'The role of experience in the construction of social theory: an essay in reflexive sociology,' *Sociological Review*, 21, 1.

Eagleton, Terry (1976), *Criticism and ideology*, New Left Books, London.

Escarpit, R (1958), *Sociologie de la litterature*, Paris.

Hoggart, R (1973), 'Literature and society' and 'The literary imagination and the sociological imagination', in *Speaking to each other*, 2, Penguin, Harmondsworth.

Jameson, Fredric (1972), *The prisonhouse of language*, Princeton, New Jersey.

Kuhn, T (1962), *The structure of scientific revolutions*, Chicago.

Laurenson, D and Swingewood, A (1972), *The sociology of literature*, Paladin, London.

Leenhardt, Jacques (1967), 'The sociology of literature: some stages in its history', *International Social Science Journal*, XIX, 4.

Lowenthal, Leo (1967), 'Literature and sociology' in James Thorpe (ed), *Relations of literary study*, New York.

Nisbet, Robert A (1968), *Tradition and revolt*, Random House, New York. (Excerpts reprinted in K. Thompson and J. Tunstall (eds), *Sociological perspectives*, Penguin, Harmondsworth 1971.)

Rockwell, Joan (1974), *Fact in fiction*, Routledge, London.

Sartre, J-P (1967), *What is literature?*, Methuen, London.

Sartre, J-P (1973), *Politics and literature*, Calder & Boyars, London.

Watt, Ian (1964), 'Literature and society' in R. N. Wilson (ed.): *The arts in society*, Prentice-Hall, New York.

Williams, R (1971), 'Literature and sociology', *New Left Review*, 67.

Williams, R (1973), 'Base and superstructure in Marxist cultural theory', *New Left Review*, 82

Williams, R (1973), *The country and the city*, Chatto and Windus, London.

Williams, R (1976), 'Developments in the sociology of culture' *Sociology* 10, 3.

The sociology of literary response

David Coward

Shakespeare, of course, never goes out of season. Each generation
discovers him afresh and isolates vital meanings which were previously
obscure or unimportant. Each age elects its own spokesmen and
reinvents for itself the incumbents of the permanent literary pantheon.
The literary historian defines the phenomenon of constant re-discovery
as a continuing process of re-evaluation. But it does not seem quite as
straightforward to those who find new gods or who look at old ones from
a suddenly 'new' angle.

What is true of generations is here true also of the individual reader
who may feel – perhaps several times over in his lifetime – that he has
entered into a particular personal relationship with Tolstoy or
Flaubert. We discover them as we imagine Columbus discovered
America. Their voice speaks to us alone, as though *Hamlet* or *Anna
Karenina* or *Madame Bovary* were written exclusively for us. At regular
intervals we may reinvent them as our own values and priorities change
and we catch hitherto unheard echoes of our evolving private
preoccupations. Or we may, so to speak, fall out of love with them and
forget exactly what it was that quickened our blood and led us to enter
their world which was also magically our world.

The literary text is therefore a notoriously elusive and shifting object.
A sonnet may be preserved within the pages of a book for centuries and
yet have no existence: it exists only when the volume is opened and the
lines are read. At that moment, there occurs an inter-reaction which is
as unpredictable as it is fortuitous. A thought or an emotion is conjured
and it is difficult to say whose thought, whose emotion it is. An author
may speak, but we do not listen passively for we add our commentary to
his monologue. The act of creation may be autonomous, but the
communication of a vision requires a reader and this reader is subject to
endlessly changing perspectives which the text is required to match. A
poem is a fantastic garment which must fit us exactly and feel new; even
though others make claim to have worn it before us, we are likely to
believe that they were mistaken. Reading is as much an act of
appropriation as a gesture of surrender, and in a sense to read is to re-
write what has already been written. Words have dictionary definitions
but we give them a context: we give them colour and mood and
meaning and their combinations acquire a significance which their first
orderer may not have envisaged. We always assume, of course, that we
always add a valid extension to our author's vision and that we are

8

mysteriously in tune with his mind. This need not be so. By responding, we may fail to hear what he has to say and instead of the intimate friend we take him to be, it is likely that he will remain a total stranger. It is a difficulty which has long been recognised and Madame de Stael expressed it clearly:

> A book is always written within the framework of some scheme of things which sets the author at a distance from the reader. The general temper of the author may be perceived, but his talent cannot but erect a kind of falseness between him and us.[1]

We fall victim to our own fabulation and may mistake our lyricism for his. What we imagine to be an act of complicity may equally be an act of betrayal. Shakespeare – who has been claimed by many generations – remains inaccessible and our reaction to him is necessarily selective, arbitrary and biassed.

What this means is that our response to literature is inevitably but not hopelessly subjective. Orwell used this position to argue that all literary criticism is a fraud. The only valid critical comments are: I like this book, or, I do not like this book. The rest is a rationalisation of a fundamentally personal reaction. D. H. Lawrence expressed the same viewpoint even more trenchantly:

> Literary criticism can be no more than a reasoned account of the feeling produced upon the critic by the book he is criticising. Criticism can never be a science: it is, in the first place, much too personal, and in the second, it is concerned with values that science ignores. The touch-stone is emotion, not reason. We judge a work of art by its effect on our sincere and vital emotion, and nothing else. All the critical twiddle-twaddle about style and form, all this pseudo-scientific classifying and analysing of books in an imitation-botanical fashion, is mere impertinence and most dull jargon.[2]

The critic can no more explain his liking for Jane Austen than his taste for pickled onions.

These reminders of the nature of basic value judgements are salutary. And yet to say that our response to literature is instinctive is no more final a statement than to say that conscience is the permanent and final regulator of moral matters. Our personalities and therefore our tastes are unique, but they are shaped by factors some of which impinge on us all, and our literary likes and dislikes, like our political or moral opinions, are not autonomous. They are inevitably determined by the experience we have, the social and ethical climate, by cultural priorities and other existential phenomena which affect our judgement and our feelings as readily as an attack of gout. For example, sentimentality is

9

currently out of fashion and rational approaches to all kinds of questions are preferred. We no longer feel that it is enough to weep for the poor; we now attribute to the State – on grounds of social justice, efficiency and the inadequacy of charity – a general responsibility for welfare. It is for analogous reasons that Rousseau's emotional novel, *La Nouvelle Héloise*, sticky with that sensibility which won the loyalty of readers for a hundred and fifty years, has fallen from grace. Nowadays it is Laclos' *Les Liaisons Dangereuses*, with its lucid dissection of human relationships, which is considered to be the greatest of eighteenth century French novels. On the wider front, the emotional response argument is not sufficient in itself to explain why we no longer respond warmly to epic and tragedy, though these two genres were, until the end of the eighteenth century, the most noble and elevated of literary productions. Cultural and aesthetic changes must be adduced if we are to explain how the emotions which these kinds of writing catered for entered into other literary forms – predominantly into the novel which, in the last century, emerged as their natural heir. What this means is, as Michel Foucault argues, that art does not reflect nature but contemporary thought structures. If rather obvious projections of this sort can be made for individual books or literary genres, it would seem that while our response to literature is as personal as Orwell and Lawrence believed, it is personal in a rather more collective way than they would perhaps have allowed. Our reactions might *feel* pristine and unique, but they are determined by any number of variables which shape what we imagine to be a personal choice. Our experience is our own, our prejudices are not.

Many attempts have been made to rationalise our response to literature, and they have normally taken the form of a recourse to authority. Laws have been laid down for the writer and the reader has been given clear guide-lines. 'Criticism', said Dryden, 'as it was first instituted by Aristotle, was meant as a standard of judging well'. The standard was guaranteed by a charter which was outside the work being criticised. In seventeenth century France, the classical doctrine prescribed rules for writers governing the choice and treatment of their material and, for readers, a code of reactions which collectively represented Taste. After the *Querelle des Anciens et des Modernes* at the turn of the century, the authority of the ancients was somewhat diminished but was replaced gradually by a mixture of reason and sentiment which, though hard to define, every ranking work of art was required to express since they were considered to transcend any individual writer or his writings. Conformity to these vague prescriptions was considered to be a greater virtue than originality or imagination (or 'enthusiasm', as it was called) and they were soon linked with values which were thought to be eternal: *'le beau est le même dans tous les temps, parce que la nature et la raison ne sauraient changer'*, claimed La Harpe. Winckelmann's discovery that art is not an imitation of nature but an always imperfect realisation of an ideal beauty made the notion of authority even safer because it became semi-mystical: the greatness of a work of art lay in its conformity with standards which were elusive and yet immediately recognisable to the trained observer. The concept of the beautiful, the good and the true remained as the essence of taste until the beginning of the twentieth century and the notion of 'beauty', as Duvignaud points out (Duvignaud 1973: 23-5), remains one of the most persistent barriers to the personal appreciation of literature.

But already in the nineteenth century, this idea of Taste came under attack as society changed, though the respect for authority continued undiminished. By 1830, feeling had replaced reason and it was believed that truth was to be apprehended by submission to more spontaneous sentiments – compassion, exaltation and a heightened sensibility. But the shift from the general to the individual excluded the possibility of any consensus view of taste and the nineteenth century turned into a collection of schools and -isms. The aloof 'Art for Art's Sake' group gave way to the realists who democratised art and allowed it to have absolute goals: a description, however impersonal, was an implied moral or social comment behind which lay the eternal values of truth and justice. Zola willingly fell in with Taine's analysis that everything concerning man and society may be explained in terms of heredity, environment and the moment, and though his success is to be measured by his individual gifts rather than by the success of this theory, Zola set about pinning human experience to the scientist's bench as a lepidopterist classifies his specimens.

The twentieth century has jettisoned the concepts of harmony, the sublime, the beautiful, the good, the eternal, 'nature' and 'taste'. But we are no less eager to refer to some form of authority which will enable us to judge what we read on what we hope will be solid and reasonable grounds. In spite of the intellectual adventurousness of Joyce or B. S. Johnson, the encouragement of reading by formula, so to speak, is as firmly rooted now as it was in the seventeenth century – though the number and variety of formulae give us the impression of emancipation from any particular view. Attempts are made to relate literature to external determinants which may be psychological (the collective unconscious) or social (the class struggle) and they derive their criteria from scientific or historical theses which are as much outside literature as Aristotle ever was.

The Freudian approaches books much as Freud approached case-histories. A poem or play has a 'contenu manifeste' and a 'contenu latent' like any other dream, and the psychocritic sets out to analyse his text with a view to passing through the outer image to the hidden mechanisms which lie beyond. The act of creation is the result of the working out of frustrations which may be defined in terms of obsessions. For Bachelard, these obsessions are communicated via 'imaginary' images through which we perceive 'fundamentals'. By analysing those images which correspond with imaginative reality (in which we all participate), he helps readers to relive the author's dream. Barthes offers a 'pre-criticism' which enables us to read an author in terms of the author's 'coherence' and he charts the semiological indicators by which we perceive his vision. The Marxist critic resorts to a view of history which helps to explain the framework of human and social relationships in a work of art in terms of the permanent dialectical process. He will account for the emergence and evolution of 'types' by relating them to more general social and economic categories in a systematic way. These ideas and ideologies and approaches do not, however, cease to be authoritarian. If we have abandoned the beautiful and the good, we have not yet relinquished the true and the absolute.

For much modern criticism barely conceals a desire to be philosophical. Forms of literary expression have always interested philosophers, since literature in many ways intrudes into philosophic territory: art is an apprehension of experience which seeks to interpret the phenomena of existence. Theories of criticism – from Leavis to Marxism and structuralism – are indeed properly philosophical matters since they are attempts to define abstract principles on the basis of logic and experience. A pragmatic reader is likely to find such approaches insufficiently literary and wonder whether they amount to criticism at all or whether they do not constitute a new concept of literature itself.

Yet even this pragmatic reader – or writers like Lawrence – does not escape other and in practice more coercive forms of authority which direct our appreciation of a literary text. Fashion is an imperious master and one which is as powerful as any. It may well prove crucial in directing us towards the books we read and certainly affects the way in which we read them. There is, for instance, a kind of law of popularity which states that an author reaches his peak audience immediately after his death and subsequently lapses into a decline from which he may or may not recover: both Dylan Thomas and Camus are currently 'unfashionable'. On the other hand, Jean Rhys had few readers until the feminist movement created a general interest in women's condition. Denton Welch or T. F. Powys have a similar small band of devoted followers, but they have not benefitted from any such upturn of fashion and we shall have to wait for other times than ours before they have much to say to us. And what is true of subject matter is true also of literary form. There may linger a few authoritative trappings of earlier aesthetic theories, but the evaluation of style and technique has been influenced more by market forces than by genre studies or the study of linguistics and stylistics. The impact of cinema and television (a growth area in aesthetics) has been very great. Novels have grown shorter and they contain less description and more dialogue. At one end of the spectrum, Robbe-Grillet has turned to the 'ciné-roman'; at the other, Steinbeck's 'play-novelette' has arrived. While it is for us to seek out Barthes or Lukács, fashion winkles its way into our way of looking at things. It is in spite of ourselves that the traditional written culture is in the process of being replaced by a visual culture. Many fashions – the twentieth century predilection for the defeated rather than the triumphant hero, for example – may be explained in terms of moral, economic, social and cultural changes and in explaining them, the sociological critics help us to understand ourselves. Other fashions may be described only in the permanent search for the new and remain inexplicable. But fashion prods us mercilessly and must be reckoned with as a form of authority of a peculiarly inescapable kind.

But our response to literature is also determined by factors outside the authority syndrome. The area of personal preference remains qualitatively large, for not all our reactions are to be explained by the collective psyche or the decay of capitalism or semiological responses. As readers we make assumptions about art and life and use them as a basis for private, idiosyncratic attitudes. Epistemological processes need not be invoked, for we are experimentally aware of our individuality and of the protean nature of individualism. For each of us, the centre of the universe is behind our eyes and it is from inside our skulls that we watch the world. Art provides an opportunity of seeing over someone else's shoulder and reading means looking into someone else's sensibility. Art as a means of escaping the self perhaps feeds the universal appetite for stories – though it does not explain why we believe some and not others.

Fiction provides us with vicarious experience and we accept it on the dubious ground of 'authenticity'. The authenticity we demand is not that of fact but that of a picture of the world which in some way is consistent with our own. The degree of our involvement is unpredictable, difficult to measure and subject to many variables: the man who reads westerns may have his emotions stirred in as profound a way as the sophisticated theatre audience at a performance of *The Cherry Orchard*. We are prepared to be seduced and we surrender our disbelief because we are persuaded by what we imagine to be real rather than by reality. Before we accept the political implications of B. Traven's 'jungle' novels, we have to be convinced by his picture of Mexican society in the early years of this century. Even if we go to infinite pains to verify his picture – and verification will not be definitive given that history is not a science – we shall find it impossible to prove that what he wrote was true. And yet we accept it as such because Traven convinces us in some ultimately mysterious way that his universe is credible.

This means that the writer is, at best, creating something that is by the conventions of social discourse untrue and, at worst, telling a lie. Diderot's *La Religieuse* began as a lie. Knowing that a sensitive acquaintance, the Marquis de Croixmare, was concerned with the fate of a nun who had attempted to break her vows in the law-courts, Diderot undertook to keep him informed of events while he was away from Paris. Diderot invented a series of letters which affected the marquis so deeply that Suzanne Simonin had finally to be killed off. But Diderot himself had become so involved with the character and plight of Suzanne that he proceeded to compose a novel which, when it was published in 1796, was received as an attack on the convent system. But we who read *La Religieuse* might well wonder whether the book is an artistically authentic portrait of an individual in a particular situation or whether it is a falsehood compounded by Diderot's easily provoked tears. It does not help to say that we are convinced because Diderot himself was so utterly involved, for this would be to imply that the artist has only to attain a level of self-deception to deceive his reader: the best lies are told by people who believe them implicitly. Nor can we explain our involvement by making Suzanne a 'type' and relate *La Religieuse* to other eighteenth century novels which deal with the same social problem: Diderot's novel might be shown to be better, but it cannot be shown to be good. Diderot may indeed have attained no more than a spurious authenticity but such is his power of persuasion that we are swept up into the world he creates. Objectively, other anti-clerical campaigners may be more true, but their factual arguments strike us less forcibly because they do not feel as true.

It is at this level that the mystery occurs. There may be conscious reasons – political beliefs, moral principles – why a reader should by rights dislike an author's books and yet read him with much delight. There are many who are out of sympathy with Evelyn Waugh's patrician values and still take pleasure in his sardonic humour or the evocation of a world which, because it is consistently and plausibly drawn, appears to be authentic. *Les Liaisons Dangereuses* has been discussed in terms of Laclos' intentions and the ethos of the late eighteenth century. Marxists have taken it as an illustration of the class struggle. Feminists have viewed it as a statement about the position of women in a male dominated society. The Gidean notion of the 'acte gratuit' has been used to explain the indifference to moral responsibility which the novel at times seems to celebrate. Existentialist readers have interpreted the boredom of Valmont and Madame de Merteuil as evidence of the 'absurd' and their petty acts of seduction as gestures of revolt. But whether we share Laclos' moral concerns, are fascinated by his portrayal of evil, view him as a 'révolté', or take him as a cipher for some social or political thesis, our valuation of his fable will depend on a personal involvement which remains beyond the reach of analysis. Before we can take his picture of the world seriously, we have to believe in it, and we can only do this for reasons which remain unclear even to ourselves.

The sociology of art is no more able to explain the crucial subjective element in our response to literature than the traditional literary criticism. For if Orwell and Lawrence were right, the new sociologies of literature are just as much *post facto* rationalisations as the conventional concern with characterisation, technique, style and form. Of course, a sociological critic is aware that although literature exists objectively, it exists principally in our response to it. Yet too often the assumption is made that our response is to all intents and purposes a collective response. It goes without saying that we cannot discuss literature at all without a common frame of reference and the history of criticism is a succession of passing 'authorities'. The uncommitted literary historian makes patterns of the past – by means of chronology, sequentiality, etc. – on the experimental nature of the evidence and seeks to explain shifts in taste or follow the fortunes of a 'type' or a *genre* in terms of events. His impulse is ideographic and he does not feel the need to relate these patterns to *a priori* generalisations which state a particular view of man and his history. Philosophically, we have learnt to take an empirical view of external reality. There is no reason why we should not learn to take a pragmatic view of literature.

The business of sociology is with abstract concepts which are used to express general notions about social behaviour, relationships of all kinds and the processes which govern change and inter-action. It is concerned with expressing the particular in terms of the general and, like French classicism with which it has much in common, it proposes technical solutions to matters of argument and opinion. Its data derive from survey methods – quantification, categorisation, comparison, etc – which have not always avoided the danger of pre-structuring the results of their enquiries. Marxist interpretations of the picaresque hero – a 'type' to be set against a socio-economic backdrop – may leave us wondering whether Moll Flanders or Jacob or Julien Sorel are symbolic effects or causes of the society they inhabit. Categorisation, that is the attempt to isolate the effective psychological and social infrastructures underlying a literary text, has in the study of literature no more – and no less – value than it has for the study of history. It defines the dominant ethos in which a book was written, but it is not required to differentiate between good and bad books save on a quantitative basis. Indeed, the rise of historical realism could as well be discussed in terms of minor novels (like Restif de la Bretonne's *Le Paysan Perverti*) as in terms of the more famous books which a consensus view of literary excellence has handed on to us. A sociological approach to recent feminist writing would perhaps reveal less about the social status of women and the concept of womanhood than the many magazine stories which in recent years have become more explicit about sexual attitudes and social problems generally; but it would not explain – save by, say, recourse to a structuralist approach which, like traditional criticism, would show why we ought to like a book – the reasons we might have for preferring this novel to that.

The sociological approach, being essentially comparative, has widened the horizons of criticism and broadened historical perspectives in a most challenging way. Yet an '*esprit de système*' does not appear to be the most appropriate of approaches to the problem of literary response. It presupposes the existence of final values which are as elusive as the notion of beauty. It assumes that some correlation may be found between social experience as a whole and the experience of a particular epoch, and that there is a relationship between the individual writer and the age in which he lives. In practice, there is a wish to impose these broad concepts universally, though they are as limited and unsatisfactory as the seventeenth century idea of good taste which forced nature instead of apprehending it. Classical taste preferred types to individuals ('l'ambitieux', 'le méchant', 'le misanthrope', etc.) just as a sociologist critic might class Rastignac in the category of 'achievement-orientation'. If we still respond to Phèdre or Rastignac, it

16

is for reasons which are not the reasons of authority. Lanson, for the old school, might analyse Corneille's dramatic technique or his mastery of psychological conflict; the new criticism might point up the inner 'coherence' of his plays or relate them to the socio-economic climate of the 1640s. But both types of commentary on Corneille's 'discourse' are descriptive and not prescriptive. They help us to exteriorise our reactions, but the important decision to like or dislike will already have been taken by our most private emotions.

University of Leeds

NOTES

1. 'Un livre est toujours fait d'après un système quelconque qui place l'auteur à quelque distance du lecteur. On peut bien deviner le caractère de l'écrivain, mais son talent même doit mettre un genre de fiction entre lui et nous.' (Madame de Stael, 1810: *Préface* 8.)

2. Quoted by H Coombes (1972: 8).

REFERENCES CITED

H. Coombes (1972), *Literature & Criticism*, Penguin, Harmondsworth.

Jean Duvignaud (1972), *The Sociology of Art*, Paladin Books, London.

Madame la baronne de Stael-Holstein (1810), *Lettres et pensées du Maréchal Prince de Ligne publiées par Madame la baronne de Stael-Holstein*, 3rd edition, Paris.

The interpretation of literature in society: the hermeneutic approach

Janet Wolff

In the social sciences in general, though there are no doubt arguments still to be heard in the debate about *Verstehen*, the simple confrontation between naive radical positivism and extreme anti-positivism, which argues that there is a crucial epistemological division between the natural sciences and the cultural sciences, has certainly been superceded. Conceptions of natural science itself have been radically modified with advances both in science and in the philosophy and sociology of natural science. Contemporary sociologists and historians, similarly, recognise that a subject matter of human behaviour, meanings and intentions does not necessarily mean that a systematising theory is impossible or that generalisations cannot be made or causes ascertained.[1] In other words, there has been a degree of convergence on a notion of social science as 'scientific' according to an altered conception of science.[2] With the exception of particular writers and schools of thought, the role of interpretation and *Verstehen* in sociology is no longer felt to be an impediment to social theory and social investigation.[3] This is less true in the case of the sociology of literature, partly because the study itself is still new enough to be entangled in a variety of problems of method, of the status of its theory, and of the definition of its proper object,[4] and partly because the question of interpretation is necessarily central to a discipline whose object is a *text*, of one sort or another. The sociological study of literature presupposes an understanding of the literature studied. If its objective is to propose a theory of literature and society, or to perceive a relationship between them, it must start from a comprehension, explicit or implicit, of the works of literature themselves. The problematic nature of this preliminary understanding is the subject of this article.

It is, I suppose, possible to study literature positivistically. One might undertake a survey of a given group of authors and their social background, or of a group of novels or plays and their conditions of production and reception. Sociological studies of the effects of developments in printing and book production on readership would also come into this category.[5] Such studies are often extremely useful and informative, but they take for granted two fundamental points: that the literature itself is unproblematic, and that therefore what is generally referred to as 'literature' in everyday life may be the subject-matter of a sociology of literature. This cannot simply be assumed.[6] Nor

18

can it be taken for granted that the sociologist's understanding of the novels, poems or plays is correct, or adequate. This is most clearly the case with the literature of the past or of another society, and the obvious immediate problem is that of understanding or translating the actual language correctly – not only from French to English, but also from Chaucerian or Shakespearean English into contemporary language, where the same words do not always have the same meanings or connotations. The kind of studies I have just referred to do demonstrate some of the connections, and often important ones, between works of literature and their social context. I would argue, however, that they do not amount to a sociology of literature. This must be the result of a threefold exercise. It must comprise the understanding (i) of the works of literature in their own right and on their own terms; (ii) of these works as expressions, in some sense, of a world-view or ideology of a social group or of a society; and (iii) of that ideology, here expressed in aesthetic form, as originating in social processes, class relations, and structural features of society. The operation which is generally, if somewhat vaguely, called *Verstehen* plays a part in all three levels of understanding and explanation, but in the first it raises problems which are peculiar to the study of literature. With a view to outlining some of these problems, and suggesting how they might be solved, I shall look at the work of a number of writers in the hermeneutic tradition, with particular reference to their views on the hermeneutic interpretation of literature.[7] I shall go on then to suggest briefly that the hermeneutic approach can be no more than a preliminary, albeit an indispensable preliminary, to a sociology of literature.

The hermeneutic tradition as it has developed has been of two broad types. One is illustrated by the works of Gadamer and of Palmer; the other by the writings of Betti and (in a somewhat different way) of Hirsch. According to Palmer, 'hermeneutics is the study of understanding, especially the task of understanding texts' (Palmer 1969:8). Palmer argues that in hermeneutic theory, and particularly in the work of Hans-Georg Gadamer, we can discover the best approach to literary interpretation. Contemporary American criticism is severely limited, he feels, and must undertake a rigorous re-examination of the presuppositions upon which its conception of interpretation is based (*ibid*: 221). Hermeneutics in Gadamer's work 'constitutes the basis for a creative re-examination of literary interpretation theory' (*loc. cit*). Gadamer is by no means the founder of the hermeneutic tradition, but he has been one of its most influential exponents in the twentieth century, and it is useful to start with his version of hermeneutic theory.

Janet Wolff

Other writers I shall consider, like Emilio Betti, E. D. Hirsch Jr, and Richard Palmer, have taken up Gadamer's arguments in order to reinforce them (Palmer) or to disagree with them (Betti and Hirsch, and members of the Frankfurt School). Although Gadamer's interest is primarily in philosophical questions of the cultural sciences and in ontology, and only secondarily in aesthetics as one among the cultural sciences, hermeneutic theory as conceived by him provides an excellent starting point for an account of its contemporary variants.[8]

The cultural scientist, and in particular the historian, works with a subject-matter which is imbued with meanings. The task of history and the other *Geisteswissenschaften*, therefore, is one of understanding and interpreting those meanings. Like Dilthey and other earlier writers on hermeneutics, Gadamer argues that the meanings of the past, of a text, or of a tradition must be grasped in their own terms and in their own historical context. The historical subject must be understood to some extent as he or she understood himself or herself. But Gadamer insists that the ability to recreate a world, a life, an experience, in this way is strictly limited by the very fact that the historian (and, by the same token, the sociologist) is also located in history and in the world. Understanding is always and necessarily from the point of view of the person doing the understanding. The historical context of the observer plays as large a part in *Verstehen* as that of his or her subject-matter, and the process of interpreting is one of a fusion of the two 'horizons' of subject and object, or historian and subject-matter. A historian must work with an 'effect-historical conciousness' (*wirkungsgeschichtliche Bewusstsein*[9]), a conciousness which recognises equally the historicity of self and of subject, and which comprehends the fusion of the two standpoints, or horizons, in the act of historical understanding.

The notion of the 'hermeneutic circle', already found in the writings of Schleiermacher and Dilthey, describes a particular process of *Verstehen* in Gadamer's philosophy, and takes account of the dual nature of historicity. A historian approaches his material with certain presuppositions, drawn from his own experience and life situation. At the same time, however, it is important that a proper 'open-ness' to the text or the object is retained; as Gadamer puts it, the text must be allowed to speak for itself, to answer the questions put to it by the historian (or literary critic). Thus, the original presuppositions are revised in the light of the initial contact with the material. The openness to the material ensures that any wrong or distorting presuppositions will be abandoned, for they will not be allowed to conceal what is really there in the material. The circular progress of the hermeneutic method is one of projecting anticipations on to the material, revising those anticipations as a result of a confrontation with the material, then a new projection and correction, and so on. There are two important points to notice about this. First, Gadamer is not apologetic about the methodological role of prejudice, or presupposition, in understanding. He argues that this is necessarily part of any understanding. Thus he inveighs against the scientific and positivistic tradition, deriving from the Enlightenment, whose ambition it has always been to eliminate the subject in knowledge. For Gadamer, this is to succumb to a false objectivism and to ignore the real nature of knowledge. It is always an historical subject who knows, and his or her historicity must be acknowledged, not only methodologically, but also in the construction of the object of knowledge. The second point follows from this, and concerns the notion of 'objectivity'. Gadamer talks about objectivity in understanding but re-defines the concept to mean, not the absence of subjective elements, prejudices and values from knowledge, but the verification achieved by working them out in the circular process of hermeneutic investigation (Gadamer 1965: 252). *There is no point of view outside history.* Therefore any knowledge is historically bound, and (despite its 'objectivity' as defined by Gadamer) relative. To refer specifically to the understanding of literature, this means that we cannot talk of any single 'true' interpretation of a text. The interpretation will change with the situation, society and period of the interpreter. It is always a form of *re*-interpretation.

Gadamer's denial of any absolutely valid interpretation of texts earns him the criticism of E. D. Hirsch Jr, who labels Gadamer's position 'hermeneutical skepticism' (Hirsch 1967: viii). According to Hirsch, the hermeneutic method is the best method for literary interpretation, but hermeneutics can, after all, be objective. Hirsch is not the only writer on hermeneutics who holds this view. Emilio Betti is an historian of law and a greatly respected authority on the theory of interpretation[10] who has taken issue with Gadamer (Betti 1962: 38-64). His criticisms are taken up by Gadamer in the Preface to the second edition of *Wahrheit und Methode* (1965). The main point of contention, again, is the possibility of objective interpretation. Against Gadamer, Betti argues that we can devise reliable criteria for correct and valid interpretation (Betti 1962: 41). He agrees with Gadamer that it is impossible for a historian to abandon entirely his or her own standpoint – to be 'outside history' – but his less radical view is that the present (the historian's own *Dasein*) directs the interest of understanding, but stays out of the process of understanding itself (*op. cit.* 46). In his eyes, the

Janet Wolff

abandonment of historical knowledge to relativism is not only wrong but unnecessary. He proposes four canons of objective understanding which hermeneutic theorists must follow. His intention is to distinguish between interpretation and the supererogatory act whereby the interpreter confers meaning on the object. Interpretation consists in 'a recognition and reconstruction of the meaning that (the) author, using a special kind of unity of materials, was able to embody' (Palmer 1969: 57). The first canon of interpretation is that of the 'hermeneutic autonomy' of the object of study, which ensures against the imposition of an alien system of meanings on the part of the interpreter (Betti 1962: 14). The second canon is that of 'meaningful coherence': the object, or text, must be understood within its totality of context. The third canon, of 'actuality of understanding', relates and adapts the act of interpretation to the interpreter's own situation. And the fourth canon, of 'adequacy of meaning' (*op.cit.*:53), insists that the interpreter bring his own living topicality into close co-ordination with the ideas emanating from the object, so that they 'resonate together'. However, this does not mean that *Verstehen* is a mediation of past and present, as Gadamer had argued. The first canon gives clear priority to the original meaning of the subject-matter, over the perspective of the historian or student of texts. (Betti contrasts these with lawyers for whom the contemporary application of the texts is more relevant and of practical import. *op.cit.*: 44). Objective understanding is attained by discovering the 'morphological laws of cultural creation' which lie behind ways of thought, texts and institutions. This goes beyond a narrower psychological interpretation, and reveals the processes whereby meaningful forms, including literature, develop on a macro-social level. This morphological analysis, in conjunction with the canons of interpretation, yields an understanding which meets the demands of adequacy of meaning and provides an interpretation which is valid.

For Hirsch too a valid interpretation of texts and meanings is possible within the framework of a hermeneutic theory. A valid interpretation, according to Hirsch, consists in discovering what the author meant. It is not a question of the significance of the text for contemporary readers, which occupies the attention of Gadamer and the school of the New Hermeneutics in theology. Hirsch dismisses the followers of Eliot and the New Critics of literary theory, who thought that the meaning of a text was somehow independent of its author (Hirsch 1967: 1) – the notion of the 'semantic autonomy' of a text. He considers and rejects a number of arguments which claim to prove that the text might mean something which its author did not mean, or could not have meant: for example, the idea that the text changes its meaning over time for the author (which he denies), or the idea that the author's meaning is inaccessible (which he argues is not usually true, except in the obvious sense that we cannot directly know another person's mind). He does raise the possible objection that the author himself often does not know what he means (Hirsch 1967: 19ff), but he comments that unconscious meaning is an integral part of intended meaning.

> It is not possible to mean what one does not mean, though it is very possible to mean what one is not conscious of meaning. The distinction between attended and unattended meanings is not the same as the distinction between what an author means and what he does not mean. No example of the author's ignorance with respect to his meaning could legitimately show that his intended meaning and the meaning of his text are two different things.
> (Hirsch 1967: 22).

So the author's intended meaning, conscious or unconscious, is the object of hermeneutic discovery. Its recovery produces an objectively valid interpretation. This meaning is something determinate, and hermeneutics provides the logic of validation for its discovery. Hirsch says there are two moments to the interpretive act: the divinatory moment and the critical moment (*ibid*: x). The first is 'unmethodical, intuitive, sympathetic'. It is an 'imaginative guess without which nothing can begin'. The second submits the first to a high intellectual standard, by testing it against all available relevant knowledge. It thereby raises the interpretive guess to the level of knowledge. His book is chiefly concerned with the second moment in interpretation. In other words, it attempts to outline the methods necessary for the weighing of evidence in favour of particular interpretations of texts.

The meaning to be recovered by Hirsch's method is the verbal meaning of the author, and it is determinate (*op.cit*. Chapters 1 and 2). He recognises the historicity of all interpretations, but he denies that this implies that the meaning of a text itself varies from age to age. If it is properly understood, there is only one meaning, though it is true that different ages will need different modes of interpretation in order to grasp that meaning. This, Hirsch says, is because 'each different sort of audience requires a different strategy of interpretation' (*op.cit*.: 137). Despite these necessarily varied styles of exposition, the real meaning of the text is timeless and unchanging. Hirsch devotes the rest of his book to a discussion of how evidence is collected and evaluated, and thus how a 'valid' interpretation may be approximated to, and how we may eventually give 'objective sanction to a particular interpretive hypothesis' (*ibid.*: 169). The interpretation always remains a probability (*ibid*: 180), but one which is supported by evidence, and which appears to be more probable than alternative hypotheses in the light of the evidence. He makes no claim that we can ever know absolutely that we have perceived the true meaning of a text, although he thinks that we may occasionally achieve a correct interpretation, without being able to know this for sure (*ibid.*: 173). This does not matter. What does matter is that we attempt to reach the most probable conclusions 'in the light of what is known'. He outlines a number of principles which must govern decisions about the use of interpretive evidence. In particular, extrinsic evidence may be admitted as relevant 'whenever it helps to define a class under which the object of interpretation (a word or a whole text) can be subsumed, or whenever it adds to the instances belonging to such a class' (*ibid*: 197). He adds that the weight of the evidence increases with the relative narrowness of the class, with the copiousness of instances within the class, and with the relative frequency of the trait among these instances. The main point is that a judgment based on a narrower class is always more weighty or reliable than one based on a broader class. For example, in trying to decide between two conflicting interpretations of Donne's 'Valediction forbidding mourning' – whether the poem is about death or about departure – the reader must go beyond the internal verbal and stylistic features of the poem, and compare the poem with others on the same theme, but more particularly with others by Donne on the same theme. As a result of referring to the latter, relatively narrow, class, we appear to be safe in assuming that the valediction is not spoken by a dying person, but by someone about to depart (*op. cit.*: 193). Similarly with the occurrence of the word 'wit' in an eighteenth century piece of writing; the class we would subsume it under is that of uses of the word 'wit' in the eighteenth century, and the narrower one (if possible) of that of other uses of the word by the same author.

> By narrowing the class, we have, in effect, created a new class far more relevant to our guess than the previous one, and this narrower subsuming class always has the power to overturn (or confirm) the evidence and the guess derived from the broader class (*ibid.*: 184-5).

By using extrinsic evidence according to this principle, Hirsch maintains, we can guess with a degree of certainty what the author meant, and come to some conclusion about the validity of an interpretation (*ibid.*: 207). The critics of radical scepticism, then, argue for a determinate object of interpretation, which is comprehensible

24

within certain limits set by the contemporary situation and by the availability of evidence.

Palmer, in his book, opts for Gadamer's historicism, and rejects the notions of objectivity proposed by Betti and Hirsch (Palmer 1969: 54-65). He disagrees with Hirsch that it is possible to separate what a text meant to its author from what it means to its interpreter, and insists that Hirsch ignores hermeneutics as a philosophical theory of understanding. His unwillingness to accept the ideas of Heidegger and Gadamer, says Palmer, allows him to overlook the implications of the act of interpretation, and the essential fact that the act of understanding or interpretation is an historical event. He fails to recognise that even the notion of 'objectivity' is one which is historically relative (*ibid.*: 65). Hermeneutics is not simply a technique for apprehending the original author's probable meaning, for its scope is wider than this, encompassing a general theory of the nature of understanding itself, and one of its conclusions must be that we can no longer talk of, or indeed wish for, 'valid' interpretations, or absolute and objective knowledge of the 'true' meaning of a text. So with Palmer we have come full circle back to the hermeneutical scepticism of the radical historicists.

We have seen now the two broad types of hermeneutic theory. The first maintains that subject and object are historically situated, and the interpretation of meaning is thus doubly relative: the meaning of a literary text is bound up with the socio-historical situation of its genesis, and the recovery of that meaning by an alien or a later interpreter is unavoidably bound to his or her contemporary situation and set of meanings. Thus the meaning of a text is not constant. There is no 'correct' interpretation, but only one which is relevant to the period or society of the interpreter. Interpretation is always re-interpretation. The second school accepts the inevitable historical specificity of the interpreting subject and of the interpreted text, and also that the historicity of the former is likely to impede valid interpretation, or set limits to comprehension. Nevertheless, Betti, Hirsch and others in this tradition of hermeneutics argue that this does not mean that there can be no determinate meaning. There is such a meaning – the hermeneutic autonomy of the text (Betti) – and it is, in principle, recoverable by historians, literary critics, sociologists. This is no naive, unhistorical view, as Palmer seems to think, but an account which is well equipped to take cognisance of the complexities and ambiguities of historical knowledge and, indeed, of any knowledge or understanding of cultural products. My own view is that Hirsch is right to argue for a determinate object of interpretation. As he acknowledges, it may not be possible to grasp it properly, given the inescapability of our own perspective, but in principle it can be understood, and insofar as it is, our understanding will be the same as that of the author or of an interpreter of another age or society. At the very least, two or more interpretations must be compatible and complementary, even if they are nor identical, for if they are contradictory, they cannot all be valid. This is simply to say that recognition of the existential-historical nature of all understanding does not amount to licence to accredit multiple and indeed infinite 'meanings' to a text, for what the text originally meant does not change.[11]

I want to go on to see how the hermeneutic theory of literature may be incorporated into the broader study of the sociology of literature. To begin with, one can see certain affinities between Hirsch's interpretive theory and Goldmann's genetic sociology. Goldmann's view is that the work of literature is the expression of a collective or trans-individual subject (Goldmann 1964: 15; 1967b). It epitomises the world-view of a particular social group at a given moment in history, and expresses in literary form the ideology of that group. The author is the 'exceptional individual' (1964: 17) or 'great representative writer' (1969:59) in whom the collective subject finds expression; he (or she) is able for one reason or another to give voice to the world-view of a social class. Goldmann has been criticised for denying the author his due credit, and for relegating the role of author in the birth of a literary work to that of a midwife (Caute 1974: 222). I think this is rather unfair to Goldmann, who never denies that the individual writer actually creates and who wants merely to emphasise that only in particular individuals is the world-view of the collectivity coherently expressed and fully articulated, as a result of specific structural features of that author's social existence. As Hirsch recognises, the ideas expressed need not be consciously perceived by the writer, but they are nevertheless the product of the writer's intention (which may be unconscious) and of his creativity. There is not, in Goldmann any more than in Hirsch, any notion of some mystical spirit speaking in the text and using the writer as its mindless vehicle. But Goldmann, unlike Hirsch, wants to go beyond the grasp of the text and of its author's meaning.

It is not, of course, Hirsch's intention to give an account of why a text says what it does, or of how and where it originates. He takes the text as given and enquires how we may understand it in its own terms. As I have argued earlier, the ability to understand a work of literature should be an integral part of the sociological study of literature. Interpretation comes first. Of the philosophers of the hermeneutic tradition, only Betti goes beyond this interpretive stage in an attempt to situate the textual meanings within the broader structure of macro-cultural formations. In Goldmann's terms, too, we must cater for two distinct moments in the sociological study of literature: interpretation and explanation (Goldmann 1967a). The first consists in the intrinsic comprehension of the text, and Hirsch's account of this act, it could be argued, is as plausible as Goldmann's and rather more explicit. The second moment, of explanation, involves the locating of the literary work in its broader social structure in order to render intelligible the genesis of the work itself. (The work too Goldmann sees as a structured and coherent totality, the inter-relation of whose elements must be seen as clearly as the elements themselves.) Explaining a text means accounting for its genesis (Goldmann: 1967b) with reference to factors external to the text itself. Elsewhere Goldmann outlines the task of the social investigator thus:

> He . . . must try to link the study of the facts of consciousness to their historical localization and to their economic and social infrastructure. (Goldmann 1969: 36)

Literature too, as a 'fact of consciousness', must be viewed in the context of its social and material background, for human activity has a total character, and there is an 'indissoluble bond between the history of economic and social facts and the history of ideas' (*ibid.*: 62). Literature is fully understood and explained only by considering the social group out of which it arises, and the processes which have formed the ideology of this group.

There are a number of problems which arise if Goldmann's methodological precepts are taken too literally.[12] Furthermore, one would not always want to look for the genesis of literary structures in social classes, as Goldmann almost invariably does, or to limit the study of works of literature to the exceptional works of those whom we have come to accept in our tradition as 'geniuses'. It may be that the simple relationship – of literature: ideology: class – can be nothing more than a suggestive guide for the sociologists of literature, for clearly there is much more that can be said about literature and its social genesis. Goldmann is right to argue that the class structure of the society in which the work originates must be the starting point for any comprehension, for, as he says, literature is part of the ideological structure of a society and a period, and ideology in general arises within the social relations of society and is related to them in complex ways. What Goldmann is trying to do, it seems to me, in adding 'explanation' to 'interpretation', goes even further than Betti's recommendation of a 'technical-morphological' study of the processes of cultural creation which form the broad macro-social background to any literary production (Betti 1962: 57ff), for as well as describing cultural development, Goldmann's method attempts to discover the social and material forces behind such development. This is an essential step which must be taken if hermeneutics is to be transformed into a sociology of literature, and this is the problem with which I shall conclude this review of hermeneutics.

Analysing a text by viewing it within the whole cultural and economic context of its origin allows us to see the homologies of structure which exist between the text, world-view and social class, as Goldmann demonstrated, for example, in his study of Racine and seventeenth century French society (Goldmann 1964). But it does much more than that, for it also provides the possibility of understanding critically the literary work and the ideology expressed in it. This does not mean reading literature as a literary critic, with attention to stylistic detail or semantic content. Rather, it means exposing the systematic distortions which affect the creation and interpretation of literature, and examining the genesis and maintenance of the ideological structures and practices which effect those distortions. Here it becomes evident that the interpretation alone of literature, however adequate or 'valid', is only the first part of a sociologist's task. As I have already argued, the essential two-fold exercise which must then be undertaken is to relate the literary expression first to broader cultural factors and then to the social determinants of those cultural factors. Goldmann himself does this, although it has been argued that his account is rather too simplistic. The recent arguments of members of the Frankfurt School against hermeneutics, and especially against Gadamer, are more helpful in this respect. The comments they have made about interpretive studies in the social and cultural sciences in general apply equally to literature.

Karl-Otto Apel and Jurgen Habermas have argued that hermeneutics must be supplemented by the critique of ideology (Apel 1971; Habermas 1970, 1971). The systems of meanings, the texts, the ideas – all that is taken as the subject-matter of the social and cultural sciences – must be comprehended genetically, as well as hermeneutically. We require an objective understanding of meanings if we are to understand why these cultural products say what they do, how they came to have the meanings historians or sociologists aim to recover, and when or why these meanings change. Hermeneutics would stop at the task of interpreting a work or a tradition. The sociologist, however, will go on to look at the factors which determine that work or tradition, and to consider the genesis and determinants of cultural meaning-systems. As Apel says, we need to go beyond the subjective and historical understanding of ideology, to an *Ideologiekritik* which lays bare simultaneously the ideological factors influencing culture and the interests underlying ideology. The cultural and ideological products are no longer taken as given: they are subjected to questioning and to social scientific explanation. An analysis which is critical in this specific sense will expose the ways in which a world-view may be a distortion of the real social relations in society. Analysed critically in this way, the ideological and literary expression of a class or social group, through those who are its most articulate members ('exceptional individuals' – Goldmann), may be seen to be biassed or partial, and in line with very specific forces of ideological domination in society. Habermas has attempted to relate forms of knowledge to different types of interest, and to locate thought in the material structures of work, language and authority (Habermas 1972: 286). Without examining his account here, I want simply to suggest that the study of literature, as a form of knowledge, might well proceed on these lines too (though I would have reservations about the specific material factors Habermas takes to be primary). In other words, the critique of ideology, as proposed by the Frankfurt School, must work equally well as a critique of literature.

The hermeneutic moment is an essential preliminary step in the sociological study of literature. It allows us to treat our object with aesthetic respect – to retain an openness to the richness of its meaning. If it is true that a sociology of literature must go further and take a critical view of its object in the way I have suggested, it is equally true that it must take care not to lose this special sensitivity to semantic content and artistic qualities, to the text's own autonomous sense (Betti, Hirsch) and to its ever new significance to different readers and different ages (Gadamer). For such a sensitivity, the hermeneutic method is indispensible.

University of Leeds

Janet Wolff

NOTES

1 Even for Weber, *Verstehen* was only part of the general sociological enterprise, whose object was the discovery of causal laws.

2 In a somewhat different sense, however, Althusserian Marxism claims 'scientific' status for Marxist sociology, taking as its starting point the work of Marx and Engels after 1845 (Althusser 1969: 33-38).

3 But note the anti-systematising impulse of sections of the ethnomethodological tradition, and of certain hermeneutic philosophers, discussed below.

4 For example, the question of whether it is only 'great works' of literature which can be grasped in their social context, or which can tall us something about the social structure or world-view out of which they arise.

5 E.g. Laurenson 1972; Escarpit 1968.

6 This is something I have discussed in more general terms in another paper. (Wolff 1975c).

7 For a recent account of the hermeneutic tradition, see Outhwaite 1975. For a brief discussion of the meaning of 'hermeneutic' and the history of the term, see Palmer 1969.

8 The following is a summary of some of Gadamer's arguments in his major work, *Wahrheit und Methode* (1965).

9 Translated by Palmer as 'historically operative consciousness' (Palmer 1969: 191) and in the new English edition of *Wahrheit und Methode* as 'effective-historical consciousness' (Gadamer 1975: 267-274).

10 Betti founded an institute for interpretation theory in Rome in 1955. See Palmer (1969: 54).

11 I am here assuming that the object of hermeneutic knowledge which may be valid is, as Hirsch says, the author's (conscious and unconscious) meaning. Here I agree entirely with his arguments against proponents of the view that a text may have some other kind of non-authorial meaning. It may, of course, have some unintended *significance*, but I would argue that its significance, for instance, for contemporary problems or in its effects after it appeared are both independent of its meaning.

12 I have made some comments on this elsewhere. (Wolff 1975a: Chapter 5).

The interpretation of literature in society: the hermeneutic approach

REFERENCES CITED

Althusser, L. (1969), *For Marx*, Penguin, London.

Apel, K-O. (1971), 'Szientistik, Hermeneutik, Ideologiekritik. Entwurf einer Wissenschaftslehre in erkenntnisanthropologischer Sicht', in K-O. Apel et al: *Hermeneutik und Ideologiekritik*, Suhrkamp Verlag, Frankfurt am Main.

Betti, Emilio (1962), *Die Hermeneutik als allgemeine Methodik der Geisteswissenschaften*, J. C. B. Mohr (Paul Siebeck), Tübingen.

Caute, David (1974), *Collisions*, Quartet Books, London.

Escarpit, Robert (1968), *Sociologie de la littérature*, Presses Universitaires de France, Paris.

Gadamer, H-G. (1965), *Wahrheit und Methode*, Tubingen. (1st edition 1960). Translated as *Truth and method* (1975), Sheed and Ward, London.

Gadamer, H-G. (1971), 'Rhetorik, Hermeneutik and Ideologiekritik. Metakritische Erörterungen zu *Wahrheit und Methode*', in Apel et al, *op.cit.*

Goldmann, L. (1964), *The hidden god*, Routledge and Kegan Paul, London.

Goldmann, L. (1967a), 'Sociology of literature – status and problems of method', *International Social Science Journal*, XIX, 4.

Goldmann, L. (1967b), 'Ideology and writing', *Times Literary Supplement*, 28 September.

Goldman, L. (1969), *The human sciences and philosophy*, Cape, London.

Habermas, J. (1970), *Zur Logik der Sozialwissenschaften*, Suhrkamp Verlag, Frankfurt am Main.

Habermas, J. (1971), 'Zu Gadamers *Wahrheit und Methode*'; in Apel et al, *op.cit.*

Habermas, J. (1972), *Knowledge and human interests*, Heinemann, London.

Hirsch, E. D. (1967), *Validity in interpretation*, Yale University Press.

Laurenson, Diana (1972), 'The writer and society', in Diana Laurenson and Alan Swingewood, *The sociology of literature*, Paladin, London.

Outhwaite, William (1975), *Understanding social life: the method called Verstehen*, Allen and Unwin, London.

Palmer, Richard E. (1969), *Hermeneutics. Interpretation theory in Schleiermacher, Dilthey, Heidegger and Gadamer*, Northwestern University Press, Evanston.

Wolff, Janet (1975a), *Hermeneutic philosophy and the sociology of art*, Routledge and Kegan Paul, London.

Wolff, Janet (1975b), 'Hermeneutics and the critique of ideology', *Sociological Review*, 23, 4, November.

Wolff, Janet(1975c), 'The sociology of art versus aesthetics', *Occasional Paper* 1, University of Leeds Department of Sociology.

A theory of literature and society

Joan Rockwell

What is wanted is a formula which will cover every form of literary expression and can be used as the key to its place and function in every form of society. It is unlikely, however, that such a formula can be found; and certainly we may say that it never will be found by empirical quantitative methods: we will never have all the data on every type, let alone every example, of literature; and we must believe Weber when he insists that we can never really know all the data about society either, or so much as a single phenomenon within it – for

> . . . as soon as we attempt to reflect about the way life confronts us in immediately concrete situations, it presents an infinite multiplicity of successively and co-existently emerging and disappearing events both within and outside ourselves. The absolute infinity of this multiplicity is seen to remain undiminished even when our attention is focussed upon a single object . . . (Weber: 1904)

The case would thus seem hopeless. But paradoxically, it may be this infinite multiplicity of events in social reality which is the key to the nature of literature. Perhaps literature is a net which the human consciousness casts over 'reality', to catch a selected number of phenomena and arrange them in a pattern which is available to human understanding. Lucien Goldmann (1967) says something rather similar to Weber about the inapprehensibility of 'reality';

> at any given moment, social and historical reality always presents itself as an extremely complex mixture, not of structures but of processes of structuration and destructuration the study of which will not have a scientific character until the day when the chief processes have been made clear with a sufficient degree of rigour.

Since, if Weber is right, this day will never come, we must instead attempt to understand society by inductive reasoning and by model-making, the imposing (or preferably the discovery) of patterns. And it is here that Goldmann claims for literature, at least for great literature, the quality of key to the nature of the society which produces it, for he goes on to say in the next sentence:

> Now, it is precisely on this point that the sociological study of the masterpieces of literature acquires special value for general sociology.

We must start, in my opinion, not as Goldmann does with the specific analysis of particular examples of literature (if the dead speak in Homer

32

and in Greek drama, can this be said to give a reliable picture of Greek society?), but with the few universal traits of society which are agreed to exist. One of them is language, of which literature, or more precisely, narrative fiction, is a major department.

It can be argued that no human society is known to exist without language, and recent studies show consistent vocal communication among animals, in addition to the 'body language' with which they have long been credited. Equally, no society exists without some form of 'literature', although we must extend the term to include every type of fictional narrative such as legends, folk-tales and ballads, and compressed forms such as proverbs or sayings. Travelling people like the Gipsies, who claim to have no literature, have a number of legends and exemplary tales in which traditional beliefs of their origin are preserved, and their social values are expressed.

What reasons can be found for this near universality of some form of literature? The universal fascination of narrative has often been noted, by persons otherwise as widely divergent in their views as Somerset Maugham and Ernst Fischer. Fischer asks in *The Necessity of Art* (1959:7-8) with reason but without really answering the question, why

> countless millions read books, listen to music, watch the theatre, go to the cinema. Why? To say that they seek distraction, relaxation, entertainment, is to beg the question. Why is it distracting, relaxing, entertaining, to sink oneself in someone else's life and problems? . . . Why is our own existence not enough? Why this desire to fulfil our unfulfilled lives through other figures, other forms, to gaze from the darkness . . . at a lighted stage where something that is only play can so utterly absorb us?

Why indeed? This is a basic question, which can hardly be answered by an analysis of particular works, whether 'great' or 'trivial'. I think the answer may be found in the nature of language, real human language as distinguished from animal communication. The distinguishing feature of human language is *words*, which makes possible, as Chomsky points out, the open-ended quality of human speech: words may be put together in an infinite number of ways and new ones are constantly being invented to cover new things and new concepts – and these words are understood by any other speaker of the same language. This makes it possible to have communication about people who are not present to be indicated by a grunt or nod (the dead, the ancestors, the unborn, the enemy village), about right and wrong behaviour, about any subject whatsoever which cannot be covered by immediate indication or agreed signals.

33

Marxists, following Engels, are infatuated with the notion that the origin of language lies in the necessity of co-operative *work*. Animals, however, also co-operate, and communicate by signals when doing so: in hunting for example, in changing place at the head of a flying V of geese, in taking turns guarding the herd – without the use of language in our sense. It is also impossible to suppose that primitive man, or hominids, had a concept of *work* equivalent to our own – as a specialised activity, necessary but disagreeable. *Work* in our sense was presumably not more necessary than religious observance or not breaking the taboos, for the maintenance of life. Nevertheless this notion of *work* as the origin of language persists among Marxists to this day: thus Fischer says:

> Only in work and through work do human beings have much to say to each other. Language came into being together with tools.
> (1959:23)

This over-simplified view of the origin of language (the 'yo-heave-ho theorem') is an effective stumbling-block to some Marxist studies of the social function of literature. Experience tells us that human beings have plenty to say to each other on other subjects than work, and the rare appearance of work as a theme in literature is only one proof of it.

What people do in fact talk about, and what is a persistent theme in literature, is their own personal relationships, and other people and their behaviour. Virginia Woolf says, somewhere, of biographical accounts of eccentrics, that this type of account is read because 'it makes us know our species better', and so it does: gazing from the dark at the lighted stage, we can see other human beings in action, and see the results of their actions. Although most of us are aware that the stories are made up, and the actors are not *really* suffering or triumphing as they pretend to be, what we see on the stage or what we read does affect us as a sort of persuasive experience.

The universal existence of censorship ought to be a proof that all societies, or at least the policy-making rulers, believe that representations of human action, even when known to be fictional, may have some potentially dangerous influence on people's beliefs, and consequently (possibly) on their social behaviour.

For certainly literature is very closely associated with changes in social behaviour. Thus in the two or three hundred years when feudal society was giving way to the pressure of bourgeois capitalism – from, say the beginning of the 17th century to the first quarter of the 19th – the theme of the right of young people to choose their own marriage partners was a dominant one in literature. It started as a tragic theme, as in *Romeo and Juliet* (such attempts were not likely to be successful in feudal society). Later it became the ubiquitous topic of novels of every grade of excellence, (and a major reason why they were consistently denounced as immoral) and the successful outwitting of parents and guardians was ever-present on the stage of the comedies, not only of the English Restoration, but of Holberg in Denmark in the 1720s, and the stage comedies of the period in France and Germany as well.

The immorality of this theme consisted not only in the justification of the rights of sexual and personal attraction, but that it set children up against their parents in the matter of marriage-choice, a point mentioned mockingly by Jane Austen, probably the last important writer in England to use the theme seriously (in *Mansfield Park*). For by 1820 it was hardly a serious theme any longer: the previous social norm of arranged marriages had been subject to that 'process of structuration and destructuration' mentioned by Goldmann, and replaced by the bourgeois value of self-choice in this matter, so much better suited to the bourgeois ideal of individualism and the bourgeois requirement of individual action and self-aggrandisement.

This theme is one of the most striking examples of a correspondence in literature to a great nodal change in a basic social institution which was happening at the same time. Doubtless the situation, as a fit subject for literary treatment, 'arose from' the fact that it was observably present in society at the time; and doubtless also, the total about-face in morality from assuming that the establishment of marriage and the family are arrangements which must be made in the interests of stability and the preservation of property, to the radically different one which now prevails, that marriage must be based on romantic love, and that any lesser basis is degrading and immoral, was helped along and consolidated by the support it got from literature, and the influence this had on the values and moral requirements of many generations of readers.

It is this didactic power of literature which in my opinion is the most interesting aspect, and certainly the one which has attracted the most attention both from authority and from those who wish to upset authority. Literature has often been compared to a mirror, which as Stendhal expressed it, reflects 'the blue of heaven and the mud in the ditches', holds vice up to scorn and virtue up to praise, and all the rest of it. But it seems to me to be far more than a mirror, in fact to be an essential part of the social machinery, as much an institution as any other, and to have been so from the very earliest times when human beings were human and in possession of language. For language, as we have seen, does very greatly extend the possibilities of communication, and it is thus possible to *tell* something to another without acting it out. This is of course very important in the socialisation of infants, and in human society, unlike animal society, they are indoctrinated into the behaviour and norms of their society not only through the exemplary behaviour of their elders but also, and very largely, through language. And not only through language, but especially through narrative fiction.

For how are the traditions of a society expressed? Children, as a practical guide to their behaviour, have nursery tales, little songs, proverbs and the like. More formally we have Legends, Heroic Epic, History, the Law, and Religion. In all of these, the lesson to be learned and the ideas to be presented are expressed not as abstracts but as representations of actual human action and its consequences, from which it is possible to draw the conclusion of what sort of behaviour is right and what is wrong. I have no doubt that the earliest taboos – against cannibalism, against incest, against shedding kindred blood – which were necessary to make it possible for human groups to live together for any continuous length of time, were expressed as narratives of what would happen if . . . Perhaps the very tales of which a faint echo has come down to us in such themes as that of the Curse on the House of Atreus.

For there does seem to be a limitation in the ability of even the most advanced human brain to express abstract ideas without personifying them or at least turning them for purposes of consideration into some sort of object, – that is, reifying them. Thus Socrates, wisest of the Athenians, could find no better definition of Virtue than 'that which a good man does', and even in modern natural science, in a field so abstruse as nuclear physics, we have testimony of a hankering after the concrete or visual. On nuclear research Martin Deutsch wrote (1959):

> The human imagination, including the creative scientific imagination, can ultimately function only by invoking potential or imagined sense impression. I cannot prove that the statement I have just made is true, but I have never met a physicist, at least not an experimental physicist, who does not think of the hydrogen atom by evoking a visual image of what he would see if the particular atomic model with which he is working existed on a scale accessible to sense impression.

Hume said we move from a phenomenon we know to one we know not, and by an association of similarity are thus able to grasp a new concept. But a corollary to that seems to be that we can grasp concepts in the abstract, or those concerned with the splendours of philosophy or the majesty of religion, only if they are initially presented in human terms, in the form of human characters (allowing animals to deputise for humans in many folk-tales and children's stories), and a narrative of imagined human action.

The invention of narrative fiction seems thus second only to the invention of language, as a mode of transmitting the bearing ideas of a society to new members, especially the pliable young, and also of reinforcing them in established members of the society and, in apparent contradiction to this, renewing them in periods of change. Thus it is that the content of Religion, religious observance, as well as religious teaching, is stories of the deeds of the Gods; the Law, even when it is not specifically using case histories as exemplary tales of what the law is and how it should be enforced, is expressed, and can only be expressed, in terms of what an imagined 'reasonable and prudent man' would do; while History, and its related areas such as Legend and Heroic Epic, offers a socially binding view of the social entity whose history it is, by means of a chronicle of the actions of the former great persons of the group. This creates a social bond on the basis of the tendency of human beings to identify with and imitate the observed action of others: originally, no doubt, before language, the imitation of the teaching animal or hominid. But *with* language and narrative, the merely described example is enough.

The Athenian drama, furthermore, which is well known to derive from religious ritual, offers something more: exemplary tales of crime and punishment, in which the principles of Justice are demonstrated ('so long as Zeus holds sway/The doer suffers'). The emotions of the public are engaged so that they are, as Aristotle said, 'purged of Pity and Terror' in much the same way as in a public trial and execution – but without killing anyone. I have discussed this at some length in *Fact in Fiction* (Rockwell: 1974). In this way, literature is not only an interpreter of the life and norms of a society, but functionally a substitute or shadow version of them, and this is of fundamental importance in repeating and indoctrinating the norms, old or new.

But having admitted that literature is didactic, we must also grant that it is many other things besides. Partly a real mirror of society, but certainly also partly a mirror of wishes and dreams, which make life tolerable for many. And while this may have the quietistic effect of soothing the populace as well as informing them, thus reducing the potential of social upheaval (otherwise it is hard to know why so many governments subsidise TV and radio), it must be said that the enjoyment of even imaginary pleasures is a good thing. If a dying man in a strait-jacket dreams that he is taking a walk in the woods, he is likely to be happier than if he knew the real situation; and his apprehension of 'reality' is valuable to him.

It has often been noted that the fantasies of fiction, like the forms in which it presents them, show a surprisingly consistent relationship to the type of society which produces it. Giambatista Vico noted in *The New Science* (1744) that different literary forms were attached to eras: specifically the Heroic Epic, such as the Homeric Poems, appear in clan societies in which the ruling strata are heroic warriors, the basic value is honour and reputation (*arete*), the economic basis is self-sustaining agriculture, in large households, and there is continual traffic in overseas trade and raiding expeditions. To this we may add that the Icelandic Sagas, which are very similar, are attached to a society with many identical traits, including that of 'competitive excellence' of the warrior heroes in many skills not now considered particularly distinguished – such as the ability to plough a straight furrow, one of the proud boasts of Agamemnon, King of Men.

This consistency of form holds also with other societies: thus peasant and in general small-scale groups have traditional exemplary tales, and also a massive body of practical advice in the form of proverbs and sayings ('Hoot-im-hand, geht durch das ganze Land'), the drama appears with the city-state where an audience can be collected (and all Greek cities had a theatre), the picaresque is typical of the breakdown of social relationships at the end of the middle ages, while the novel appears with printing, cheap paper, the spread of literacy, and all the related phenomena which accompanied the rise and establishment of bourgeois capitalism. Ian Watt demonstrated this in an absolutely convincing way in *The Rise of the Novel* (1957) and also the relationship of the values of the novel to the philosophical individualism which preceded, accompanied, and is characteristic of the bourgeois view of the world. Cinema, radio and TV – the mass media – are also of course characteristic of advanced industrial societies, both because of their technological complications, and because of the massive investment necessary to establish them and keep them going.

The relation of form to types of society is relatively easy to establish; what is rather more difficult, and also more important, is the relation of values. Vico went so far, in 'The Search for the True Homer' as to say that Homer as an individual poet never existed, but the so-called 'Homeric' poems were rather the expression of the genius of the whole Greek people over a period of several hundred years. The miasmic view of literature–that it 'arises' like a mist from society in general–is an unfortunate reification of the true perception that literature has a real and regular relationship to society. Scholars have been at pains to point out the complex structure and formal literary devices of epic poetry, including the Saga literature, and come to a conclusion, equally fallacious in my view, that these are individual works of literature, similar to modern novels, and attributable to poets who had no particular social purpose but were producing simply 'superior entertainment'.[1] With respect to this type of literature, I think a more reasonable view must be that traditional material, family or historical chronicles, were shaped by a poet or series of poets into the form which has come down to us, but that it is absurd to say that Snorri Sturlusson 'wrote', for example, *Egils Saga* in the sense that Tolstoy wrote *War and Peace*; and that these stories, by describing in narrative the actions of human beings and implying or stating what was right and what was wrong, transmitted these norms to their own people, and thus give us a clue as to what the norms were for them.

We can never hope to understand wholly the values of a society so radically different from our own as, say, classical antiquity in Greece and Rome, and still less the vast cultures of the Orient. We too are bound to our own time, although we have a wider spectrum of possible comparison. We view other cultures and their literature through our own ideas of what constitutes 'reality', and also what constitutes 'morality'. The monstrous events in the house of Atreus – child-sacrifices, cannibalism, the murder of a husband by his wife and of a mother by her son – could hardly appear in our society except in terms of criminal pathology; while two other crimes in the same series, considered most grievous by the Greeks: the seduction of a brother's wife and the abuse of a guest 'while he crouched a piteous suppliant at his hearth' – a breach of the Law of Host and Guest and thus tantamount to a crime against the gods, or blasphemy – we can hardly take so seriously. The *way* this guest was abused, by being tricked into eating his own children's flesh, is almost inconceivably serious to us – but we would hardly count it as blasphemy. Our first task in approaching such themes must be to note their profound differences from the values of our society, and the second must be to refrain from trying to judge them by our standards. That is, we must support the proposition that literature is attached to its *own* society.

At the same time, we must note what topics are selected for literary treatment in various societies, and draw some conclusion from this. The novel, for instance, which deals with ordinary life, depicting as Dr. Johnson said 'accidents that daily happen in the world, and influenced by passions and qualities which are really to be found in conversing with mankind' is said to be realistic, in contrast with the chivalric romance, the epic, or other previous forms. However, it takes very little observation of the content of the novel to show that it is an art form, which unlike the real world with its infinite multiplicity of phenomena and events, selects a very small range out of the myriad possibilities, to deal with. The majority of all novels written are stories of courtship and marriage – the standard conclusion of the majority of novels could be expressed as 'and then they lived happily ever after'. This means that on the whole they deal with a few years in youth and early adulthood at most, though sometimes, especially in the 19th century, they begin in childhood, and sometimes in our own time especially they begin *after* marriage and are concerned with a rearrangement of partners. This is very unrealistic, in terms of the average normal life-expectancy. Another theme of the novel is success – establishment in life in terms of the acquisition of money, coinciding on the whole with success in courtship. Thus Tom Jones inherits a fortune and gets the girl, and in our own day Lucky Jim gets a super-job and gets the girl. This again does not correspond to any average norm of what really happens to most people. What it does correspond to, though, are the bourgeois norms of individual aggrandisement, individual choice in marriage, the individual private conscience as the final arbiter of right and wrong (in contrast to the heroic society where *reputation*, or what is said by others, is the final arbiter). The novel, too, is full of realistic touches, descriptions of daily life, although very rarely of daily work (we see Mr. Morel at home, but never follow him down the mine) and credible conversations and relationships. A closer look, however, will show us that this apparent casual transcription of life is not neutral: it is highly selective for emotionally loaded or significant communications, presented in an artful way to further the purpose of the story – to let the young people get on with their courtship, the villains plot, and so on. In other words, far from being true to reality with its infinite jumble, it is no more realistic than troubadorial poetry, which also had a social basis in the fact that women were really locked up.

Like troubadorial poetry, the heroic epic, or any other literary form, the novel is a faithful reflection of the norms of society, and the vast quantity of tendentious literature shows that it is also available as a means of changing them. But its so-called realism is really only a reflection of the fact that one of the bourgeois norms *is* a 'realistic', pragmatic, hard-headed view of the world, so that the supporting details of novels generally try to be convincingly realistic, and in the

18th century novels were presented as true narrations: but this realistic detail is merely a top-dressing for the real content, which is the values of bourgeois society.

Literature, then, in my view, is not a luxurious extra, a decorative frill on society, or a segment of the 'superstructure' which is purely passive. On the contrary, it has consistently been a very powerful didactic force. It has this power because people learn from the actions of other human beings, whether real or imaginary. Literature appears in various forms consistently corresponding to various societal patterns, and thus can be said to 'arise from' various types of society; nevertheless, as Raymond Williams (1973) pointed out, culture has also its own traditions. It often is 'about' previous societies: the story is placed in the past, so that it cannot be checked by the reader against daily life. Moreover literature has its own tradition and develops in terms of the influence of one literary work on another, without necessarily dipping down into society. In any case all fiction, including the realistic novel, is an art-form with its own requirements, and thus never an accurate transcript of 'reality' – it selects for its own purposes from the myriad phenomena available in the world. Yet this selection is consistent within the normative framework available to the writer because of his life-experience within a particular society. Similarly, his audience is subject to various constraints of acceptability which also correspond to the societal norms. Therefore, although literature cannot be said to give a blue-print of society or nature at any given time, it can give us a certain amount of practical information (such as the state of technology, laws and customs in use at the time) but more importantly it gives us a chance to perceive, if not always to understand, the values and accepted behaviour of its own time and place.

University of Reading

NOTE

1 See, for instance, Magnus Magnusson's introduction to the Penguin edition of *Njals Saga.*

Joan Rockwell

REFERENCES CITED

Deutsch, Martin (1959), 'In Nuclear Research' in D. Lerner *Evidence and Inference*, Free Press, Chicargo.

Fischer, Ernst (1959), *The Necessity of Art*, Penguin, Harmondsworth.

Goldmann,Lucien (1967), 'The sociology of literature; status and problems of method' *International Social Science Journal*, 19, 4.

Rockwell,Joan (1974), *Fact in Fiction: the use of literature in the systematic study of society*, Routledge & Kegan Paul, London.

Watt, Ian (1957), *The Rise of the Novel*, Chatto and Windus, London.

Weber, Max (1904), Essay in *Archiv fur Sozialwissenschaften und Sozialpolitik* quoted by J. E. T. Eldridge 1971 in *Max Weber: the Interpretation of Social Reality*, Nelson, London, 78.

Williams, Raymond (1973), 'Base and Superstructure in Marxist Cultural Theory' in *New Left Review*, 82 (November/December) 3-16.

Structuralism

John Rutherford

A feature common to many of the different critical movements that have developed in the course of this century is a move away from the concentration on the author, his life and times, which marked nineteenth century criticism, to a concentration upon the work itself. Very few would now deny that this development was an important advance which has produced valuable results. After all, one can hardly expect to discover much about any phenomenon other than by examining it closely. Emphasising the author usually produced a rather peremptory type of criticism which, regarding the text as occupying a secondary position as an extension of the author, customarily talked about it in a vague, impressionistic way, lacking the methodological equipment to analyse it closely. Russian Formalism, Practical Criticism in England, New Criticism in the United States, and (somewhat late on the scene) the French Nouvelle Critique were all direct reactions against the often naive historicism that marked earlier thinking about literature.

Literary structuralism is a further development of this modern trend. It grew up in Paris during the early 1960s out of the Nouvelle Critique movement (it also has close links with Russian Formalism). Its principal instigator was Roland Barthes, who remains its most prominent figure amidst the numerous other students of literature who, in France and elsewhere, are now called structuralists. Literary structuralism's antecedents are not only to be found in other critical movements: it has also derived ideas and techniques from certain non-literary disciplines that have enjoyed spectacular advances in the twentieth century, in particular linguistics and anthropology. Structuralism has had but small influence on literary studies in England, where its insistence on the necessity for abstract theoretical thinking arouses grave suspicion, and indeed outraged hostility and steadfast incomprehension.

It is difficult to give an accurate brief summary of a movement as heterogeneous, recent, and large as structuralism. Literary structuralists themselves have never agreed on any coherent overall programme. Consistency and judiciousness have not been prominent among the virtues of a movement whose strength is its suggestion of exciting new ways of thinking; and so, understandably enough, it has tended to encourage the issuing of pronouncements that are as grandly sweeping as they are insecurely founded. Structuralists value stimulation above soundness, and regard being sometimes wrong as a less fearsome danger than being bored (and boring); and the project of shocking a firmly entrenched, complacent literary establishment has its own powerful attractions. Rather, then, than undertaking the impossible task of describing the whole movement, or even the work of one or two of its members, I shall try to extract certain interesting common tendencies from the often perplexing diversity of structuralist practice.

Structuralism is a general way of thinking that is by no means confined to literary studies. There are, perhaps, two ways in which it can be defined.

It can be seen as the conscious application of the notion of structure to the object of study. 'Structure' itself is a term that has been frequently used in literary criticism in general. It has often been made vaguely synonymous with 'form' as opposed to 'content'; but as understood by structuralists the word has a different, more precise meaning, embracing both 'form' and 'content', and establishing a much more complex relationship between them – for no rough-and-ready dichotomy of this kind can possibly be sufficient to describe the multifarious complexities of literature. Structure is not form, some kind of vessel into which content is poured, but rather an organised functioning system built up of interrelated elements. The structural study of anything consequently takes it as a system, attempts to distinguish its elements and to examine them in terms of the network of relationships within which they exist and which, to a large extent, defines them.

If structuralism is seen thus, then all natural sciences and many other disciplines (mathematics, logic, musicology) are structuralist activities by their very nature. Modern structuralism could more precisely be seen, perhaps, as the application of these principles to the study of cultural phenomena, where they had not previously been applied: first of all in linguistics, with Saussure; then in anthropology, with Lévi-Strauss; and now in literary studies, with Barthes.

An apparently quite different definition, which is now more commonly accepted, is 'the application to studies of literature and other cultural constructions of models developed in linguistics.' In fact this definition is quite close to the first one. No-one would deny that the inspiration of linguistics in the development of general structuralism has been powerful, indeed decisive, or that many of its most fruitful concepts have come from that source. This is natural enough: linguistics was the first and most clearly successful of the new disciplines to develop from structural principles. And literature is, after all, made of language. But according to the first definition, literary structuralism develops from a direct application of basic structural principles to the study of literature, working out its own methods from there, and regarding linguistics as one potential source of ideas among others. The second definition makes it all, in theory, immediately and exclusively dependent upon linguistics. Many structuralists have claimed that language is such a fundamental human process that it necessarily precedes all other cultural activity, and that linguistics must consequently be at the heart of all cultural studies. On the other hand, one can point to features of structuralist practice that do not support a definition purely in terms of linguistics – for example, the presence of ideas derived from music in Lévi-Strauss's work, and the influence of many of Lévi-Strauss's own ideas upon literary structuralists.

All structuralists at least agree in regarding literature as a sign-system. Their work, then, falls within the general science of semiology (or semiotics): that is to say, the study of the principles that make it possible for conventional sign-systems to carry meaning. Literary structuralism, is, in other words, a descriptive, theoretical poetics. And just as linguistics distinguishes between the shared general code that makes communication possible, and the specific acts of communication that take place – known respectively by Saussure as *langue* and *parole*, by Chomsky as competence and performance – and regards the former as the goal of investigation, so structural poetics is concerned with the general literary code, or set of unwritten rules and conventions that enable people to write and read poems and novels: in short, with literary competence. The institution of literature depends in the first instance, of course, on language; but linguistic competence alone is clearly insufficient for the comprehension of a literary text. Modern poetics is principally concerned with the elusive quality of 'literariness', which distinguishes literary discourse from all other uses of language.

A literary work is seen, then, not as a unique, autonomous structure, but as belonging within, and dependent upon, the general system of literature; for however much of an individual genius an author may be, he still has no choice but to use the interpersonal mediating sign-systems of language and literature. The discussion of the organisation or structure of a text is not, then, in itself necessarily a structuralist activity, even though it is often mistakenly presented as one. Structuralism is no mere haphazard tracing of isolated pretty patterns. The properly structuralist analysis conforms with certain requirements; above all, it attempts to discover general principles characterising literature as a whole, in order that it may bear upon the theory of literature that structuralism is elaborating; at the very least, then, the terms of the analysis should be able to lay some claim to general applicability and relevance. So structuralist enquiry is distinguished from other modern critical methods in that it pushes on beyond the individual text towards the general shared code of rules and conventions upon which all texts depend. Close textual analysis is essential; but not for its own sake, or as an attempt to define the special characteristics of each text or author, but rather as a step towards a general understanding of the functioning of literary discourse. Theoretical considerations take priority; hallowed critical procedures like interpretation and evaluation are regarded as of merely ancillary concern – the goal is not to offer new interpretations and evaluations, but rather to find out about the operations involved in such procedures.

It is important to note that literary competence, like linguistic competence, is to a great extent possessed and practised intuitively. Whether an author consciously intended a given effect, or indeed had any precise awareness of the means of achieving it, is of very little interest, simply because people do not need to know how a system works in order to be able to use it efficiently. This is not to deny the creative skills of writers. It is just that the poetician will normally wish to avoid speculation about immediate causes, without necessarily denying that other kinds of literary scholars may well find it worthwhile to study them. This approach is, in terms borrowed from linguistics, synchronic rather than diachronic; he wants to know what makes it possible for the system to work, regardless of the historical developments that have given rise to the system. And structuralists regard the literary message from the standpoint of its reception rather than its production, since the notion of literary competence is much more readily approached through the reader's performance than through the author's.

It will be clear by now that structuralism vigorously opposes what might be called the 'reverential' approach to literature, which regards it as something too singular and ineffable to be subjected to close analysis or theoretical discussion. There is a move in structuralism, indeed, towards objectivity and precision in method, towards a markedly scientific approach. Its vocabulary is not only ideally (though not always in practice) precise, but also often technical, abstract, difficult and innovatory. It has frequently been attacked on these grounds, quite unreasonably; literature is a rich and complicated phenomenon, and there is consequently no reason to believe that simple, straightforward, matter-of-fact talk about it, using the vague vocabulary under which literary criticism has long laboured, can carry us very far towards a fuller understanding of it. In this respect, and in many others, there is much in modern poetics that goes radically against some of the basic assumptions of traditional, and indeed recent literary criticism. Yet the structuralist enterprise can incorporate much work done by non-structuralists, and in doing so give it new relevance.

Although the ultimate aim of poetics is the elucidation of the concept of 'literariness', it has to make its approach through the analysis of individual texts. Several different kinds of approach have been tried. One is to view the text from the standpoint of a completed reading and see it as a whole structure possessed of a certain unity (but not, of course, of any autonomy). Such a structure is inevitably so complex that it is necessary to break it down into various constitutive substructures for separate consideration: so that a poem can be seen as an interplay of patterns of sound, metre, syntax, imagery, and so on; and a narrative text can be broken down into components such as character, description, and story. Story, particularly, has attracted much structuralist attention, probably because it is a relatively firm, positive and definable aspect of narrative literature; and the idea of the 'grammar' of story has provoked much discussion. Such a grammar sets out formally and explicitly the principles that inform literary stories; they guide readers' intuitions about, for example, whether a narrated sequence of events constitutes a complete and well-formed story, and shape their expectations of any new narrative work they begin to read. In very broad terms, stories involve a succession of conflicts between human situations and actions which threaten to alter them, all held together in a tight chain of causality; this is the pattern which we have absorbed as a result of exposure to literary stories and which we keep in mind as we read any new story, assigning appropriate roles to characters, situations and actions accordingly, and so stringing the whole narrative together. Structuralists, and Russian Formalists before them, have analysed this particular aspect of literary competence in great detail.

Another structuralist approach to a text is to explore the various mental operations a reader performs on it (usually unconsciously) as he reads through it, in order to make it make sense to him. In the particular case of story structure I have already indicated the lines upon which such a reading proceeds. There are some more general fundamental literary conventions which inform our expectations of any text we read and hence our reading of it. One is, of course, that a literary text has unity, that its different parts fit together somehow to form a coherent, satisfying whole. Another is that a text has meaningful things to say about experience; that the fictional world it describes stands in some special way as a microcosm of the world of real experience. As we read, then, we seek to organise the text around an abstracted core of themes (that is to say, more or less universal features of human experience) which we find manifested in the text in various guises; a literary reading is, then, thematic and symbolic, and revolves around the construction of networks of associations. Furthermore, and most importantly, such a reading proceeds under the expectation that these patterns of theme, symbol and association will be particularly rich, intense, and cohesive; it will seek not just unity and meaning, but indeed the greatest possible degree of both.

The code of literature is, of course, very much more complex and interesting than I have been able to suggest. I have only, in the most general and approximate terms, mentioned some of its obvious fundamental rules. These are the broad outlines of the kinds of expectation that experienced readers of literature take to poems and novels, and that are, on the whole, amply satisfied in what structuralists call 'classical' texts (in general terms, those of the seventeenth, eighteenth and nineteenth centuries). Literary reading is, then, itself a process of structuring, of finding in one text a repetition of patterns found previously in other texts; we always attempt to make any succession of words labelled 'poem' or 'novel' conform to such patterns. The reader could almost be envisaged as a machine programmed by his experience of 'classical' literature to fit a text together like some kind of superior mental jig-saw puzzle that, once solved, gives a special, privileged access to Truth. Such a notion has given rise among structuralists to a fascination for texts that in some way actively resist such structuring, rather than encouraging it (and so imply less confident or optimistic views of the meaning of life). Much twentieth-century literature has been of this unco-operative, uninterpretable, or 'unreadable' type: works that readers find deeply disconcerting because they defy basic expectations, and will not allow themselves to be seen as neatly patterned constructs embodying clear, comprehensible meanings.

The struggles between many modern poems and novels that refuse to 'read' easily, and the determined, undismayed pattern-seeking of their readers, are certainly most revealing. Confronted by, for example, Lorca's famous *Romance sonámbulo* ('Sleep-walking ballad'), critics have been most unwilling to take the author's word for it that 'there is a strong sense of things happening, an acute dramatic atmosphere, and nobody knows what is happening, not even me, because the mystery of poetry is a mystery, too, for the poet who communicates it and who is often in the dark about it.' The ballad starts:

Verde que te quiero verde.	(Green I want you green.
Verde viento. Verdes ramas.	Green wind. Green branches.
El barco sobre la mar	The ship upon the sea
y el caballo en la montana.	And the horse on the mountain.)

It continues in enigmatic, apparently allusive language; all that is clear is that three people are involved; a gypsy girl waiting on a moonlit balcony for a young man, who arrives, wounded, and unsuccessfully begs a second man in the house for shelter. The ballad ends with the girl in a pool and the Civil Guard knocking at the door. Story grammar, however, requires more detailed specification of states and actions, and of the relationships between them; and critics feel a clearly irresistible compulsion to make the ballad tell a definite story, in other words to impose a closed, determinate narrative structure upon it. But the narrative possibilities of the text itself are so open – so little is given – that there are almost as many stories as there are critics. And so a young smuggler is caught in the mountains by the Civil Guard and wounded escaping from them; they follow him to his girlfriend's house where her father refuses to hide him, and she kills herself in despair (or, in variant versions, falls into the pool while sleepwalking, or while under the hypnotic influence of the moon). Or a husband finds out about his wife's adultery, waylays and mortally wounds her lover in the street without revealing his identity, returns home and drowns his wife, and then torments the lover when he comes to spend his dying moments in the company of his beloved. Or two men (Lorca himself and his close friend Salvador Dali, we are confidently assured by one critic) find their relationship threatened by the woman, who is therefore disposed of. And so on. Reading the ballad at the level of narrative is, in all these examples, a process of searching for, and finding, at any cost, one specific structure of character, situation and action that conforms with the rules of story grammar; each critic, I note in passing, furthermore feels impelled to claim that his story is the real story.

But the structuring activities of readers go further than this. A text must not only tell a story; it must also say something definite and important about life. This text is about a dream world, to be sure, and that is a way of explaining its illogicalities; but this explanation is by itself insufficient, since it says nothing about the particular nature of the illogicalities of this text; why 'verde que te quiero verde' and not 'negro que te quiero negro'? So critics proceed to make it meaningful, by constructing themes and symbols in it; and since the rules for these operations are rather more permissive than those for story construction, the results of the exercise are even more diverse. Hence the colour green symbolises strength, vigour and vitality; and the lines I have quoted become the girl's thoughts about her lover (who will arrive either in a boat or on horseback). Or green is the colour of nature, and the lines are the narrator's description of an idyllic coastal scene. Or green is the colour of death, and the lines are spoken by the grief-maddened husband as he contemplates the body of the beloved wife he has just murdered. Or green is an earth-symbol, and the poem expresses a chthonic view of life as a circular, earth-bound process. Or green represents equivocal sexuality, or fatality, or coldness, or hope . . .

A structuralist might conclude that some of these readings are more in accordance with the conventions of literary discourse than others (a full study of the whole text would be necessary to indicate exactly in what ways); but that all these critics are equally mistaken in their hurry to construct definitive interpretations, since this is, precisely, an 'unreadable' text – one which presents an interplay of many darkly suggested possibilities, none of which is confirmed. To single out any one of these possibilities is to do violence to the text, to impose a closed order on a structure which is essentially open, and which rejects the very principles of order. It is not only, in fact, modern texts which resist definitive interpretation in this way; there is in all literature an element of 'unreadability', a core of resistance to the mind's longing for precise patterns, soothing symmetry, absolute order, and clear meaning; the principle of resistance has been intensified rather than invented by modern writers. For literature is essentially the discourse of doubt rather than of affirmation. And the extraordinary ingenuity of interpretations by critics intent on reducing rebellious texts to structured and meaningful conformity is itself eloquent testimony both to the patterning powers of the human mind in general and to the energetic vitality of literary competence in particular.

These last considerations provide an interesting illustration of the complex relationship between structural poetics and other disciplines that study man and his activities. In one sense the structuralist development in literary studies moves them away from neighbouring disciplines in its vision of literature as a system of signs rather than a reflection of the world or an expression of man. Its reaction against historicism also seems to dehumanise it, and obviously makes it a target of attack from the Marxist viewpoint. Yet at the same time it does insist that literature is a social institution rather than pure individual creation; and it does finally return to historical considerations such as the concept of the 'classical' text as an expression of a confident general outlook characterising particular societies during a certain stage in their development. All this suggests that structuralism does not so much seek to sever relationships with sociology and history as to destroy an inadequate, simplistic historicism and put in its place the possibility of a more sophisticated and accurate definition of the social functioning of literature. What structuralism does reject is the view, so often found in sociological approaches, that literature is a more or less simple, passive reflection of society. This cannot be correct, for literature has a life of its own; it is a separate, active sign-system with its own principles and conventions. It is essential, therefore, to analyse the internal workings of this system with great care before attempting to trace its inevitably complex relationships with other systems, such as that of society. If this condition is satisfied, there is no reason why the structural analysis of literature should not lead on to valid and interesting discussion of its relationships with social structures, relationships which are necessarily hidden to more casual, unsystematic approaches. For example, structural analysis isolates and defines a text's core of themes, distinguishing them from the other areas of human experience to which it also refers, but which the analysis can show to be merely accessory. These themes, alone powerful enough to generate the text, can be expected to represent dominant cultural codes and to express social values. And generally structuralism attempts to demystify literature, and so makes it possible to show in precise detail how it can propagate the views of certain social classes, whether its creators intend it to or not. This propagation is particularly powerful and insidious because the traditional view of literature holds it up as something sacrosanct and above mundane concerns. Poetics, refusing to stand back in reverent awe, is evidently by no means incompatible with Marxism, after all. Its emphasis on the primacy of synchronic study does not exclude the possibility of historical work. This is a methodological point, which is taken from linguistics: that for any tracing of the historical development of a system to be possible, analyses of that system at different points of time have first to be made, and then compared. And, to return to the concept at the heart of structuralist poetics; though it may be that literary competence has some inherent, universal characteristics (this itself is not above dispute), it is quite clear that it is to a very large extent historically conditioned, changing with social changes.

But if the structuralist enterprise is, as its enemies claim, anyway misconceived, then none of its results is likely to have any validity, and it is irrelevant to discuss whether they point to a close relationship between literature and society or to a tenuous one. And if structuralist poetics is to be taken seriously, then anyone concerned with literature from any viewpoint would want to take it seriously, even if it pointed towards negative conclusions about his own particular approach. Is structuralism, then, merely a passing fad, or on the contrary an important, radical advance in our thinking?

Many structuralists have seemed to make the case for literary semiotics rest on their claim that it is no less than a new human science. Pursuing the analogy with studies of language, they argue that just as theoretical linguistics is the science of language, so structuralist poetics is the science of literature. Poetics is clearly not a science at the moment, in any accepted sense of the word; there is far too little general agreement about methods, aims, and terminology. But these are very early days. Might poetics continue to flourish, consolidate, and finally develop into a science, as many structuralists hope? The thought is attractive in many ways; but it seems to me highly improbable that any such thing will happen. For so much in literature (in fact nearly all of what is most interesting and particular) is incorrigibly elusive and ambivalent. I have already referred to the convention that literary discourse is peculiarly rich and intense; poems have been described as 'language at full stretch'. This plurivalence, which we look for when reading literature and which is a central feature at least of 'classical' texts, is in large part based on figurative usages like symbol, metaphor, and irony. Such usages all have in common the fact that they always involve processes of interpretation that are not only extremely complex but also – and here is one of the poeticians' most challenging problems – apparently open-ended. In all these processes the associative meanings of words are more important than their conceptual meanings: that is to say that the word 'toad', for example, appearing in the context of literary discourse, is likely to stand for qualities that in our experience are common to toads (baseness, ugliness, repulsiveness, wretchedness, and so on) in the first place, and only secondarily for a tailless amphibian of the genus Bufo; green, as we have noticed, seems in a literary text to mean anything but the neutral concept of 'that colour which is placed on the spectrum between yellow and blue'. In scientific discourse, on the other hand, conceptual meaning is dominant over associative meaning; everyday discourse tends to mix the two fairly indiscriminately. Indeed, association is commonly so dominant over conceptualisation in literary texts that the rules of conceptual meaning are continuously contravened in order that associative meaning may assert itself more freely. Metaphor, for example, works in this way – to say that someone is a toad is nonsense in terms of conceptual meaning. Now conceptual meanings are relatively stable and intuitively clear – though linguisticians have found that even these are resistant to scientific study. Associative meanings, on the other hand, vary considerably from individual to individual, society to society, age to age: for they depend upon people's knowledge and belief about the universe. The study of literature, then, in which associative meanings are essential, even arguably definitive, therefore necessarily involves considerations so disparate and limitless – quite simply the whole of experience – that it cannot ever become scientific. No study can be scientific that cannot be delimited and defined.

It is, of course, true that associative meaning is by no means a completely random phenomenon; nor is literary interpretation a totally subjective activity. It is constrained by certain conventions within the public system of literature, and by the particular features of whatever text is being interpreted: both central concerns of structuralist analysis. But after such analysis has shown certain interpretations not to be permitted by the rules of literary discourse, there is still bound to remain a large area of doubt, about which nothing definitive can properly be said, and which must ultimately be surrendered to the intuitive reactions of the reader. And no science can be based on intuitions. At the centre of the system of literature there is an unassailable secret redoubt of mystery and fascination, which ensures the system's continuing vitality.

Such negative conclusions about the scientific pretensions of some structuralists need not lead us to the other, despairing extreme: to the view that no worthwhile or meaningful discussion of literature is therefore possible. Students of literature can and sometimes do test their results by airing and discussing them, and consensuses can be reached; structuralism encourages such tendencies. And linguistics itself may, after all, also depend ultimately on intuition since, like poetics, it is concerned not with material objects but with cultural phenomena, which only exist as such in so far as they mean something to people. Having said this, I must go on to state that a linguistician does, in practice, work with sentences about whose meaning and 'well-formedness' there is no serious disagreement, since he usually chooses to examine simple and corrected forms of everyday speech. He thus works with the kind of fixed, solid, positive, definable data on which a science can be based. This is not true of the poetician; and so it seems to me that here the analogy between linguistic and literary studies breaks down. If we ignore the references everyday language makes to the world in order to be able to study it scientifically as a self-contained system of signs, as the theoretical linguistican does, there is still quite enough left – syntax, phonetics, semantics – to make such a study worthwhile and interesting. The processes of reference and association are so essential to the workings of literature, however, that to simplify it by leaving them out of consideration would remove so much at its centre as to denature it; and the results of any approach that does so can consequently be expected to be, at best, partial and modest in scope.

Studies of very restricted areas of literary concern – like, for example, stories, about whose 'well-formedness' people are able to come to firm conclusions, and which do have a system of internal relationships that it is worth studying in isolation – can, then, perhaps aspire to some kind of scientific status. But literature, as a whole, is a type of phenomenon that is not studiable scientifically. We need not be at all dismayed by this conclusion. Scientific knowledge is not the only valid kind of knowledge; in any case, none of the social or human sciences is, of course, a science at all in the way that natural sciences are; and the ideal of perfect objectivity and absolute rigour cannot be fully achieved even in the latter. The question, made in absolute terms, whether a given discipline is scientific is perhaps not the appropriate one to ask; maybe we should rather ask the relative question about how much use it is able to make of scientific methods.

Certainly a most salutory move in the direction of scientific method is one of the achievements of literary structuralism. It recommends that we be as objective, rigorous and systematic as we can in our observations, and as precise and explicit as possible in our recording of them. I regard this as a highly desirable corrective in a subject which suffers from a tradition of uncontrolled, self-indulgent impressionism, loose, vague terminology, and lazy thinking.

The simultaneous broadening and intensification of vision that is a result of structuralism's insistence on the importance of theory is also, I feel, welcome and needed. A consequence I have been unable to consider is the concern in structuralism to subject the conventions of its own discourse, as well as those of literature, to constant critical scrutiny. Traditional literary studies have been for too long complacently content to concern themselves with matters that are of merely esoteric, incidental interest. For the most part they have succeeded only in amassing sundry information about the writers of literature and their works, producing as the result of far more accumulated scholarly toil than I can or would like to imagine a vast anthology of anecdotes, a sprawling mountain of unordered material; amidst all this haphazard erudition, any advances towards an explanation of the literary phenomenon itself have been modest and inconspicuous. Literary studies were badly in need of the challenge of this new, exciting, and demanding approach, whose difficulties should be regarded as a merit rather than as a defect, and whose theoretical basis brings them into profitable contact with those other disciplines that are concerned with cultural phenomena. Ultimately the various semiological activities offer us the prospect of a better understanding of ourselves, in their vision of man the sign-maker, the pattern-maker, the sense-maker.

One of the attacks most commonly made on structuralist poetics is that it destroys literary values by examining them too closely and coldly. To retort that values which cannot withstand close examination are false values that ought to be destroyed would perhaps be a little unfair (but only a little). Yet by encouraging us to concentrate on specifically literary qualities, to explore the inner workings of the literary sign and pay less attention at first to its mimetic aspect, structuralism can enhance our reading. Reading, in the structuralist view, is a confrontation between the possibilities of the text and the expectations and needs of its readers; that is to say it is activity, construction, play, rather than passivity, reception, contemplation. We should therefore allow the text to play its special and fascinating game with us for as long and as fully as may be, postponing the foreclosure necessarily entailed by definitive interpretation. Pre-structuralist criticism's concentration on the text itself was an important advance upon concentration on the author. Yet it can be argued that it did not go far enough. For a text only comes into being as literature when it is read; it cannot by itself say anything; it is no more than what its readers make of it. By focussing attention on the processes of reading, structuralist poetics can increase both our understanding and our enjoyment of literature.

The Queen's College, Oxford

John Rutherford

NOTES ON FURTHER READING

Jonathan Culler (1975), *Structuralist Poetics*, Routledge & Kegan Paul, London. By far the best general introduction to the subject. It presents a full discussion, critical but fair, of all the major issues. Essential reading.

David Robey, ed., (1973), *Structuralism: An Introduction*, Oxford University Press. A series of papers, some of great interest, delivered as a course of lectures by structuralists in various fields.

Roland Barthes (1970), *S/Z*, Seuil, Paris. An analysis of Balzac's *Sarrasine* in terms of the reader's structuring activities as he progresses through the text. Probably Barthes' most important single contribution to literary structuralism.

Tzvetan Todorov (1969), *Grammaire du Décaméron*, Mouton, The Hague. A stimulating brief work on story grammar.

Jonathan Culler (1974), *Flaubert: the Uses of Uncertainty*, Paul Elek, London. An often brilliant application of structuralist and Sartrean ideas.

Roland Barthes and the English Tradition

Philip Thody

Roland Barthes is often considered a difficult author to understand. This is mainly because he chooses to write in a curious, alembicated style, with a wealth of neologisms and a plethora of subordinate clauses. It is also, for an English or American reader, because his frame of cultural and literary reference is so exclusively French, and because even there he disdains to make his points by reference to the better-known works of French literature. When, for example, he wanted to attack the view that Balzac's novels were realistic in the sense that they gave an account of what life was really like in Restoration France, he did not talk about *Le Père Goriot* or *Eugénie Grandet*. He discussed a minor and not very well known short story called *Sarrasine*, and devoted a whole book – *S/Z* (1970) – to analysing the way that it merely projected the illusion of reality by conforming to the ready-made notions already existing in the readers' minds. In point of fact, however, Barthes's ideas on literature are not particularly hard to grasp, and are not, for an English reader who knows his Eliot or his L. C. Knights or for an American reader with even a nodding acquaintance with the 'New Critics' of the nineteen-thirties, particularly original. Where he is nevertheless interesting is in the link which he establishes between literary criticism and the more systematic ways of looking at human experience embodied in the ideology of Marxism, the ideas of Freud, and the new intellectual disciplines of structuralism and semiology.

Thus in 1968, Barthes published an article rather grandly entitled *La Mort de l'Auteur* (The Death of the Author). In it, he declared that the 'scriptor' (*'scripteur'*) – he refuses to use the term 'author' on the ground that it implies an acceptance of the bourgeois view of the individual as all-important – has in him 'neither passions, humours, feelings or impressions. Only this immense *écriture* (writing, verbal activity) which can never cease' (Barthes 1968: 12-17). The terms may be unfamiliar but the idea is not. T. S. Eliot expressed the same attitude in 1920 when he pointed out in *The Sacred Wood* that 'Impressions and ideas which are important for the man may have no place in his poetry, and those which become important in his poetry may play quite a negligible part in the man, the personality'. Neither is Barthes's idea, when translated into more comprehensible language and illustrated by specific examples, a particularly contentious one. Strindberg's *The Father* would be no better and no worse as a play if Strindberg the man had been the happiest of husbands. Indeed, the dismissal of the neo-Romantic view that a work of art is good if it sincerely expresses what the author himself actually thought and felt has been a truism in Anglo-Saxon literary criticism for some sixty years.

It is in a way a reflection of the intellectual insularity of French literary culture that Barthes should be regarded as a revolutionary thinker for stating such obvious notions. When placed in the context of French post-war philosophical discussion, however, he does fit into quite an interesting general development, and shows how close the relationship is in France between literary discourse and philosophical thinking. To begin with, he carries on where Lucien Goldmann left off. Thus Goldmann had argued, both in his discussion of Jansenism in *Le Dieu Caché* (1955) and in his book on the modern novel, *Pour une Sociologie du Roman* (1964) that it was totally mistaken to see the individual as the sole or even the main creative force as far as works of the imagination were concerned. When Pascal sat down to write the *Pensées* or Racine *Andromaque*, the former may have thought he was trying to convert people to Christianity and the latter may have been convinced that he was emulating Euripides. In fact, however, both were expressing something which quite transcended them as individuals: the contradictory situation in which the *noblesse de robe* (legal nobility) had been placed by the King's decision to deprive them of their earlier importance by entrusting the government of France to the new class of permanent civil servants known as the *Intendants de Justice, de Police et de Finances*. Similarly, Alain Robbe-Grillet may have thought he was exercising a predominantly aesthetic preference by choosing to write about objects rather than people. In fact, however, he too was merely the articulate midwife ensuring the intellectual delivery of something much larger than him personally: the decline in importance of individuals under the impact of the technocratic bureaucracy of late capitalist civilisation.

Barthes does not acknowledge these similarities, but they are obvious to any outside observer. So too is the coincidence between his vision of the disappearing author and the statement which Michel Foucault made at the end of *Les Mots et les Choses* in 1966: 'Man is an invention which the archaeology of our knowledge can easily show to have been of recent origin. And which may also shortly disappear' (Foucault 1966: 398). Like Claude Lévi-Strauss, who stated in *Le Cru et le Cuit*, in 1964, that his aim was to show 'how myths thought themselves out in men, without men knowing what was happening' (Lévi-Strauss 1964: 20), Barthes is a structuralist in that he takes it as axiomatic that the way men think is much more important than what they think. Thus his principal thesis in his book on Racine, whose publication in 1963 was later to spark off a major row in French literary and academic circles[1], was that the underlying patterns in Racine's play are all reducible to the same basic model. At the beginning of human society, he argues, men lived in tribes. Only the chief, the original father, the leading dominant male, had the right to possess and enjoy the women, and his sons (or other junior members of the tribe) did so very much at their own risk. The more aggressive sons naturally rose up against this tyranny, and tried to establish their independence through a revolt against the father. The more submissive obeyed his rule, albeit reluctantly, and waited until he was weak before trying to challenge the Law which he incarnated. The more audacious rebelled before the time was ripe, and were, as Barthes elegantly puts it, *'impitoyablement tués, châtrés ou chassés'* (pitilessly slain, castrated or driven out) (Barthes 1963: 20).[2] When the old man is eventually killed, quarrels break out among the sons for the possession of his wives and authority.

The basic relationships within primitive early society were thus those of power, possession, jealousy, rivalry, punishment and revolt; and, argues Barthes, it is precisely this structure which provides the emotional underpinning for the imaginative universe which Racine created in his plays. If, he maintains, one looks at Racine's plays as they really are, phenomenologically, one might say, and thus without any preconceived ideas as to his debt to the Greeks, his relationship to Port-Royal, his supposedly tumultuous private life, his acceptance of the neo-classical doctrine of the three unities, one always sees the same pattern emerging: there are those who are identified with power and are truly virile – even, he maintains, if they are (like Agrippine in *Britannicus* or Roxane in *Athalie*) biologically female; and, in contrast, there are those who are weaker, but who nevertheless try to escape from the Old Law, from the Authority of the Tribe, and establish themselves as sons, fathers and human beings in their own right: Pyrrhus in *Andromaque*, Pharnace and Xipharès (albeit in contrasting ways) in *Mithridate*, Néron in *Britannicus*.

Naturally, Barthes maintains, the pattern does not recur in absolutely the same form in every play. It is nevertheless always accompanied by the 'typically Racinian' situation in which A has all power over B – Pyrrhus over Andromaque, Mithridate over Monime, Roxane over Bajazet – but is not loved by them in return. This is, indeed, a transposition of the kind of primitive emotional universe Barthes describes, since one can easily imagine cases in the primitive human horde when the younger women were not all that keen on being reserved exclusively for the Old Man of the Steppes. But the fact nevertheless remains – according to Barthes – that the fundamental structure of Racinian tragedy varies only superficially from play to play: it always contains relationships characterised essentially by force and authority; and it deals with a revolt that is frequently accompanied by feelings of guilt. For, argues Barthes – clearly if unconsciously following Freud – the son who rebelled against the father for the possession of the women generally felt guilt at what he was doing. Similarly, in *Phèdre*, the main character feels guilty over her love for Hippolyte – she, too, of course, is presented as an aggressive, masculine-type woman, of the kind which Barthes describes as *viriloide*–and so interiorises her guilt that she commits suicide. If we follow these recurring patterns in Racine's plays, suggests Barthes, we shall in fact discover a gradual rejection of the idea of revolt, culminating in the punishment of Athalie (another virile, rebellious woman) and the triumph of the authority figure of Joad. So that if we, as readers of Barthes's essay, insist on reverting to the old-fashioned idea of the author as a real person and link this pattern to Racine's own career, we can see this rise, fall and punishment of the rebel as a reflection of his own initial attempt to escape from Port-Royal and his final repentant return to the fold.

If we use *Sur Racine* as a basis for defining Barthes's version of structuralism, we shall arrive at something like the following statement: What matters in a work of art is not the author's conscious intentions; these are irrelevant, as are most of the objectively ascertainable facts of his life and the aesthetic which he thought he was adopting. What matters are the patterns which recur in his work, its fundamental emotional structure, and this is something over which the author himself, in the last resort, has very little control. The patterns and structures in Racine's plays depend for Barthes upon the survival in the writer of the kind of collective unconscious which Jung identified as lying at the heart of the myths and legends which are common to all people. Any value which we may find in an author's work depends, in the aesthetic implied by *Sur Racine*, not on its similarity to our own experience and certainly not on the skill of the author in creating characters. It does not stem from the beauty of his language or the persuasive power of the images and metaphors he uses, from his ability to recreate a vanished epoch or depict the true workings of society, from his psychological perspicacity, or from the originality of his moral vision. It is not a result of his power to evoke emotions in the reader's mind of the honesty and perception with which he analyses and comes to terms with his own past experience and it certainly has nothing to do with his ability to use established literary forms. In the case of Racine, for example, Barthes dismisses his skill in handling the alexandrine as a mere epiphenomenon. What really matters is the reproduction, in apparently original terms, of the earliest psychic history of mankind. Almost by definition, this is something of which Racine's conscious mind could have known absolutely nothing. The theory of the 'primitive horde' is a late nineteenth century, post-Darwinian concept, and there is every reason to believe that Racine shared Bishop Bossuet's view that the world was created in exactly 4004 B.C. It is nevertheless from the basic situation whereby individuals define themselves in terms of their loyalty towards the most ancient discipline of the tribe that Racine's theatre derives what Barthes presents as its greatest aesthetic quality: its coherence. Barthesian structuralism would thus seem to be the search for the repetition of coherent but unconscious patterns in an author's work, irrespective of his conscious intentions. It celebrates 'the death of man' and 'the death of the author' by showing how little control an individual has over his creations.

Even in *Sur Racine*, however, Barthes is not a particularly original thinker. He himself admits, in a footnote at the beginning of the book, that he owes a good deal to the work of an earlier, Freudian critic called Charles Mauron. This is indeed obvious the moment one opens Mauron's *L'Inconscient dans l'Oeuvre et la Vie de Racine* (1957) and finds the same insistence on violent, possessive, Jocastian females, fleeing Oedipal sons and inadequate fathers. Where an unrepentant Anglo-Saxon empiricist such as myself finds Mauron's approach preferable to Barthes's is in the fact that Mauron does not believe sufficiently in 'the death of the individual' to ignore the fascinating question of why these unconscious patterns recurred in the work of so apparently conscious an artist as Racine. Mauron exploited the well known facts about Racine's life – he was an orphan, brought up by an aunt in the austere moral atmosphere of the Jansenist stronghold of Port-Royal-des-Champs; he expressed his defiance of the values inculcated into him during his childhood by writing for the theatre but eventually returned to the fold – to substantiate the validity of the Freudian approach, and this attempt to prove a case by specific facts makes Mauron's book a good deal more convincing than Barthes's. It can, of course, be an interesting experiment to write about an author while pretending to know nothing at all about his private life or conscious intentions. It may even be a valuable corrective to the insistence of some academic critics on trying to explain everything in an author's work by reference to his glands, his marriage, or his childhood vision of something nasty in the woodshed. But Barthes's approach, especially but not solely in the Racine book, has one enormous disadvantage: it greatly reduces the reader's and the critic's intellectual curiosity. It is all very well to consider a work of art as a machine. This is the view implied by the definition which Barthes gave of the structuralist approach in 1964: to provide a working model which made the more complex patterns of the original artefact more fully comprehensible (Barthes 1964: 214). But even machines are sometimes ingenious and beautiful enough to invite legitimate speculation about the men who made them.

It is perhaps a mark of the intensely French nature of Barthes's intellectual make-up that he should carry the Eliot/New Criticism attitude to such extremes. Where an English critic suggests that it might be more useful to concentrate more on the poem and less on the man, Barthes unhesitatingly condemns as bourgeois any hint that the biographical approach of earlier scholars might have anything at all to be said in its favour. The same similarity of general approach, coupled with the same contrast in intellectual attitude, recurs in the second way in which Barthes's ideas on literature reflect, in a more strident and intolerant form, views which have long been commonplace in English literary criticism. Thus the general argument in *S/Z* runs very close to the opinions expressed by L. C. Knights in 1930 in his famous lecture *How many Children Had Lady Macbeth?* Both critics reject what one might call the mimetic illusion: the view that literature works because it reproduces events or emotions which actually occur or occurred in real life; and both substitute for it the attitude which Dr. Knights expressed when he wrote that 'a poem works by calling into play, directing and integrating certain interests'.[3] But whereas Dr. Knights quotes Hugh Walpole's remark that 'the test of a character in a good novel is that it should have existed before the book that reveals it to us began, and should continue after the book is closed' to illustrate the view he is rejecting, Barthes gives his readers no such help. Instead, he divides Balzac's *Sarrasine* into 561 *lexias*, or units of reading, and analyses each of them in terms of the five codes into which he claims that the statements in the short story can be classified. He also gives each of these an impressive neo-classical abbreviation: HER stands for hermeneutics: the art of deciphering mysteries. SEM is short for *sème*, the unity of meaning in semantics. SYM stands for the symbolic value of a word or phrase. ACT involves both action and what the Greek rhetoricians called the proairetic, the ability to think before taking action. REF, for referential, describes sentences which work by virtue of an accepted code. His basic idea, however, is much less complicated than his terminology seems to imply, and can be most conveniently explained by an example from economics. When paper money was first introduced, its value was officially guaranteed by the gold and silver in the possession of the bank or government issuing it. Nowadays, however, this fiction has been abandoned. The value of a pound note depends on the belief which people have – or, more frequently, do not have – in such complex factors as the productive capacity of British industry, the Bank note, the likelihood of future inflation or of industrial unrest. A solid guarantee to pay twenty silver shillings has been replaced by a structural network of beliefs and acts of faith, by the ability of pieces of paper to act as meaningful counters within an accepted monetary code. There is nothing behind a pound note to guarantee its purchasing power. This stems solely from its acceptability within a particular financial system.

Similarly, within the history of the novel, readers can be supposed to have begun by believing in the story because its authenticity was guaranteed by what actually happened in real life. Early novelists encouraged this idea by presenting their story as something 'found among the papers' of a real person, or told by a particular narrator. In the nineteenth century, the readers of *Le Père Goriot* were solemnly assured by Balzac that 'All is True', and evidence of how widely accepted this particular belief continues to be can be found in the immense amount of industry and critical ingenuity that has been spent by critics of Flaubert's or Proust's work in endeavouring to discover who the 'real' Madame Bovary or the 'real' Baron de Charlus were. A more sophisticated awareness of how fiction works has nevertheless begun to take the place of this out-dated belief that the authenticity of the story is guaranteed by a solid core of real truth, in the same way that the gold in the vaults of the Bank of England guaranteed – in happier days – the value of the pound sterling. We now see – and this is where Barthes and L. C. Knights converge – that stories work, as money works, by reference to a general code. We understand what happens in a novel less because of our experience in the real world than because we have read a lot of other novels. We know, in other words, what to expect when the novelist presents us with a mysterious old man, a beautiful girl or a handsome, misunderstood young man. Like money, the codes of fiction circulate because of a general belief in their meaning and validity, because of the consistency of the structure within which our mind works, because of the network of presuppositions within which we are accustomed to make sense out of our own experience. If we look critically for what actually happens in a novel, all we shall find is an emptiness, what Barthes calls, in *Critique et Vérité*, '*le sens vide qui les supporte tous*', (the empty meaning which supports them all) (Barthes 1966: 57). We are like the Peer Gynt who thought that he could find the centre of the onion by stripping off the overlapping layers of skin but found, in fact, that there was nothing there. Like onions, works of literature exist by virtue of the inter-relationship of their constituent parts, not because a solid centre forms a strong support for everything that they contain.

Another way of realising how relatively unoriginal Barthes's theory of the novel is in *S/Z* is to reflect on the activities of the Sherlock Holmes Society or on the state of mind of those listeners to the BBC who write and ask whether they can spend their holidays at Ambridge. In both cases, the mimetic illusion on which Barthes claims that earlier theories of literature were based is being called into question: in the first case with conscious humour, since nobody really believes that a flesh and blood Holmes actually lived at 22B Baker Street; in the second, by a rather pathetic belief on the part of people whose normal life needs to be made more interesting by the conviction that a pastoral idyll is based on empirical facts. We are frequently encouraged, according to Barthes, to take the illusions of literature for normal reality by the dishonest way in which the writer tells his story. Time and again, in Barthes's submission, the eminently cultural activity of telling a story is presented by the writer as absolutely natural. The writer endeavours to reproduce ordinary language, introduces swear words, makes his characters speak ungrammatically, and generally does everything possible to disguise the fact that all modes of story-telling are equally unnatural in the sense that each is profoundly influenced by the culture in which both the writer and his presumptive readers happen to be living. This is a form of cheating which Barthes denounced in the very first book he published, *Le Degré Zéro de l'Ecriture* (1953), and for which he proposed the remedy implied by the words which the Roman actor carried on his mask: *Larvatus Prodeo* (I come forward pointing to my mask). Writers should, in other words, constantly accept and proclaim the artificiality of their calling, and for once there is an excellent illustration in Barthes's own work of what he means by this. It is contained in the first essay, "*Le monde où l'on catche*", in what is still the best and most comprehensible of all his books, *Mythologies* (1957). It is in this essay, an analysis of all-in wrestling as brilliant in its own way as the famous description in Kingsley Amis's *Girl 20*, that Barthes's interest in popular culture coincides with his views on literature, and that he illustrates, with a clarity found nowhere else in his work, just what he means by semiology.

The principal point which Barthes makes is that it is wholly misleading to see the actions and gestures performed by the all-in wrestlers as in any way reflecting a real struggle. They do not indicate something which is really happening in the way that the stroke made by a cricketer is integrally bound up with his decision to send the ball through the slips rather than through the covers. Like the gestures made in the traditional *Commedia dell' Arte*, they form part of a highly formalised system of communication in which there is never any serious pretence that the events depicted on stage are really taking place. They are, to use two of the many words of Greek origin to which the popularity of Barthes's work has given new currency in France, diacritic and not mimetic in nature. They do not imitate reality. They sketch out patterns. And they represent themselves from the very beginning as wholly arbitrary and artificial. No all-in wrestler expects the audience to believe him when he performs the ritual of stamping on his opponent's face, or writhing in agony when hit in the stomach, only to recover fast enough to win victory by an aeroplane twizzle two minutes afterwards. He is, to take up the classical reference already mentioned, exactly like the Roman actor whose motto was *Larvatus Prodeo:* I come forward pointing to my mask. The great virtue of all-in wrestling, from a Barthesian standpoint, is that it perfectly epitomises the famous Saussurean principle of the arbitrary nature of signs. Since there is nothing behind the gestures which the all-in wrestlers make, no real pain or genuine violence, then there is absolutely no reason why delight should not be expressed by tears, or fury by a broad smile and an enthusiastic hand-shake. No reason, that is to say, apart from the need to make the audience understand, to enable the spectators to rejoice in a world that is, for once, absolutely legible and wholly unambiguous.

Quite whether all-in wrestling matches should be taken as a paradigm for all future literature is perhaps a more open question than Barthes's literary criticism would sometimes imply. Indeed, one of the great problems for English readers of Barthes's work is that of deciding when he is using language in a descriptive or prescriptive sense. There can be few authors whom one would more willingly send to read philosophy at Oxford in the hope that they might learn the difference between 'is' and 'ought', and it can be truly said of him that he raises far more problems than he or anyone else will ever be able to solve. Perhaps, however, this is a mark of an original thinker in what are

Philip Thody

nowadays called, in an interesting Gallicism, the human sciences. The down-to-earth methods of the English empiricists are doubtless right, but they sometimes tend to seem a trifle dull. Barthes, in contrast, has a flash and flamboyance which make you think.

University of Leeds

NOTES

1 In 1965, Raymond Picard published a pamphlet entitled *Nouvelle Critique ou Nouvelle Imposture* denouncing *Sur Racine* for its inaccuracies and pretentious obscurity. The attack evoked a considerable amount of comment in the literary press, and Barthes replied in 1966 with *Critique et Vérité*. A full account of the quarrel is included in my forthcoming book, *Roland Barthes: a conservative estimate*, Macmillan. Especial consideration is given to the claim frequently advanced by Barthes's admirers who alleged that Picard's attack was part of a right-wing plot to eliminate any new tendencies in French criticism and maintain the bourgeois ideology prevailing at the Sorbonne. I share the view expressed on 23.6.1966 by the reviewer in the *TLS*: Picard was concerned not with politics but with accuracy.

2 Barthes's own preoccupation with castration is a partial explanation for his decision to analyse *Sarrasine*. Balzac's short story describes how an eighteenth-century French sculptor fell in love with a beautiful Italian known as La Zambinella only to be horrified by the discovery that 'she' is a *castrato*.

3 L. C. Knights's pamphlet was based on a lecture given in King's College, London, and published by the Minority Press, Cambridge in 1933. It does not seem to have been republished.

REFERENCES CITED

Barthes, Roland (1953), *Le degré zéro de l'écriture*, Editions du Seuil, Paris. (English edition, *Writing degree zero*, Cape, London, 1967).

Barthes, Roland (1957), *Mythologies*, Editions du Seuil, Paris. (English Edition, *Mythologies*, Cape, London, 1972).

Barthes, Roland (1963), *Sur Racine*, Editions du Seuil, Paris. (English Edition, Hill and Wang, New York, 1964).

Barthes, Roland (1964), *Essais critiques*, Editions du Seuil, Paris. (English edition, Northwestern University Press, Evanston, Illinois, 1972).

Barthes, Roland (1966), *Critique et vérité*, Editions du Seuil, Paris.

Barthes, Roland (1968), 'La mort de l'auteur', *Mantéia*, 5, Marseilles.

Barthes, Roland (1970), *S/Z*, Editions du Seuil, Paris. (English edition, Cape, London, 1975.)

Foucault, Michel (1966), *Les mots et les choses*, Gallimard, Paris. (English edition, *The order of things*, Tavistock, London, 1970).

Roland Barthes and the English Tradition

Goldmann, Lucien (1955), *Le dieu caché*, Gallimard, Paris. (English edition, *The hidden god*, Routledge & Kegan Paul, London, 1964).

Goldmann, Lucien (1964), *Pour une sociologie du roman*, Gallimard, Paris. (English edition, *Towards a sociology of the novel*, Tavistock, London, 1975).

Lévi-Strauss, C. (1964), *Le cru et le cuit*, Plon, Paris. (English edition, *The raw and the cooked*, Harper & Row, New York, 1969).

Mauron, Charles (1957), *L'inconscient dans l'oeuvre et la vie de Racine*, Editions Ophrys, Gap.

NOTES ON FURTHER READING
OTHER WORKS BY BARTHES

Barthes, Roland (1954), *Michelet par lui-même*, Editions du Seuil, Paris.

Barthes, Roland (1967), *Elements of semiology*, Cape, London.

Barthes, Roland (1967), *Système de la mode*, Editions du Seuil, Paris.

Barthes, Roland (1970), *L'empire des signes*, Albert Skira, Geneva.

Barthes, Roland (1971), *Sade, Fourier, Loyola*, Editions du Seuil, Paris.

Barthes, Roland (1975), *The pleasure of the text*, Hill and Wang, New York.

Barthes, Roland (1975), *Roland Barthes par Roland Barthes*, Editions du Seuil, Paris.

WORKS ON BARTHES

There have been a number of critical studies on Barthes in French. The best of these, Stephen Heath (1974), *Vertige du déplacement: lecture de Barthes*, Fayard (Collection Digraphe), contains an excellent bibliography. The special number of *Tel Quel* (47, Autumn 1971) on Barthes also has a very full bibliography. So too does the special number of *Le magazine littéraire*, 97, February 1975. Other critical studies include L. J. Calvet (1973), *Roland Barthes. Un regard politique sur le signe*, Petite Bibliothèque Payot; and Guy de Mallac and Margaret Eberbach (1971), *Barthes*, Editions Universitaires.

Of particular interest are the two articles which Barthes devoted to biblical texts and which have not yet been reprinted in Barthes's work: 'L'analyse structurale du récit: à propos de Actes X-XI' in *Exégèse et herméneutique*, (Rapports) Association Catholique Francaise pour l'étude de la Bible. Congrès 2. Chantilly 3-7 September 1969, Seuil, 1971; and 'La lutte avec l'ange: analyse textuelle de Genèse 32, 23-33' in *Analyse structurale et exégèse biblique*, Barthes, R. et autres, Delachaux et Nietslé, Neuchâtel, 1972.

Structuralism and the revival of rhetoric

Stephen Bann

Ten years ago, the French critic Gérard Genette explained the difficulty of defining the contribution of Structuralism to contemporary critical theory in terms which still appear relevant:

> Certainly, as a method structuralism is committed to studying structures everywhere it meets them; but in the first place structures are not by any account objects which one meets, they are systems of latent relations, conceived rather than perceived, which analysis constructs in so far as it picks them out, and which it sometimes risks inventing in the belief that it is discovering them; and secondly, structuralism is not only a method, it is also what Cassirer calls a 'general tendency of thought', which others might more brutally describe as an ideology, whose function is precisely to assess structures at the expense of substances, and which may therefore overestimate the explicative value of the former. (Genette 1966: 155).

Any attempt to encompass Structuralism as a 'general tendency of thought' within the bounds of a short article is foredoomed to failure. In 1963 Roland Barthes performed the feat when he drew his map of 'structuralist activity', taking as his governing principle 'not man the possessor of particular meanings, but man the fabricator of meanings.' (Barthes 1964: 218). But this brilliant, if schematic, characterisation of *homo significans* – man the maker of signs – has been followed subsequently by a host of more detailed studies which comment upon and attempt to synthesise the overwhelming variety of structuralist work in progress.[1] In one of the most recent, Jean-Marie Benoist goes so far as to claim the existence of a 'structural revolution', as a result of which psychoanalysts, anthropologists, political theorists, literary critics and intellectual historians have all learned to take as their 'methodological presupposition' not man himself, but the *signs* which he produces.[2] Such a perspective can only be lightly indicated in a study of this kind. But it can scarcely be ignored. One of the chief reasons why debates about the utility of Structuralism in literary analysis have acquired their particular stridency in Britain is because of this latent, or barely concealed, element of ideology, which provokes defensive or over-protective responses at the very hint of the term. Yet the pious hope that the structuralist challenge will evaporate if we turn our heads resolutely in the other direction is surely no nearer to realisation. The merry-go-round of Anglo-Saxon criticism is not revolving so speedily and securely on its axis as to be able to throw off the intruder.

Precisely because of this hostility, it seems worthwhile to begin by stressing the traditional associations of the structuralist method, which can legitimately be represented not as a novelty but as a reassimilation of techniques which had dropped out of the critical armoury. Among the ways of confronting 'the problem of literary structuralism' would be an investigation of its philosophical implications, as Francois Van Laere suggests when relating Husserl's notion of 'placing in parenthesis' to the structuralist approach (Van Laere 1970: 55). Anthropology would also provide a way in, as Genette recognises when he defines the work of literary critics in terms of Lévi-Strauss's notion of 'bricolage' (Genette 1966: 145-49). Building upon the fact that Lévi-Strauss's own structural anthropology borrows many of its principles of classification from structural linguistics, we might well feel that a survey of modern developments in linguistics and semantics was essential to any fundamental grasp of the problem. Fortunately this task is performed with exemplary lucidity by Jonathan Culler in his *Structuralist Poetics* (1975). A further possibility, and the one adopted here, is the consideration of structuralism under the general rubric of 'revival of rhetoric'. This emphasis has the advantage of bringing out the considerable debt of structuralist criticism to the innovatory work of the Russian Formalists in the early part of the century.

Both Tzvetan Todorov and Gérard Genette, who as critics and co-editors of the French journal *Poétique* have played a pivotal role in the structuralist movement, have written in an illuminating way about the decline and revival of rhetoric as a technique for describing and interpreting literary texts. In his lengthy appendix to *Littérature et signification*, Todorov shows how the study of rhetoric was discarded by poets and critics, and became progressively detached from the science of linguistics, in the course of the 19th century. The assumption that there was a 'natural' language, in opposition to the language of rhetorical figures, fell into discredit with the coming of the Romantic movement. For the Romantics, 'all is natural or all is artificial, but there is no zero degree of writing, no innocent writing' (Todorov 1967: 97). Consequently, it was impossible to maintain the traditional concept of the rhetorical figure, which had been seen essentially as an elaboration of, or a divergence from, this neutral linguistic base. Genette, writing a few years after Todorov, can already point to a group of three recent studies which indicate the reversal of this decline.[3] His approach is particularly valuable because it traces the long history of 'restricted rhetoric', in which the figure of metaphor came to be employed as a general term covering virtually every type of 'image': it is followed by a subtle exploration of Proust's 'metonymy within metaphor' which amply demonstrates the utility of 'expanding' our rhetorical categories (Genette 1972: 21-40, 41-63).

Of course the development which Genette describes and exemplifies would be dubious, not to say archaistic, if it were simply a matter of resurrecting the categories that most schoolboys have learned to abandon with relief in the closing pages of Kennedy's *Shorter Latin Primer*. Indeed some of the opposition to structuralist method seems to be based on the view that it is reintroducing the tyrannical pedantry of a Renaissance rhetorician like Puttenham. In order to counter this impression, it is worth stressing the radical difference in procedure, even while accepting that many of the terms remain the same. Just as the rhetorical figure can no longer be seen as an elaboration or a divergence, so the critic's role is no longer simply one of identifying or describing it – as a choice specimen of linguistic aberration. Jonathan Culler is quite right to shift the emphasis from mere identification to interpretation; for this purpose rhetorical figures offer themselves to a critic not as descriptive categories but as strategies to be put into operation;

> Once we begin to think . . . about interpretive operations as ways of making sense, we find that we can bring under this heading all the displacements which classical rhetoric, approaching the matter in a different perspective, defined as forms of expression. Instead of thinking of metaphor, metonymy, synecdoche, etc. as ways of saying one thing and meaning another, we can take these figures as the names of possible interpretive moves one can make when confronted with a textual problem (Culler 1974: 31).

A good indication of what this distinction means in practice can be found in the comparison of two recent works which employ rhetorical categories in analysing historical texts: Hayden White's *Metahistory* and Peter Gay's *Style in History*. Gay is chiefly content to locate and quote characteristic instances of rhetorical usage in particular historians – for example, the persistent use of anaphora in Macaulay. But he stays with the implication that these are simply expressive effects, aimed at convincing Macaulay's public. White's approach, on the other hand, is to take the four major tropes of metaphor, metonymy, synecdoche and irony (so formalised by Vico) as strategies for explaining the overall organisation of historical texts. The tropes are seen not merely as local expressive effects but as methods of defining and characterising the historical field in accordance with the epistemological and critical perspective of the historian.

The fact that Hayden White also employs Northrop Frye's categories of tragic and comic emplotment brings to mind the point that the revived rhetoric owes something to American New Criticism as well as to European antecedents. Indeed one critic has suggested that Structuralism in general can be seen as reproducing the – not entirely satisfactory – approach of the New Critics.[4] But, by comparison with the New Criticism, the Russian Formalists can be shown to have had a far more comprehensive grasp of the problems of literary texts as well as having been incomparably more aware of the need to conciliate a diachronic and a synchronic approach. Those who identify Structuralism with this precedent are, often quite explicitly, choosing to depreciate both. Conversely, those who attempt to plot the convergences and continuities of formalist and structuralist practice (as Robert Scholes has done in a useful introductory article)[5] make us aware of an evolving debate which touches upon the most lively issues of contemporary criticism.

The positive arguments for considering Russian Formalism in the light of the revival of rhetorical criticism can be simply enumerated. Lubomir Dolezel, who has traced important links between the Russian group and their precursors in Germany, puts the point with precision:

> Both the German and Russian representatives of 'compositional' analysis were firmly convinced that in literary scholarship solid *description* is preferable to far-fetched interpretations. 'Immanent' poetic devices and structures, rather than the poet's intentions or the reader's responses should assume the central place in the study of literature. It is precisely in these features that 'compositional analysis' manifests itself as a 'rhetorical' and, more generally, 'Aristotelian' trend. (Dolezel 1974: 82).

Tzvetan Todorov, who himself introduced the French public to the Russian Formalists in a collection of translated texts dating from 1965, pays no attention to this German precedent. But he also notes the significance of Formalism as a Neo-Aristotelian tendency, remarking that the first published anthology of the Russian group reintroduced to currency the Aristotelian term of *Poetics*. For Todorov, the initial determination to view literature in terms of its 'literariness' leads to the possibility of establishing a genuine 'poetics', that is to say, 'the system of literary discourse in so far as this is the generative principle behind any and every text' (Todorov 1973: 9). Todorov's own immensely fertile work, together with the journal which he and Genette chose to call *Poétique*, are dedicated to this objective.

Stephen Bann

To illustrate the implications of this programme, and its reference to the precedent of Formalism, we must look briefly at two of Todorov's own studies. *Littérature et signification*, which incorporates the discussion of the revival of rhetoric as an appendix, is in effect a study of Laclos's *Les Liaisons Dangereuses*. But Todorov uses this 18th century novel – composed according to the convention of successive letters sent between the protagonists – as a pretext for examining the models of communication in the fictional work. His scheme of *enunciation*, which breaks communication down into the elements of sender, receiver, context and contact, derives from the linguistic theories of Roman Jakobson, an original member of the Russian group: his 'homological model' for representing the intrigue of the novel is taken from Lévi-Strauss's analysis of myth (with some demur). It is also fair to add, as a counter to those who claim that the structuralists are ignorant of British intellectual life, that Todorov employs Austin's notion of the *performative* in his differentiation of types of discourse.

Clearly a reader who expects to gain a vivid impression, let alone an evaluation, of *Les Liaisons Dangereuses* from this study will be disappointed. What he will gain, however, is an acute sense of the basic problems of literary signification, which the epistolary novel, by its very nature, brings to the forefront. Another of Todorov's important works, the *Introduction à la littérature fantastique*, builds on the investigation of genre distinctions pioneered by the Formalists, and in particular takes up Jakobson's challenge to investigate 'transitional genres' (Scholes 1973). Todorov subtly discriminates between the categories of the 'fantastic', the 'uncanny' and the 'marvellous', on the principle of what degree of 'reality' a reader is impelled to attribute to the events described in a series of 18th/19th century narratives. But whereas the 'uncanny' and the 'marvellous', are shown to be 'pure' genres, the 'fantastic' is defined as the product of 'a certain hesitation, felt by reader and character alike':

> . . . they have to decide whether or not what they perceive has its source in 'reality', as this is commonly understood. At the end of the story, however, the reader, if not the character, does come to a decision, he opts for one solution or the other, and by so doing he abandons the domain of the *fantastic* (Todorov 1970: 83).

Todorov's distinctions not only serve as an adequate instrument for contrasting and comprehending the set of stories under review. They also help to refute the claim that structuralist method is unhistorical.

For it is precisely the life and death of an unstable genre, in its particular epistemological context, that is rendered meaningful by Todorov's scrupulous attention to the nuances of response.

Todorov's debt to Jakobson, in particular, among the Russian Formalists leads us to investigate in however summary terms the contribution of this long-lived and remarkable scholar to the heritage of Formalism and Structuralism. Apart from his famous definition of 'literariness',[6] Jakobson has contributed both general procedures and analytic instruments of extreme precision to modern critics. Among the former, his discrimination between the metaphoric and the metonymic modes of discourse holds a place of importance. In advance of Genette's conclusion that the rhetorical figures have been reduced to the sole category of metaphor, Jakobson suggested in 1962 that there are basically two orders of discourse: the metaphoric – in which associations by substitution predominate – and the metonymic – in which syntagmatic associations predominate. To the former category belong, for example, Romantic and Symbolist works, Surrealist painting and the films of Charlie Chaplin; to the latter, the epic, the Realist narrative and the films of D. W. Griffith. Of course the central purpose of this distinction (in line with Genette's view of the overvaluing of metaphor) is to draw attention to the fact that the analysis of metonymic discourse has been virtually ignored; or rather, that as yet the metonymic character of such crucial categories of work has not in itself become the basis of analysis.

As Roland Barthes claims in his *Elements of Semiology*, Jakobson thus opens up one of the most fruitful possibilities for the passage from linguistic concepts to the critical analysis of types of discourse in society (Barthes 1967: 60-61). One could also maintain that, in drawing attention to metonymy not simply as a figure, but as an associative procedure for achieving the unity of particular types of discourse, Jakobson is challenging literary critics to explore that 'endless labyrinth of linkages' which Tolstoy declared to be the 'essence of art'. (Shklovksy 1973: 71).

Jakobson's development of phonological analysis in the investigation of poetry is perhaps the most highly evolved aspect of his critical method. Yet serious objections have been made to the validity of this technique of applying minute linguistic analysis to a text without paying adequate attention to the structures generated by the act of reading. Jonathan Culler puts the case in the following way, when he discusses Jakobson's critique of the Shakespeare sonnet, 'Th' Expense of Spirit':

If one assumes that linguistics provides a method for the discovery of poetic patterns, then one is likely to blind oneself to the ways in which grammatical patterns actually operate in poetic texts, for the simple reason that the poems contain, by virtue of the fact that they are read as poems, structures other than the grammatical, and the resulting interplay may give the grammatical structures a function which is not at all what the linguist expected (Culler 1975: 73).

It is probably fair to say that Jakobson's concern to illuminate the 'innermost ties between sound and meaning' is vindicated most successfully when his chosen text offers relatively simple grammatical and thematic structures. Thus his analysis of a poem by the 13th century Portuguese troubadour Martin Codax has the force of a genuine revelation, precisely because his disclosure of the symmetrical distribution of phonic and grammatical elements helps to concentrate our reading attention on the simple variations and repetitions which constitute the poem (Jakobson 1973: 20-25).

Apart from the continuing research of Jakobson, the existence within the Soviet Union of a flourishing school of 'Neo-Formalist' criticism is a further sign of the way in which Formalism continues to nourish contemporary investigations. In the field of poetic analysis, the contribution of Iouri Lotman has been outstanding. Lotman has been a professor at the University of Tartu (in the former territory of Estonia) since 1963: his work builds upon the critical theories of Formalist precursors like Propp and Brik, as well as those of Jakobson. Starting from a definition which situates art within the total spectrum of linguistic usage as 'a remarkably well organised generator of languages of a particular type'. he proceeds to develop a semiotic interpretation of literary texts which is capable of extension to any system of signs fulfilling an artistic function.[7]

Another important aspect of contemporary work in the Soviet Union is the analysis of narrative structure pursued by such scholars as Y.K. Scheglov, which is now becoming available to British readers through the admirable periodical *Russian Poetics in Translation*. A direct precedent for this type of systematic analysis can be found in the work of M. A. Petrovsky's seminar on narrative composition which flourished in the 1920s. A. A. Reformatsky's analysis of a short story by Maupassant, which results in a detailed 'formulaic scheme' of the development of the plot, is explicitly designed to contribute to the formation of a 'poetics' which has not yet reached the stage of generalisation (Reformatsky 1973: 85). If we compare it with Scheglov's 'Towards a description of detective story structure', we can immediately note the transition from particularised study of narrative craft to the construction of generative models underlying a whole range of examples (in this case, the Sherlock Holmes corpus). Scheglov has made good use of recent research in descriptive and transformational linguistics in order to establish models for the development of narrative structures (Scheglov 1975).

The formula which Scheglov employs for plotting the derivation of the 'general Conan Doyle theme' against the *genre* constraint of the detective story (Scheglov 1975: 10-11) calls to mind the audacious precedent of the Formalist Vladimir Propp, whose influential study of the morphology of folktales involved the reduction of a large group of narratives to a limited series of 'functions'. In Propp's case, the presupposition that these 'functions' combined in different ways to create the apparent diversity of the genre led him to posit the existence of a 'single source' or 'unitary schema of composition' from which the individual variants could be derived. Propp's scheme has been attacked, by Lévi-Strauss among others, because it fails to make clear whether this 'single source' was a concrete one, in the historical sense, or merely a methodological presupposition. Scheglov's use of transformational schemas, which are obviously the latter and employ sophisticated concepts like 'concretisation' and 'intensification' for tracing the generative path, effectively avoids this objection.

In all events, the problems posed by Propp's methodology are not directly applicable to literature, since (as Todorov has emphasised) the conditions of production for a folktale and a literary text are significantly different (Todorov 1971: 17). This does not, however, invalidate the contribution of the great Formalist critic Viktor Shklovsky, who constantly varies his rhetorical analysis of the literary text with the introduction of narratives and motifs from folklore. Shklovsky's formulations are often deliberately paradoxical, and he provokes strenuous opposition in his ostentatious emphasis on 'devices' (that is to say, rhetorical strategies) to the detriment of 'content' (Shklovsky 1973: 71). But if his vivid and idiosyncratic essays lack the systematic qualities of the work of the Petrovsky seminar, they still continue to provide imaginative fodder for critics.

A specific case of his influence can be found in *Littérature et signification*, where Todorov introduces his formulation of the rules which govern human relationships in two widely differing works: Boiardo's *Orlando Amoroso* and Pushkin's *Eugene Onegin*. Shklovsky discerns in both of these narratives the pattern: 'If A loves B, B does not love A. When B begins to love A, A no longer loves B.' As Todorov insists with reference to his own similar rules for *Les Liaisons Dangereuses*, it is through exact formulations of this kind that we can begin to undertake comparison between the 'laws which govern the universes of respective books' (Todorov 1967: 66). Shklovsky's analysis may seem to be merely an exercise in reduction. But the dividend in this technique, as in all his rhetorical analyses, is that it enables a direct correlation between the expectations of readers and the formal features of the fictional 'plot'. As Jonathan Culler recognises, Shklovsky is always asking the vital question: What kind of structure satisfies our formal expectations? (Culler 1975: 223). The question could serve as an epigraph to Culler's own study of the problem of 'making sense', in which the various rhetorical strategies are seen as 'interpretive' rather than descriptive (Culler 1974: 36). Obviously Shklovsky's decision to remain on the interpretive level dispenses him from the type of criticism which Culler aims at Jakobson.

One of the most productive elements in Shklovsky's approach is his use of frequent transitions between the 'device' or specific rhetorical effect and the large-scale design of plot (or *syuzhet*). This is indeed the major theme of one of his most challenging articles: 'On the connection between devices of *Syuzhet* construction and general stylistic devices' (Shklovsky 1973: 48-72). In this study, Shklovsky is primarily concerned with the formal devices which he labels retardation, parallelism and 'staircase construction'. But the principle of transition from what might be called the 'micro-rhetoric' of specific figures and usages to the 'macro-rhetoric' of overall narrative construction is an endlessly fertile one. Awareness of even the traditional rhetorical categories as possible keys to overall structure, as well as to thematics, can disclose consistent patterns in an author's work. For example, I have argued elsewhere for the application of the figure of *chiasmus* as an interpretive strategy in analysing the stories of Kipling (Bann 1973: 62-83). The formulation of this figure as an ABBA structure provides a clue not only to certain recurrent themes (the 'deal' or exchange), but also discloses certain plots as 'mechanisms of exchange' (e.g. 'Dayspring Mishandled') and finally models Kipling's basic schema of communication. Such a strategy can also help in the elucidation of the links between different artistic enterprises of the same author. Ellipse would appear to be the recurrent figure employed in the poems and the novels of Meredith, though in the narrative form it reveals itself in the form of complementary tensions between *adjunction* and *suppression*, accumulation and loss.[8]

Of course the various aspects of formalist and structuralist method that have been isolated in the previous discussion are in no way mutually exclusive. It is evident that a contemporary critical analysis can make use of several in combination, together with other procedures that may or may not belong to the same arsenal. A summary of the different techniques which I have used in the study of a single text, Thackeray's *Henry Esmond*, may help to illustrate this point. *Henry Esmond* involves, so it would appear, a system of stable relations between recurrent terms which recalls Genette's schematic presentation of the relations between materials in Baroque poetry (Genette 1966: 34). The terms Sun/Moon/Stars form a triangle, from the basis of which other related terms take their place in the semantic universe of the novel. For example, the term 'Moon' can either be associated with the colour 'yellow', through the intermediacy of the moon goddess Diana, or, by association with its homonym 'Mohun' (the villain of the novel) with the colour of blood. A schema of this kind, albeit a simplification of textual complexity, has explanatory value in the sense that it underlines the metonymic connections between recurrent terms that Thackeray exploits throughout the novel. Far from representing a static reduction of the plot, it generates possibilities of 'shifting', as when the young heroine Beatrix's degeneracy is identified with her moving away from the beneficent influence of the Sun (her mother) to the sterile sign of the Star (the old Countess of Castlewood): the moment is marked by her wearing of the family diamond (also associated with 'Stars').

Use of a schema of this kind is therefore a way of coming to terms with the metonymic shifting which, in Thackeray at any rate, seems to be highly systematic. But the overall design of the plot can only be further understood if we describe the *relational functions* of the characters in a system which recalls, for example, Todorov's 'rules' for the characters of *Les Liaisons Dangereuses.* These functions can, I suggest, be formalised as a series of three possibilities of relationship:

I. A is linked to B (and B to C etc.) by the intermediacy of a pre-existent hierarchy (genealogy of the Esmond family: existing order of society etc.)

II. A is linked to B (and so on) in such a way as to pose a threat to this hierarchy (e.g. A, presumed superior to B, avows that he is his inferior, or *vice versa*).

III. A is linked to B by the intermediacy of a transcendent hierarchy (end of the novel, at which point Esmond has renounced his loyalty to the House of Stuart and emigrated to America) (Cf. Bann 1972: 75-76).

The formalisation of relationships within the novel in terms of these three successive functions helps us to see why certain apparently innocent details (such as the motif of confusion between mother and daughter) are actually integrated with the overall theme of the novel (Esmond's passage from subjection to liberty). Yet this pattern also leads us to question the generic status of the work as a 'historical novel'. Thackeray can be shown to have established his generic consistency precisely through an inversion of the terms of the Scott historical novel, briefly through replacing the fundamental motif of 'acceptance by the king' (cf. *Quentin Durward, The Fortunes of Nigel*, etc.) by that of 'renouncing the pretender'. Thackeray's reasons for 'emptying' the historical novel of its significance in this way require moreover to be considered further in the light of the relation of genre to historical context (as in Todorov's placing of the 'fantastic'), and finally in that of Roland Barthes' conception of the 'plenitude' of the classic text (Barthes 1970: 206).

The mention of Roland Barthes renders unavoidable a discussion of the role of this remarkable critic and writer in the general movement which has been traced up to this point. Although he has often applied himself to a specific pedagogic function – in *Elements of Semiology*, for example, or in the brilliant 'Par où commencer' with which he launched the first number of *Poétique* – Barthes has succeeded in mobilising opposition from sections of the academic profession where Todorov and Genette have largely avoided this. His *Critique et Vérité* was written in response to a forthright attack by the Sorbonne professor Raymond Picard. Picard's assault was primarily directed, as indeed have been several of the attacks on Barthes, against one of his first structuralist works, *Sur Racine*. But any tendency towards acceptance through familiarity has been corrected by the fact that, as Michel Butor puts it, Barthes always succeeds in writing the book which no one expected. Of his more recent works, the exhaustive analysis of a short story by Balzac, published under the title *S/Z*, is perhaps the most fruitful from the point of view of critical method. Conceived and to a great extent composed in the context of Barthes's seminar at the Ecole Pratique des Hautes Etudes, it subjects every sentence of Balzac's story to minute analysis in terms of five basic codes, while interrupting the commentary from time to time with passages of fascinating speculation. Reference is explicitly made to the medieval functions of 'scriptor', 'compilator', 'commentator' and 'auctor' which Barthes has duplicated in this extraordinary exercise.

If *S/Z* mirrors a pedagogic situation, Barthes' next major work, *Sade, Fourier, Loyola*, is offered as a subversive text from the point of view of academic conventions. Ideology–not the ideology of 'structuralist activity' proposed in 1963, but a so-called ideology of 'theft' establishes the unifying approach to the texts of Sadism, Socialism and Mysticism. Barthes is ready to claim, in a passage which recalls the attitude to bourgeois ideology defined in *Mythologies* (Barthes 1973: 139).

> 'In effect, there is today no place for language outside bourgeois ideology: our language comes from it, returns to it, remains shut in it. The only possible riposte is neither confrontation nor destruction, but solely theft: fragmenting the ancient text of culture, science, literature and disseminating its features according to unrecognisable formulae, in the same way as you paint over a piece of stolen merchandise...The intervention of a text in society (which is not necessarily accomplished at the time when the text appears) cannot be measured by its popularity with its audience, or by the fidelity of the socio-economic reflection which is inscribed in it or which it projects in the direction of a few sociologists anxiously on the look out, but rather by the violence which allows it to *exceed* the laws which a society, an ideology, a philosophy provide themselves with in order to be self-consistent in a beautiful movement of historical intelligibility. This excess has a name: *écriture.*' (Barthes 1971: 16).

Barthes' definition clearly represents a position far beyond any formal statement of structuralist 'method'. At the same time, in its concentration on the 'excess' of '*écriture*' (writing), it also takes as its first premise that primacy of the *signifier* over the *signified* whose very possibility of formulation refers back to Saussure's original binary distinction. And even if Barthes's virtuoso display of linguistics, rhetoric and personal *écriture* defies – is calculated to defy – formal presentation, it is worth noting that Julia Kristeva, of the French *Tel Quel* group, proposes a similar primacy of *écriture* while manipulating a formidable battery of theoretical concepts in her *Révolution du Language Poétique.* For Julia Kristeva, this emphasis has a specifically psychoanalytic justification, since it is the property of *écriture* to 'reach back into space-time previous to the phallic stage . . . and grasp the becoming of the symbolic function . . .' (Kristeva 1974: 131).

Both explicitly in Julia Kristeva, and implicitly in Barthes, the critical review of a text has come to depend upon a framework of advanced theoretical knowledge which incorporates the Neo-Freudianism of Lacan and the Marxism of Althusser as well as contemporary developments in linguistics. It is not surprising, in consequence, that Julia Kristeva should reveal herself as a critical as well as a perceptive commentator on the legacy of Formalism. This is the case in the preface which she wrote in 1970 for the French edition of the Formalist Bakhtin's study of Dostoevsky, and which she significantly entitled 'The ruin of a poetics' (Kristeva 1973: 102-19). For Julia Kristeva, Bakhtin's criticism was inevitably hampered because of the lack, in 1929, of a satisfactory theory of the language user. Her own work on the poetry of Lautréamont and Mallarmé is massively influenced by I. Fonagy's linguistic studies which reach beyond verbal communication to a 'more archaic language' which the poet accedes to through his use of rhythm and sound (Kristeva 1974: 258).

With Barthes and Julia Kristeva, we come inevitably to a stage at which the structuralist critique is not simply the 'analysis' of structures described by Genette but the inseparable concomitant of a 'tendency of thought'. Indeed the formidable backing of linguistic, psychoanalytic and political concepts which underlies the notion of *écriture* as it is instanced and practised by Barthes and the *Tel Quel* group almost inevitably summons up a reaction. Their critique is so total, so all encompassing, that it provokes the almost paranoid retreat into prepared positions. George Watson's article on 'Old Furniture and "Nouvelle Critique"', with its uproarious suggestion that we should prize Lévi-Strauss for his 'refined aphoristic mode', is a good example of this tendency (Watson 1975: 48-54). His choice of the title 'Old Furniture' for his attack is unexpectedly appropriate, since it leads us to infer, in the words of Hardy's poem of the same name:

> The world has no use for one today
> Who eyes things thus – no aim pursuing!
> He should not continue in this stay,
> But sink away.

George Steiner, who certainly could not be accused of underestimating the relevance of linguistics to literary criticism, has at the same time made successive attempts to redress the balance against what he sees as the excesses of Structuralism. In his essay, 'In a Post-Culture', he refers specifically to the debate about '*écriture*', praising 'the vivacity, the sheer critical intelligence with which such questions are being posed' but identifying them nonetheless with 'an unmistakable Byzantinism and malaise' (Steiner 1972: 170). In another context, he has attacked the disproportion between what he regards as the minor text of Balzac's *Sarrasine* and the excessive volume of Barthes' commentary. Finally, in a recent review of the structuralist Michel Serres' *Esthétiques sur Carpaccio*, he has roundly condemned 'the essentially exploitative stance, the use of a painting, a literary text, ethnographic situation towards ends which are solipsistic' (Steiner 1976: 243). Citing a number of critical questions which come to mind in the reading of Serres' text, he deplores that the tone of the argument militates against their resolution: he notes 'the appetite for normative universality which drives out, almost rules out such queries'.

Steiner's argument is essentially an ethical one, in favour of a sense of proportion, even decorum. To his complaint that the saddling of a short story with a monstrous critique is out of all proportion, the Barthes of *S/Z*, and certainly the Barthes of *Sade, Fourier, Loyola*, would respond with his definition of '*écriture*' as 'excess'. This would not satisfy Steiner, but at least it would establish unambiguously the ground of difference. In the case of Serres, the problem is less unequivocal. Steiner raises the question of whether the method used in relation to Carpaccio might not work, in so far as it does work, for other painters, and, if so, whether the urge for 'normative universality' has not allowed the critic to bypass what is specific in his subject. The question must remain open, since in fact it reproduces at another level that very question of the possibility of a 'poetics', a system underlying specific discourse, which the structuralists have chosen to explore. To be fair to Serres, it is worth recording that other aspects of his voluminous recent work, for example his essay on Turner, achieve a more equable balance between the proportions of the critique and those of the material treated.

If Steiner is concerned to expose the polar opposites in the 'great gap' between approaches to the text in Britain and on the Continent, he is also willing to admit the existence of a *via media* – a middle path formed by a group of critics who neither lapse into British 'inertness' nor indulge in French 'Byzantinism'. It is an encouraging feature, no doubt, that recruits to this *via media* can be found on both sides of the Atlantic. They might include Genette himself, whose absorbing 'essai de méthode' on Proustian discourse concludes with an invocation of the British instrument *par excellence*, Occam's razor, with reference to the multiplication of theoretical terms: they would surely also include Henri Meschonnic, whose *Pour la poétique* builds upon a measured assessment of American New Criticism and Russian Formalism, and Philippe Lejeune, a recent recruit to the editorial group of *Poétique* who announces his intention of conciliating poetics and criticism, theory and reading, at the outset of his sensitive study, *Le pacte autobiographique* (Lejeune 1975: 7). On the other side of the Atlantic, candidates for inclusion would certainly comprise the formidable Harold Bloom, whose *Map of Misreading* not only sets out a comprehensive rhetorical scheme for the analysis of poetic influence, but supplements it with a schema of Freudian defence mechanisms, on the basis that the defence mechanism is concerned to 'trope against death, rather in the same sense that tropes can be said to defend against literal meaning' (Bloom

1975: 91). They might also comprise Bloom's colleague at Yale, Geoffrey Hartman, whose admirable paper, 'The Use and Abuse of Structural Analysis', takes up Michael Riffaterre's article on Wordsworth's 'Yew-Trees' but does so in such a balanced way that the genuine dividends of structural analysis are allowed to appear, as well as its presumed defects so far as the 'understanding of words as a temporal medium' is concerned (Hartman 1975: 170).

That structuralist methods are destined to be absorbed into new critical syntheses seems hardly open to doubt. But it would be too sanguine to imagine that these examples afford the basis of a compromise which is wholly acceptable within the British milieu. It is not so much Genette's reservation about the risk of inventing structures, or Steiner's concern with ethical proportion, that is the root objection, as the radical doubt in the possibility, or utility, of a rhetorical criticism, a poetics. British empiricism holds tenaciously by the dubious, or at least provisional, categories of the individual poem, or novel, or author: the 'system of literary discourse', or indeed that concept of 'New Literary History' so impressively debated in the American journal of the same title, are both antipathetic to this point of view. In *The Popular Education of France*, Matthew Arnold thought it legitimate to temper the laissez-faire inclinations of his countrymen with a defence of executive power, confident that it would not be welcomed to an alarming extent in that uncongenial milieu. On the same principle, we might argue that in Britain a little *'écriture'*, however excessive in its native context, could hardly come amiss.

University of Kent.

FOOTNOTES

1. See Roger Poole, 'Structures and materials', in *20th Century Studies* 3 May 1970, for a balanced account of the contribution of Foucault, Lacan and Barthes.

2. Jean-Marie Bénoist, *La revolution structurale*, 1975; a useful summary of the same author's approach in an English version can be found in 'The end of Structuralism', *20th Century Studies* 3, May 1970.

3. The most comprehensive of these is J. Dubois et al., *Rhétorique générale*, Paris, 1970. This is a most useful source for locating types of rhetorical usage.

4. See Alastair Fowler, 'The selection of literary constructs', in *New Literary History*, Autumn 1975, 40-41: 'Thus, French literary structuralism and Nouvelle Critique, however inventive in their idiosyncratic applications, may turn out when firmly grasped to be belated imitations of Anglo-Saxon formalisms.' It is hard to see what exactly is meant by 'may turn out' in this context.

5. Robert Scholes, 'The Contributions of Formalism and Structuralism to the Theory of Fiction', in *Novel*, 1973: see also Todorov's article, 'L'héritage méthodologique du Formalisme', in *Poétique de la Prose*, Paris, 1971.

6. 'However, up to now historians of literature have invited comparison with a certain type of police detective who intends to arrest a culprit but is quite prepared to seize hold of anything to be found in the room where the crime was committed and even the people passing by in the street below. Literary historians were totally indiscriminate; they used the evidence of their own life, of psychology, politics, philosophy and what have you. A conglomeration of unrelated trades was substituted for literary research . . .' (Todorov 1973:8). 'Literariness' is thus defined negatively, as what is proper to literature, and nothing else.

7. The definition relates once again to Jakobson, who maintained that the artistic message is precisely that which is recognised not by its form or content but by its *function*, which is to direct attention to the 'message for its own sake' (cf. White 1975: 107).

8. See the general definition of *metataxis* given in *Rhétorique générale*: metataxis is the name for the class of procedures under which ellipse is listed.

REFERENCES CITED

Bann, Stephen (1972), 'L'anti-histoire de Henri Esmond', in *Poétique* 9, 61-79.

Bann, Stephen (1973), 'Il compenso di Kipling', in *Paragone*, Oct., 62-83.

Barthes, Roland (1964), 'L'activité structuraliste', in *Essais critiques*, Paris, text originally published 1963 in *Les Lettres Nouvelles*, and translated into English in *Form* 1, Summer 1966, 12 & 13.

Barthes, Roland (1966), *Critique et vérité*,Paris.

Barthes, Roland (1969), *Elements of Semiology* (trans. Annette Lavers & Colin Smith).

Barthes, Roland (1970), *S/Z*, Paris, (English translation 1975).

Barthes, Roland (1971), *Sade, Fourier, Loyola*, Paris.

Barthes, Roland (1973), *Mythologies*, (selected and translated by Annette Lavers).

Benoist, Jean-Marie (1970), 'The end of Structuralism', in *20th Century Studies* 31-54.

Benoist, Jean-Marie (1975), *La révolution structurale*, Paris.

Bloom, Harold (1975), *A Map of Misreading*, New York.

Culler, Jonathan (1974), 'Making sense', in *20th Century Studies* 12, 27-36.

Culler, Jonathan (1975), *Structuralist Poetics*.

Dolezel Lubomir, 'Narrative composition – a link between German and Russian poetics', in S. Bann & J. E. Bowlt, *Russian Formalism*, Edinburgh 73-84.

Dubois, Jacques *et al.* (1970), *Rhetorique generale*, Paris.

Fowler, Alastair (1975), 'The Selection of Literary Constructs', in *New Literary History*, Autumn, 39-55.

Gay, Peter (1975), *Style in History*.

83

Stephen Bann

Genette, Gérard (1966) *Figures*, Paris.

Genette, Gérard (Oct. 1966), David MacDuff, in *Form* 10, 4-11.

Genette, Gérard (1972) *Figures III*, Paris.

Hartman, Geoffrey (Autumn 1975), 'The Use and Abuse of Structural Analysis: Riffaterre's Interpretation of Wordsworth's 'Yew-Trees'', in *New Literary History* 165-86.

Jakobson, Roman, 'Letter to Haroldo de Campos on Martin Codax's poetic texture', in Bann & Bowlt, *Russian Formalism*, 20-25.

Kristeva, Julia (1973), 'The ruin of a poetics', trans, in Bann & Bowlt, Russian Formalism, 102-19.

Kristeva, Julia (1974), *La révolution du language poétique*, Paris.

Laere, Francois van, (May 1970), 'The problem of literary structuralism', in *20th Century Studies* 3, 55-66

Lejeune, Philippe, (1975), *Le pacte autobiographique*, Paris.

Lotman, Iouri, (1973), *La structure du texte artistique*, Paris.

Meschonnic, Henri, (1970) *Pour la poétique*, Paris.

Scholes, Robert (1973), 'The Contributions of Formalism and Structuralism to the Theory of Fiction', in *Novel.*

Scheglov, Y. K. (with A. K. Zholkovskij), (1975), 'Generating the literary text', *Poetics in translation*, I

Shklovsky, Viktor (1973), 'On the connection between devices of *Syuzhet* construction and general stylistic devices', in Bann & Bowlt, *Russian Formalism*, 48-71.

Steiner, George, (1972) *Extra-territorial – Papers on literature and the Language Revolution.*

Steiner, George, (27 Feb., 1976), Review of Serres, *Esthetiques sur Carpaccio*, in *Times Literary Supplement*, 243.

Todorov, Tzvetan, (1967), *Littérature et Signification*, Paris.

Todorov, Tzvetan, (May 1970), 'The fantastic in fiction' (abridged and translated version of *Introduction à la littérature fantastique*), in *20th Century Studies*, 76-92.

Todorov, Tzvetan, (1971), *Poétique de la prose*, Paris.

Todorov, Tzvetan, 'Some approaches to Russian Formalism', in Bann & Bowlt, *Russian Formalism*, 6-19.

Watson, George, (Feb. 1975), 'Old Furniture and "Nouvelle Critique"', in *Encounter*, 48-54.

White, Mayden (1973), *Metahistory*, Baltimore.

Marxist Literary Criticism

Terry Eagleton

Marxist criticism begins, naturally, with the work of Marx and Engels themselves. Yet what their critical writing actually consists in is not a simple question to answer. There is a familiar corpus of explicit literary comment to be extracted from their work – fragmentary, eminently anthologisable comments on form, realism, 'typicality', commitment, to be culled from texts treating largely of other matters.[1] Yet it is questionable whether it is at this relatively obvious level that Marx's own most substantial contributions to an aesthetics are to be found. For it was inevitable, given Marx's running debate with German idealism, that the concept of the 'aesthetic' would never be far beneath the surface of his scientific pre-occupations, infiltrating apparently quite different forms of discourse. It is not simply overt critical comment, but art as a category within some putative anthropology, which we find in the early Marx; it is less the scrutiny of particular literary texts (of the kind Marx undertakes at excessive length in *The Holy Family*) than the relevance of aesthetic production to some general 'theory of super-structures', which is most suggestive. The literary fragments have been duly canonised and ritually reproduced: two letters of Engels to indifferent novelists have become *(faute de mieux)* as memorable as whole treatises in bourgeois aesthetics. Yet as Mikhail Lifshitz has shown, the question of the aesthetic is active within a whole range of Marx's theoretical positions. (Lifshitz: 1973). It appears, for example, as a subordinate but significant factor in his analyses of material production, the division of labour and the product as commodity; its submerged influence can be detected in the concepts of value, fetishism, sensuousness, abstraction. If Marx's letter to Ferdinand Lasalle or his dissection of Eugène Sue's *Mystères de Paris* are clearly 'literary' texts, it could equally be claimed that the richly suggestive remarks on the political uses of symbolism and mythology which open *The 18th Brumaire of Louis Bonaparte* are even more pertinent. It is not easy merely to point to the 'aesthetic' in Marx; the extraction and cataloguing of isolated 'literary' comments is itself an ideological displacement of its true significance.

Granted that Marx and Engels had rather more important tasks on their hands than the construction of a complete aesthetics, it is still remarkable how many of the issues now central to the development of a Marxist criticism emerge in embryonic form in their *oeuvre*. The material basis of cultural practices; the relations between aesthetic 'super-structures' and material history; problems of the historical or transhistorical status of aesthetic 'value'; the relations between 'textual' and 'authorial' ideology, and the question of 'commitment' in art: there is hardly a topic in subsequent 'Marxist criticism' which does not make its shadowy appearance in the work of the founders of historical materialism. Yet it is naturally not the case that 'Marxist criticism' is no more than an extended footnote to that work; it is not a matter of Marxist criticism elaborating each empirical literary insight of the masters, binding them into a total structure. It is the materialist method of the *Grundrisse* and *Capital*, not hints gleaned from the 'literary criticism', which must form the basis of anything worthy of the title of a 'Marxist criticism'.

And yet this raises an obvious problem. For what is precisely lacking in Marx and Engels's own work is any elaborated theory of ideological 'superstructures' – of that realm of significations which occludes and represses real history in the act of 'mediating' it. The problem for Marxist criticism, cast in its most generalised form, is how it comes about that history produces (and reproduces) that set of ambiguous significations which we term the literary text. The problem, moreover, is that how you address yourself to that question depends upon your own particular historical epoch, and your mode of insertion into it. The first point to grasp about the history of Marxist criticism is its *history:* the specific historical conditions of its production, how it flares, fluctuates, fades in complex relation to the mutations of history itself. This is not to argue for some reductive historicism, dissolving Marxist literary science into the white heat of its contemporary 'moment'. For Marxist criticisms – and we should properly speak in the plural, abandoning the idealist notion of some unitary essence unfolding through time – belong to a conjuncture of historical moments, complexly (and sometimes contradictorily) combined. I want to demonstrate this by attempting in this essay to sketch the barest outlines of a 'structural-historical' understanding of Marxist criticism – historical, in that it returns Marxist literary science to its historical determinants, but structural in that it grasps this history, not as a simple linear unfolding, but as a series of conjunctures of various critical modes which are permanent within the corpus of Marxist criticism.

Let me make clearer what I mean by taking the most important historical moment in the whole of Marxism, and indeed, in a sense, in the whole of human history to date: the Bolshevik revolution. The Bolshevik revolution can be viewed as a seismic event which lays bare, and compacts against one another, a set of 'strata' permanent to

Marxist criticism. Before the revolution, Marxist criticism was nurtured largely in the shadow of the later Engels. The dominant Marxist aesthetician – Georgi Plekhanov – inhabits that distinctively Engelian world of anthropological scholarship and 'dialectical materialism'. (Plekhanov 1953). However sporadically illuminating his texts, their academicist inertia betrays the absence of the aesthetic as a concrete issue of revolutionary practice. Instead, a sluggish sociologism combines, in classic Second International style, with a contemplative neo-Kantianism: 'literary facts' correspond mechanically to 'social facts', but the *appreciation* of art is sealed off into the sphere of the privatised Kantian consumer of the 'beautiful'. We may contrast this intellectual *Menshevism* – in which, since all must wait upon economic development, speculative theory is the order of the day – with the activist, materialist, politically engaged aesthetics of the so-called 'revolutionary-democratic' school (Belinsky, Chernyshevsky, Dobrolyubov). Their aesthetic successors are Lenin and Gorki – the Lenin of *Party Organisation and Party Literature*, calling for a committed literature, and the Gorki of *The Mother*, written after 1905 to keep the revolution alive. That novel was to become the founding text of 'socialist realism', the concept of literary partisanship to degenerate into the theoretical nullity of *proletkult* and its Stalinist aftermath;[2] yet in Lenin's texts on Tolstoy, a contemplative Plekhanovian concern with the 'aesthetic', and vulgar political propagandism, are both definitively transcended. (Lenin 1952). Those texts, as Pierre Macherey has argued, represent an urgent *political* intervention between the two Russian revolutions (Macherey 1966); but precisely because they thus scrupulously address themselves to the contradictions of Tolstoy's fiction, they mark, inseparably, a genuine *theoretical* advance. The simple 'reflectionism' of Plekhanov's work, in which cultural history directly mirrors mutations in the class-structure, is now inevitably forced into some more subtle (although still insufficient) concept of partial, refracted, contradictory reflections.

The ground, then, is prepared for that fierce collision of critical modes which occurs after the 1917 revolution – a collision which plays within the space of Trotsky's *Literature and Revolution*. *Proletkult*, idealism, Formalism, Futurism, Constructivism: it is in relation to each of these 'strata', these possible or permanent tendencies within a materialist aesthetics, that a 'Marxist criticism' has to construct itself. Almost all of the problems which have haunted Marxist criticism since are thrown violently into the theoretical arena. The epistemological problem: is art reflection, refraction, creation, transformation, reproduction,

production? The political problem, inseparable from the first: what is the relation between art and the masses, between producer, product and audience, literature and cultural reconstruction, poetry and propaganda? The historical problem: is bourgeois culture to be destroyed or assimilated, cultural 'tradition' to be 'sublated' or scrapped? The related problem of aesthetic value: how far is 'value' the product of, how far in contradiction with, historical progressiveness? If literary value survives its ideological contexts, how is this to be explained without recourse to mere aestheticism, or to a mystical idealism of the literary 'genius'? If, on the other hand, value is internally bound up with art as progressive material practice, how is this to avoid a mere technologism of art (the artist as 'engineer') and a tyrannic over-politicisation of the artefact?

What won the day, of course, was neither an authentically materialist aesthetics nor any one of its post-revolutionary competitors but the spiritual catastrophe of 'socialist realism'. Throughout the long trauma of Stalinism, Marxist aesthetics of any value were historically forced back–back to Marx and Engels themselves, as in the work of Lifshitz, but also back beyond them, to Hegel. The revolutionary proletariat as the inheritor of the great classical, rational bourgeois lineages, bearer of the 'universal', 'human' values of non-alienated, non-reified 'totality' of which artistic realism is a supreme expression: it was in such neo-Hegelian terms that Georg Lukacs attempted to nurture, through the medium of aesthetics, a muted critique of Stalinism impossible in the sphere of politics.[3] It was in similar terms – of art as formal 'transcendence' and 'negation', an implicit critical refusal of a reified reality – that the neo-Hegelian Marxist aestheticians of the Frankfurt School of the 1930s (Adorno, Fromm, Marcuse and others) formulated their aesthetic theories.[4] But once a rational, scientific, materialist criticism has been confiscated and dissolved by 'vulgar' Marxism, the idealist opposition was bound to dissolve also, deprived by its enemy of the instruments it needed. The mystical irrationalism of the later Lukacs's aesthetics; the petty-bourgeois disillusion of the scattered remnants of the Frankfurt School, and of Lukacs's chief acolyte Lucien Goldmann:[5] it is hardly surprising that those for whom the proletariat was in any case primarily a philosophical category should so quickly fall prey to the bourgeois mythology of its effective dissolution.

But there were other trends also. If there is the moment of Lukacs, there is equally the moment of Bertolt Brecht and Walter Benjamin, whose work strives to relocate Marxist aesthetics on a genuinely materialist basis – who turn from the sealed realm of art as mere 'form' and 'consciousness' to the question of aesthetic forces of production and their attendent social relations.[6] The question of 'commitment' is thus radically re-posed: the artistic producer's engagement with historical progress is now situated, not merely at the level of his 'views' and 'values', but at the level of his material practice in so reconstructing the modes of aesthetic production as to transform the relations between producer(s), performers, product, audience. It is not a position free of 'technologism', in its sometimes unguarded equation of the 'progressive' forces of aesthetic technology (film, gramophone record, photography etc), with political progressiveness; but it signifies a 'stratum' of Marxist aesthetics powerfully compacted against a neo-Hegelianism which would reduce the artefact to mere mental signification, dislocating it from its material determinants and social relations of production.[7] One might mention, too, in this respect, the somewhat parallel enterprise in Italy of Galvano Della Volpe, who in his different way combats a Crocean aesthetic idealism by dint of a 'rational', materialist aesthetics which scrupulously analyses the semiological codes of a literary text (Della Volpe 1960).

If the project of Brecht and Benjamin harks back in some ways to that of the Russian Futurists and Constructivists, Della Volpe's studious attention to textual detail recalls the Russian Formalists, and points forward to the semiological labours of our own time. The Bolshevik conjuncture, that is to say, is once more on the agenda; there is a configuration of strata which share a history, if unevenly and discontinuously, with those strata thrown into exposure by the moment of 1917. Within this complex configuration, the encounter between historical materialism and structuralism (that off-spring of Formalism) is of particular significance. For while Russian Marxism recognised, in the scientific, systematic, anti-subjectivist methods of Formalism, a school of critical theory obliquely akin to its own ambitions, it was never able fully to incorporate that tenacious attention to the very language of the text for which Formalism is so rightly distinguished. What was historically forestalled by Stalinism was the possibility of a conjuncture between three permanent, recurrent structures of materialist criticism: an attention to the interrelations of literary form, value, ideology and history characteristic of the Hegelian heritage at its most productive; an analysis of literature as material practice and production, typical of the best work of the Futurists and Constructivists, and surviving into the Brechtian school; and a critique of the textual codes and conventions which permit the production of specifically 'literary' meaning, pursued by the Formalists and elaborated by contemporary semiotics. The forestalling of that possible conjuncture has had dire consequences; as the strata have been wedged apart, each has displayed a tendency to subside internally under its own unsupported weight. The history of Marxist criticisms is essentially the history of the top-heavy, counter-productive dominance of a single one of these modes over the others.

To argue for the necessity of such a conjuncture is not to press the claims of a 'fruitful' eclecticism. Nothing could be needed less, not least in Britain. For it is, precisely, eclecticism, often in rampant form, which has characterised what paltry amount of 'materialist' criticism we have indigenously known. A structural critique of literary forces and relations of production has been ousted by feebly empiricist 'sociology of literature', mechanistically coupling empirical literary facts with empirical sociological ones; instead of a semiological knowledge of the elements governing a text's self-structuration, we have had, for the most part, a bourgeois 'practical criticism' with a materialist tinge; a form of nebulous romantic idealism has substituted itself for what is of enduring value in Hegelian aesthetics. One has only to look at the best of the English Thirties Marxist aestheticians – Christopher Caudwell – to see how a *mélange* of bourgeois empiricism, Romanticism and 'vulgar' Marxism has been made to do the work of a scientific literary method. One might formulate the problem paradoxically by saying that our best Marxist critic – Raymond Williams – is not in fact a Marxist. Yet if Williams, in his own time, was forced to make a detour around Marxism in order to produce his pioneering *oeuvre*, this is no longer necessary (in large measure *because* of that detour) for those that follow. If we are to develop a criticism which does more than 'interpret' the text (i.e., says less in trying to say more), the need for a scientific aesthetics cannot be ignored.

Wadham College, Oxford

FOOTNOTES

1. See Baxandall & Morowski (eds.): 1974.

2. For a useful account of this history, see Alan Swingewood, 1975. Part 1, Ch. 4.

3. See especially his *The Historical Novel* (1963), and *Studies in European Realism* (1972).

4. For a descriptive account of the school, see Martin Jay 1973.

5. See, for example, his *Towards a Sociology of the Novel* (1975).

6. See especially Benjamin's essay 'The Author as Producer', in *Understanding Brecht* (1973).

7. See Brecht's critique of Lukacs in *New Left Review*, 1974.

REFERENCES CITED

Benjamin, Walter (1973): *Understanding Brecht*, New Left Books, London.

Brecht, Bertolt (1974): 'Against Georg Lukacs' in *New Left Review* 84 (March/April) 39-53.

Goldmann, Lucien (1975): *Towards a Sociology of the Novel*, Tavistock, London.

Jay, Martin (1973): *The Dialectical Imagination*, Heinemann, London

Lenin, V. I. (1952): *Tolstoy and his Time*, New York.

Lifshitz, Mikhail (1973): *The Philosophy of Art of Karl Marx*, Pluto Press, London.

Lukacs, Georg (1963): *The Historical Novel*, London.

Lukacs, George (1972): *Studies in European Realism*, Merlin, London.

Macherey, Pierre (1966): *Pour une Théorie de la Production Littéraire*, Paris.

Marx, K. and Engels, F. (1974): *On Literature and Art*, ed. L. Baxandall and Morawski, S. International Publishers, New York.

Plekhanov, Georgi (1953): *Art and Social Life*, Lawrence and Wishart, London.

Swingewood, Alan (1975): *The Novel and Revolution*, Macmillan, London.

Volpe, Galvano della (1960): *Critica del Gusto*

I

Marxism and Literature

Ian H. Birchall

Marxism is a body of ideas which sees all human history as the history of
class struggle. In particular, it is concerned to analyse the dynamics and
contradictions of the capitalist system, and to show how the working
class has the historical potential to overthrow capitalism and establish a
classless, socialist society. Marxism stands or falls by its ability to
interpret existing society, and to mobilise men and women to change it.

A Marxist theory of literature – or, for that matter, of music, sexuality
or carpet-weaving – is conceivable only if situated within such a
framework. At first sight, it might not appear that the consideration of
so-called 'creative literature' has very much importance for Marxism. If
it had nothing to say on the matter, its validity as a revolutionary theory
would scarcely be challenged thereby.

In fact, Marxism has always had a great deal to say about literature
and to its practitioners. The major figures of Marxism from Marx and
Engels to Gramsci and Trotsky all wrote at length, if fragmentarily,
about literary questions. And many of the most important figures of
twentieth century literature – Sartre, Brecht, Gorky, Breton, Neruda,
Hikmet, to name only a handful – have been influenced by Marxism
and attempted to absorb its insights into their creative practice.

Many reasons have been given for this close interplay between
Marxism and literature. Meszaros attributes it to Marxism's
preoccupation with the question of alienation (Meszaros 1970: 190);
while Lukács sees literature as a particularly suitable area for the
'ideological clarification' that precedes a 'great crisis in social relations'
(Lukács 1972: 107).

Yet to many people the attempt to integrate a theory of literature
within a theory of politics seems to pose a threat to the integrity of
literature, indeed to its very essence. Most readers with anything like a
conventional literary education will suffer a momentary shock on
reading statements such as: 'No one ever wrote a good book in praise of
the Inquisition' (Orwell 1970: 92) or 'No one could imagine for a
moment that it is possible to write a good novel in praise of anti-
Semitism' (Sartre 1964: 80). It is not that empirical refutations spring
immediately to mind (they are, indeed, remarkably hard to think of); it
is rather that the apparently self-evident autonomy of literary values
has been called into question.

But the problem of the relation between literature and politics is not
something that has existed unchanged from all eternity. Nobody

complains that Shakespeare dragged politics into literature just because a certain theory of kingship is an absolutely integral component of most of his major tragedies. The idea of 'art for art's sake' – and its corollary, that political or 'committed' literature could be seen as a specialised genre – emerged only during the Romantic period, and got a firm grip in Europe after the defeat of the revolutions of 1848. Nowadays the term 'political novel' probably suggests to most people a story of adultery in the House of Commons; but that is an indictment of contemporary notions of what 'politics' means.

We live in a period when many long-held assumptions about the nature of our society and culture are being shaken. The future of literature is inextricably bound up with the future of society as a whole. It is a realisation of this that lies behind the recent growth of interest in the Sociology of Literature, a field in which much of the work done draws on Marxism to some extent.

But Marxism is not simply a fixed body of doctrine, nor is it coextensive with the work of Marx himself. It is a theory of history, but it does not stand outside history; it is a living part of the historical process. Marxism is a century and a quarter of polemics, sects, mass parties and states. It is a movement which has contained deep and fundamental divisions: Lenin against Kautsky, Stalin against Trotsky, Krushchev against Mao – in each case both sides laid claim to the orthodoxy of Marxism. What follows is an attempt to sketch – of necessity briefly and with many omissions – the main themes and problems confronted by a Marxist theory of literature and the evolution of some of the main variants of that theory.

A. Marx and Engels

Neither Marx nor Engels ever wrote systematically or at length on literary or aesthetic questions. Marx's project of a study of Balzac was never fulfilled, and he never wrote the encyclopaedia article on aesthetics that he was invited to contribute. This was not the result of any lack of interest – on the contrary, fragmentary references throughout Marx's work confirm the testimony of his friends that he had a deep and wide-ranging interest in literature. But at any given time in his life he found the demands of political activity and economic analysis too pressing.

This incompleteness of Marx's work leaves us several alternatives. We could restrict ourselves to listing the various specific literary judgments made by Marx. But such a procedure, unless intended to render Marx respectable by showing what a 'cultured' person he was, is

Ian H. Birchall

essentially trivial. Or we could argue that since Marx did not provide us with an aesthetic his work has to be complemented by an aesthetic borrowed from elsewhere – say Kant or Aristotle. But since on other questions Marx's thought is radically opposed to theirs, this would call into question the whole coherence of his thought.

The third possibility is to attempt to deduce from Marx's general comments on ideology how literature might fit into his scheme, and see if the fragmentary remarks on literature do in fact fit.

In so doing, it is necessary to remember that the problematic relation of literature to society was being widely discussed at the time Marx wrote. In Germany a whole tradition from Herder and Lessing through Hegel to Marx's friend Heine had attempted to develop a historical approach to literature. In France the Romantic school had split between those like George Sand who advocated a political literature committed to social change and the emancipation of the working class, and those like Gautier who argued for 'art for art's sake'. A little later Taine was to attempt to create a sociology of literature on rigorously deterministic foundations, seeing the factors of 'race, milieu and moment' as sufficient to account for any literary work or school (Taine 1863).

The classic statement of Marx's view of the relation between society and ideology comes in the Introduction to *A Contribution to the Critique of Political Economy* (1859):

> In the social production of their life, men enter into definite relations that are indispensable and independent of their will, relations of production which correspond to a definite state of the development of their material productive forces. The sum total of these relations of production constitutes the economic structure of society, the real foundation, on which rises a legal and political superstructure and to which correspond definite forms of social consciousness. The mode of production of material life conditions the social, political and intellectual life process in general. It is not the consciousness of men that determines their being, but, on the contrary, their social being that determines their consciousness . . . a distinction should always be made between the material transformation of the economic conditions of production, which can be determined with the precision of natural science, and the legal, political, religious, aesthetic or philosophic – in short, ideological forms in which men become conscious of this conflict and fight it out (Marx & Engels 1973: 85).

This text is so central and so often quoted that it is important to be quite clear what it does and does not say. It asserts, quite firmly, that literature and other forms of ideology are not autonomous or self-contained – they can be understood as part of the total process of man's social being. What it decidedly does not say – contrary to the belief both of some 'Marxists' and of many critics of Marxism – is that the relation of literature to the economic structure is one of passive dependence, or that ideology is simply a 'reflection' of the economic foundations. On the contrary, the essential feature of society is that conflict is central to it, and literature, art, religion etc. are among the weapons that men fabricate in order to 'fight it out'.

Indeed, Marx stresses the active nature of literary practice. In an article on the Prussian press censorship written in 1842 he declared:

> A *style* is my property, my spiritual individuality. *Le style, c'est l'homme.* Indeed! The law permits me to write, only I am supposed to write in a style different from my own (Easton & Guddat 1967: 71).

It is this stress on activity and conflict which distinguishes Marxism from such sociological theories as that of Taine. Taine is able to take an author – Shakespeare, Racine, or Balzac – and, with a good deal of insight, relate him to the social context he wrote in. What he fails to explain is how radically different ideological productions – Descartes and Pascal, Voltaire and Rousseau – come into existence in the same society at more or less the same time.

Once again, Marx does not argue that a work of literature can be simply reduced to the class position of the writer. Rather he argues that the historical position of a particular class sets *limits* within which a writer works. As he puts it in *The Eighteenth Brumaire of Louis Bonaparte*:

> Just as little must one imagine that the democratic representatives are indeed all shopkeepers or the enthusiastic champions of shopkeepers. According to their education and their individual position they may be as far apart as heaven from earth. What makes them representatives of the petty bourgeoisie is the fact that in their minds they do not get beyond the limits which the latter do not get beyond in life, that they are consequently driven, theoretically, to the same problems and solutions to which material interest and social position drive the latter practically. This is, in general, the relationship between the *political* and *literary representatives* of a class and the class they represent (Marx & Engels 1973: 84-5).

As so often, Marx's statement of the problem is pregnant but brief and cryptic. Much of the work of Lucien Goldmann on social groups and 'world-views' can be seen as a development of the ideas expressed in the above passage.

But if Marx insists that literature cannot be independent of society, that it is related to the practice of a given social class, this does not mean that he takes a relativistic position. On the contrary Marx's insistence that consciousness is inseparable from social being means a clear recognition of its cognitive role. As Trotsky was to put it: 'Art is one of the ways in which man finds his bearings in the world . . . a form of cognition' (Trotsky 1970: 86). The way in which Marx, throughout *Capital* and the *Grundrisse*, draws on a wide range of literary sources – for example, the novels of Balzac – as a source of documentation and confirmation of his economic analysis testifies to his belief that literature can have a content of objective truth.

This, of course, leads us directly to the problem of realism, which has been a central question throughout the Marxist tradition.[1] The term 'realism' acquired wide currency in French literary circles in the 1850s, and was much discussed throughout the second half of the nineteenth century. Often the term was given so broad and vague a sense that it seemed to lack meaning altogether. The main features of literature which bore the label were the depiction of middle and lower class life and an attempt to give a carefully documented portrayal of social *milieu*.

Perhaps because of the dangerous vagueness of the term, Marx scarcely ever uses it, even though the problem is at the heart of his work. Engels, however, discusses the term explicitly in a letter to the English novelist Margaret Harkness written in 1888 (Marx & Engels 1973: 115-7).[2] Here Engels makes clear that, for a Marxist, realism cannot simply be a portrayal of the world as it is. On the contrary, simply to portray the world as it is at present would mean, as Engels put it in another letter a few years earlier, to reinforce the 'optimism of the bourgeois world' and suggest the 'eternal validity of the existing order' (Marx & Engels 1973: 114).

In Marxist terms realism must mean, not simply laying bare the class antagonisms within society, but showing how these antagonisms make society open to change. Engels's main criticism of Ms Harkness's novel *City Girl* is that it shows the working class as a 'passive mass unable to help itself' (Marx and Engels 1973: 115), whereas Engels insists that 'the rebellious reaction of the working class against the oppressive medium which surrounds them, their attempts – convulsive, half-conscious or conscious – at recovering their status as human beings, belong to history and must therefore lay claim to a place in the domain of realism' (Marx & Engels 1973: 116).

Realism in literature therefore necessarily comes into conflict with the ideology of bourgeois society, which seeks to present existing social relations as unchangeable. Indeed, Marx suggests, in *Theories of Surplus Value*, that there is an even more fundamental antagonism between capitalism and art. 'Capitalist production', he states quite simply, 'is hostile to certain aspects of intellectual production, such as art and poetry' (Marx & Engels 1973: 64). Capitalism reduces all human productions to the level of a common measure, exchange value; it degrades human beings by subordinating them to objects which they themselves have created but which seem, in the mystified ideology of capitalism, to acquire a life of their own.

Marx, who rarely engaged in Utopian speculation, offers little indication of what art might be like after the overthrow of capitalism. In the *German Ideology*, however, there is the suggestion that under communism the whole nature of art as a specialised activity separate from the rest of social life would be radically transformed. 'In a communist society there are no painters but at most people who engage in painting among other activities' (Marx & Engels 1973: 71).

It is in the context of Marx's general critique of capitalist society that we should look at two other problems that have been much discussed in Marxist literary theory, *progress* and *intention*.

The standard bourgeois view of progress, a continuous upward movement towards greater knowledge, control over nature and human well-being (developed by the French Enlightenment and crystallised by Comte) seemed to Marx to be nothing more than an apology for capitalism. For Marx capitalism was both progressive – above all because it created the conditions for its own overthrow, – and at the same time regressive, because of its destruction of human and in particular aesthetic values.

In 1857 Marx wrote an *Introduction to the Critique of Political Economy* in which he discussed the abiding aesthetic value of classical Greek art, and stressed that capitalism's technological advances did not automatically equip it to surpass the aesthetic achievements of the Greeks. With sharp irony he wrote:

> Is the view of nature and of social relations which shaped Greek imagination and thus Greek (mythology) possible in the age of automatic machinery and railways and locomotives and electric telegraphs? Where does Vulcan come in as against Roberts & Co., Jupiter as against the lightning rod, and Hermes as against the Crédit Mobilier?' (Marx & Engels 1973: 136-7).

But, perhaps foreseeing that this passage would be seized up on by subsequent commentators. not as a satire against capitalism, but as proof of Marx's deep attachment to eternal aesthetic values, he put it aside and it was published only after his death.

Ian H. Birchall

Any writer who strives after realism and authentic aesthetic values will, even if on the political level he is in no way revolutionary, find himself becoming a critic of bourgeois society. This accounts for the paradox of Balzac, which Engels drew attention to in his letter to Ms Harkness (Marx & Engels 1973: 116-7).[3] Balzac, though politically a conservative diametrically opposed to the values of the French Revolution becomes, through his realism and against his own personal intentions, a valuable ally of the revolutionary cause.

The Balzac paradox is an important component of the Marxist theory of literature; but there is a danger, manifested for example in the work of Lukàcs, of giving it too central a position. Marx and Engels recognised that it was not necessary to be a socialist to be a good writer, but they believed in the possibility of a literature consciously wedded to the revolutionary practice of the proletariat. Marx was always concerned with the proletariat, not as an abstraction, but as actual living working men,[4] and he had great faith in the capacity of working men and women to develop their own culture:

> The new literature in prose and in poetry which is coming from the lower classes of England and France would prove to them that the lower classes of the people are quite capable of rising spiritually without the *blessing* of the *Holy Spirit* of *critical criticism* (Marx & Engels 1956: 181).[5]

And Marx's contacts and discussions with Heine, Herwegh and Freiligrath show clearly that he saw the future of literature as bound up with the growth of the working-class movement.[6]

B. Lenin and the Russian Revolution

The approach to literature developed by Marx and Engels was taken up and systematised by a younger generation of Marxists, notably Plekhanov. But the most important new development for the Marxist tradition was the emergence of Bolshevism in Russia leading to the seizure of power in 1917.

As an individual Lenin was far more single-minded in his devotion to organisational tasks than Marx or Engels, and his work does not contain anything like the same wealth of literary references. His wife Krupskaya tells us that he usually walked out of the theatre after the first act of a play (Lenin 1967: 236), and Gorky relates that although he was so moved by Beethoven's music that he wanted to pat people on the head, he quickly added: 'But today we musn't pat anyone on the head or we'll get our hand bitten off; we've got to hit them on the heads, hit them without mercy, though in the ideal we are against doing any violence to people' (Lenin 1967: 247).

In his articles on Tolstoy, Lenin (1967: 28-33, 48-62), follows in the tradition of Engels's treatment of Balzac by trying to 'identify the great artist with the revolution which he has obviously failed to understand' (Lenin 1967: 28). But historically Lenin's most important contribution to the debate was an article, written in 1905, on *Party Organisation and Party Literature*, in which he argues that literature must be subordinated to the political work of the revolutionary party:

> What is this principle of party literature? It is not simply that, for the socialist proletariat, literature cannot be a means of enriching individuals or groups; it cannot, in fact, be an individual undertaking, independent of the common cause of the proletariat. Down with non-partisan writers! Down with literary supermen! Literature must become *part* of the common cause of the proletariat, a 'cog and screw' of one single great Social-Democratic mechanism set in motion by the entire politically-conscious vanguard of the entire working class. Literature must become a component of organised, planned and integrated Social-Democratic Party work (Lenin 1967: 23).

As with all Lenin's writings, this must be put in context. The party Lenin was thinking of was a small voluntary association of persecuted revolutionaries, not one with its grip firmly on the state machine. He was above all polemicising against the practice, common in many socialist parties, of individuals pursuing private journalistic activity independent of any party discipline. But it is too simple to argue, as Lukács does, citing a long-unpublished letter of Krupskaya's that the article 'was *not* concerned with literature as fine art' (Lukács 1963: 7). Lenin recognised a distinction between literature and political writing – for example in his comment that aspects of Inessa Armand's pamphlet on free love would be better treated in a novel (Lenin 1967: 200) – but at the same time he was anxious to involve creative writers such as Gorky in the work of the party press (Lenin & Gorky 1973: 25).

The whole tortuous history of Lenin's relationship with Gorky brings out Lenin's sensitivity to the relationship between art and the political struggle and the tension between the demands of the political struggle and the recognition of artistic autonomy. Lenin hailed Gorky's work as an integral part of the socialist movement: 'Gorky is undoubtedly the greatest representative of *proletarian* art . . . Any faction of the Social-Democratic Party would be justly proud of having Gorky as a member' (Lenin & Gorky 1973: 219).

Even when Gorky became involved with the ideas of Bogdanov, whom Lenin was to attack violently, there is a tolerant recognition of the independence of the artist: 'I believe that an artist can glean much that is useful to him from philosophy of all kinds' (Lenin & Gorky 1973: 33). But when Gorky went so far as to sign, at the outbreak of war in 1914, a nationalistic protest against German 'barbarity', Lenin's tolerance was exhausted. Whereas he accepted that the singer Chaliapin could be seen as 'an artist and nothing more' (Lenin & Gorky 1973: 220), the nature of Gorky's work did not allow such leniency. 'Why should Gorky meddle in politics?' (Lenin & Gorky 1973: 225).

After the seizure of state power by the proletariat in 1917, the emphasis in Lenin's work shifts. The need is now for the working class to appropriate the culture of the dispossessed bourgeoisie.

> We must take the entire culture that capitalism left behind and build socialism with it. We must take all its science, technology, knowledge and art. Without these we shall be unable to build communist society (Lenin 1967: 123).

Once again, the historical context must be recalled if Lenin is not to appear guilty of a certain conservatism. The Russian working class in 1917 was small and culturally deprived; even literacy had been largely withheld from it. The first need was to take over the basic cultural tools with which the bourgeoisie had ruled.

As a result Lenin showed some impatience, mixed with a grudging respect, towards writers like Mayakovsky (Lenin 1967: 158, 214, 237, 248) who wanted to transform literature radically in the light of the revolutionary achievement:

> As I see it, the fine poetical work would be one written to the social command of the Comintern, taking for its purpose the victory of the proletariat, making its points in a new vocabulary, striking and comprehensible to all . . . and sent to the publisher by plane (Mayakovsky 1970: 21).

Perhaps the most sensitive account of the problems of literature in the immediate post-revolutionary period is given in Trotsky's *Literature and Revolution*. Trotsky is sympathetic to some at least of the literary innovators without making any compromises with the notion of a 'proletarian culture', which he believes to be impossible. He tries to steer a middle path between party control and total independence:

> Art must make its own way and by its own means. The Marxian methods are not the same as the artistic. The party leads the proletariat but not the historic processes of history. There are domains

in which the Party leads, directly and imperatively. There are domains in which it only co-operates. There are, finally, domains in which it only orientates itself. The domain of art is not one in which the Party is called upon to command. It can and must protect and help it, but it can only lead it indirectly (Trotsky 1960: 218).

C. The Age of Stalin

But Trotsky's hopes were not to be fulfilled. By the end of the twenties all hope of spreading the Russian revolution had gone; Stalin's doctrine of 'socialism in one country' had triumphed and Trotsky and the Left Opposition had been hounded out of Party and country. With the Five Year Plans the last remnants of working class power were eradicated. A massive effort to develop Russia's industrial strength was accompanied by an ever-tightening ideological grip of the Party over the state machine, culminating in the show trials of the late thirties.[7]

In Stalin's Russia the ideological control of the Party and state over literature was given considerable importance. (One result of this is the way in which the 'literary' opposition has played a much greater role than dissident writers could in Western society). The front man for laying down literary orthodoxy was Andrey Zhdanov, whose various speeches offer the most systematic exposition of Stalinist literary doctrine.

In his speech to the First Congress of Soviet Writers in 1934, Zhdanov laid down the main ideological tasks of Russian writers:

> To eradicate the survivals of capitalism in the consciousness of people means to struggle against all the remnants of bourgeois influence on the proletariat, against laxity, frivolity, idleness, petty-bourgeois indiscipline and individualism, greed and the lack of conscientiousness with regard to collective property (Zhdanov 1970: 5).

In simple terms, this was a plain indication that literature was to be subordinated to the economic goals of the regime, to the encouragement of productivity and labour discipline.

In a speech of 1946, Zhdanov stresses the importance for Soviet citizens of regular self-criticism and self-analysis, in terms that recall the 'Protestant ethic' associated with the early phases of Western capitalism (Jdanov 1970: 31). And in a lecture on philosophy the following year the basic moralism of Zhdanovism comes out clearly in a stinging attack on Sartre's journal *Les Temps Modernes* for publishing Genet's *Thief's Journal* which opens with the words: 'Treachery, theft and homosexuality will be my fundamental themes'. For Zhdanov this is

Ian H. Birchall

enough to indicate the bankruptcy of bourgeois culture (Zdanov 1970: 64).

In contrast to bourgeois culture, the official literary doctrine advocated was 'socialist realism', defined as follows:

> Socialist realism, being the basic method of Soviet literature and literary criticism, requires from the artist a truthful, historically concrete representation of reality in its revolutionary development. Moreover, truth and historical completeness of artistic representation must be combined with the task of ideological transformation and education of the working man in the spirit of Socialism (Slonim 1967: 160-1).

The doctrine was not, of course, confined to Russia. Wherever there were Communist Parties, there were party intellectuals arguing for seeing 'the re-creation of literature as a consciously and collectively planned piece of work under the leadership of the Communist Party' (Hobsbawm 1950: ii).

But the Stalin period produced at least two major contributions to the Marxist theory of literature in the writings of Georg Lukàcs and Bertolt Brecht.

Lukács's work represents a major development in the treatment of the interrelation of form and content in works of literature. His use of the category of 'totality' and the distinction between 'realism' and 'naturalism' represent important methodological advances, even if one does not always accept the particular applications made of them.

But Lukács's work remains confined within the framework of Stalinist orthodoxy as he occasionally reveals with unusual frankness for example, calling Thomas Mann's *Dr Faustus* the 'fullest artistic and intellectual confirmation' of the decree of the Central Committee of the Communist Party of the Soviet Union on modern music (Lukács 1964: 22).

This framework leads Lukács to be unduly fatalistic about the possibilities for art under capitalism. After 1848 there seems little possibility offered to writers:

> Balzac and Stendhal could dig down to the very roots of the sharpest contradictions inherent in bourgeois society while the writers who lived after 1848 could not do so: such merciless candour, such sharp criticism would have necessarily driven them to break the link with their own class. Even the sincerely progressive Zola was incapable of such a rupture (Lukács 1972: 86).

And though his critique of modernism is more sophisticated than Zhdanov's, it is equally unsympathetic: 'It is clear, I think, that modernism must deprive literature of a sense of perspective' (Lukács 1963: 33).

Brecht's theoretical work is rather more fragmentary than Lukács's and is directly related to the problems of a practising dramatist and poet. Brecht never broke politically with Stalinism; indeed, the treatment of the theme of means and ends in many of his poems and plays must be seen as a direct apology for Stalinist brutality. But unlike Lukács, his sympathies are with modernism,[8] and literary innovation. His main contribution to a Marxist aesthetic lies in his stress on changeability; he is concerned above all to stress that any account of reality is deceptive if it does not show how that reality can be changed by human practice.

D. The Present Period

In 1956 Stalin's successor, Krushchev, made his celebrated 'secret speech' in which he denounced the crimes of the Stalinist era. The speech can be criticised for not explaining how, in Marxist terms, such crimes were possible in a 'socialist' society; and the subsequent tortuous process of 'destalinisation' confirms this inadequacy. Nonetheless, within Russia and in and around the international Communist movement the new period of 'liberalisation' offered the possibility of more adventurous work in literary theory.

The official review *Communist* interpreted the new line as follows in 1956:

> The task of Soviet writers and artists is to take over all the wealth in the field of artistic skill that humanity has accumulated and to boldly increase this wealth by new creative discoveries. Socialist realism imposes no limits in this respect (Arvon 1970: 91).

In the following years debate about literature in Communist circles was able to take a more positive attitude to the problems of modernism. The blanket category of decadence was no longer seen as adequate. As the veteran Communist Ernst Fischer put it: 'We must have the courage to say: if writers describe decadence in all its nakedness and if they denounce it morally, this is not decadence' (Baxandall 1972: 233).

The Stalinist tradition had assigned such a writer as Kafka to the 'cultural dung heap of reaction' (Fast 1960: 7). More recently a variety of Marxist critics have tried to show how the Marxist framework can accommodate his work. Thus Adolfo Sanchez Vasquez:

> Some Marxists, however, have seen in Kafka only an expression of a decadent bourgeois world and, in condemning that world, have also

condemned Kafka. They have fallen into the trap of abandoning Kafka's work to the bourgeoisie, as if Kafka belonged within the narrow framework of the bourgeois world. Kafka certainly expresses, in a brilliant and unique way, the decomposition of the bourgeois world, but his expression is such that the characters in his works seem to be saying to us: behold what men have made of themselves, how they dehumanise and degrade themselves (Vazquez 1974: 140).

The weight of Stalinist dogmatism has been so great that much Marxist criticism of the last two decades has been little more than a protest against such dogmatism. But the rejection of dogmatism is not an end in itself, and easily degenerates into pure eclecticism. Take, for example, the case of Roger Garaudy, for many years an intellectual hatchet-man for the French Communist Party, but expelled therefrom in 1970. Garaudy has concerned himself with the problem of redefining realism:

> From Stendhal and Balzac, Courbet and Repin, Tolstoy and Martin du Gard, Gorky and Mayakovsky we can take and analyse the criteria of 'great realism'. And what do we do if the works of Kafka, Saint-John Perse or Picasso do not correspond to these criteria? Do we have to exclude them from realism or from art? Or do we, on the contrary, have to open up and extend the definition of realism, and discover new dimensions of realism in the light of works characteristic of our century, thus enabling us to attach these new contributions to the heritage of the past (Baxandall 1972: 253).

Garaudy here comes dangerously close to saying that 'realism' means whatever you want it to mean.

Ernst Fischer, likewise a long-serving Communist who was expelled from the Austrian CP in 1969 for persistent criticism of the Russian invasion of Czechoslovakia, takes a somewhat similar position, though his work reveals a far more thorough and honest attempt to think through the lessons of the Stalinist experience. When Fischer writes:

> We must not abandon Proust, nor Joyce, nor Beckett and even less Kafka to the bourgeois class. If we allow them, they will turn these writers against us. Otherwise, these writers will no longer aid the bourgeoisie – it will be us that they aid (Baxandall 1972: 233),

one gets the impression that he is taking as given, on the basis of criteria derived from outside Marxism, the fact that these are 'great writers'. One wonders just what the working class is going to do with Proust.

But those Marxists who remained outside the Communist Parties were not more successful in integrating Marxist literary theory with revolutionary practice. Lucien Goldmann, for example, has the enormous merit of systematising the methodological achievements of Marx and the early Lukács, and his concrete studies remain as a testimony to the comprehensive power of his method. But for Goldmann Marxism became a method and nothing else. He could write: 'Dialectical materialism is a working hypothesis which, in the works of Marx, Engels, Lukács, and even of several other authors of lesser scope, has proved itself extremely fertile and fruitful' (Goldmann 1959: 44). Goldmann's position seems to have been that, since there were no prospects of revolutionary politics in the foreseeable future, the job of Marxist intellectuals was to keep the method alive by competing with bourgeois scholarship on its own ground.[9]

For Sartre, on the other hand, practice came first. The great merit of his *What is Literature?* is its stress on literature as action. But Sartre (not wholly through his own fault) was never able to resolve the problem he posed in *What is Literature?* – how does a bourgeois intellectual, committed in principle to the working class, actually reach it without making intolerable concessions to Stalinist politics:

> The majority of the proletariat, wrapped round by a single party, encircled by an isolating propaganda, forms a closed society, without doors or windows. One means of access, and a narrow one at that, is the CP. Is it desirable that the writer should commit himself to it? If he does so out of conviction as a citizen and out of disgust with literature, then very good, he's chosen. But can he become a communist and remain a writer? (Sartre 1964: 304).

Eighteen years later Sartre's only solution was for some kind of division of labour among intellectuals:

> All we can say on this subject is that it is necessary for there to be in parties or popular organisations intellectuals associated with political power, which represents the maximum possible degree of discipline and the minimum of criticism; and it is also necessary that there should be non-party intellectuals, individually linked to the movements but outside them, which represents the minimum possible discipline and the maximum criticism (Sartre 1972: 75).

It is the greatness and the tragedy of Sartre that he could never have decided which group he would be in.

If the battle between dogmatism and anti-dogmatism can finally come to an end, it is time for Marxist literary theory to start returning to the problems it was preoccupied with before the rise of Stalinism – the relation of artistic practice to political organisation, the relation between ideology and culture. To conclude, I suggest one or two questions which Marxist literary theory should be concerning itself with over the next few years.

(i) To what extent is the 'literary heritage' as embodied in the educational system class-bound, and to what extent should it be revalued (for example, why is Jane Austen part of 'English Literature' and Robert Tressell not?).

(ii) Are the arguments used by Lenin and Trotsky against 'proletarian culture' still valid for Western Europe in the seventies, or does the very different nature of the proletariat, and the fact that the existing 'culture' consists far more of ideology than basic techniques, call for reconsideration?

(iii) How should politically oriented literary practitioners (e.g. theatre groups) relate to political organisations? How can they get orientation from them without unnecessary constraints?

If Marxists can come up with some interesting answers to these questions, they will show that Marxism is still very much a living body of thought.

Middlesex Polytechnic

FOOTNOTES

1. The one apparent exception, the Surrealists, reject realism above all in the sense of a passive acceptance of the world as it is.

2. Engels's discussion of Balzac here seems to me to make explicit what is implicit in Marx's use of Balzac in *Capital.* I see no grounds for alleging any fundamental division between Marx and Engels on this question.

3. Engels's low view of Zola, as contrasted with Balzac, should not be taken too seriously. There is little evidence that he had any wide acquaintance with Zola; and if *L'Assommoir* could be subjected to some of the same criticisms as *City Girl, Germinal* is in fact a brilliant fulfilment of Engels's criteria for a working-class novel.

4. See, for example, his letter to Feuerbach of 1844, where he urges Feuerbach to see the socialist implications of his philosophy, and adduces in evidence the high theoretical level of the discussions in the Paris workmen's meetings (Cited in Goldmann 1970: 157).

5. The 'them' refers to Bauer and followers.

6. For details, see Demetz (1967: 74-101).

7. The present writer (following Cliff 1974) believes that the view that Russia under Stalin became 'state capitalist' gives the most adequate framework for understanding the use of Marxism as an ideology in Russia.

8. Cf. for example Brecht, 1974.

9. This was the position I heard Goldmann argue at a meeting in the LSE in 1969.

REFERENCES CITED

Arvon, H. (1970), *L'esthétique marxiste*, Presses Universitaires de France, Paris.

Baxandall, L. (ed) (1972), *Radical perspectives in the arts*, Penguin, Harmondsworth.

Brecht, B. (1974), 'Against Georg Lukács', *New Left Review* 84.

Cliff, T. (1974), *State Capitalism in Russia*, Pluto, London.

Demetz, P. (1967), *Marx, Engels, and the Poets*, transl. Samons, Jeffrey L. University of Chicago Press.

Easton, Lloyd D. and Guddat, Kurt, H. (1967), *Writings of the Young Marx on philosophy and society*, Doubleday Anchor, New York.

Fast, H. (1960), *Literature and reality*, International Publishers, New York.

Goldmann, L. (1959), *Recherches dialectiques*, Gallimard, Paris.

Goldmann, L. (1970), *Marxisme et sciences humaines*, Gallimard, Paris.

Hobsbawm, E. (1950), Introduction, J. Revai: *Lukács and socialist realism.* Fore Publications, London.

Jdanov, A. (1970), *Sur la littérature, la philosophie et la musique*, Norman Béthune, Paris.

Lenin, V. (1967), *On literature and art*, Progress, Moscow.

Lenin, V. and Gorky, M. (1973), *Letters, reminiscences and articles*, Progress, Moscow.

Lukács, G. (1963), *The meaning of contemporary realism*, Merlin, London.

Lukács, G. (1964), *Essays on Thomas Mann*, Merlin, London.

Lukács, G. (1972), *Studies in European realism*, Merlin, London.

Marx, K. and Engels, F. (1956), *The holy family*, Lawrence & Wishart, London.

Marx, K. and Engels, F. (1973), *On literature and art*, ed. Lee Baxandall and Stefan Morawski, International General, New York.

Mayakovsky, V. (1970), *How are verses made?*, Cape, London.

Meszaros, I. (1970), *Marx's theory of alienation*, Merlin, London.

Orwell, G. (1970), *Collected essays, journalism and letters*, IV, Penguin, Harmondsworth.

Sartre, J-P. (1964), *Qu'est-ce que la littérature?*, Gallimard, Paris.

Sartre, J-P. (1972), *Plaidoyer pour les intellectuels* (Lectures given in Japan 1965), Gallimard, Paris.

Slonim, M. (1967), *Soviet Russian literature*, Oxford University Press.

Taine, H. (1863), *Histoire de la littérature anglaise*, Hachette, Paris.

Trotsky, L. (1960), *Literature and revolution*, University of Michigan Press, Ann Arbor.

Trotsky, L. (1970), *On literature and art*, ed. Paul N. Siegel, Pathfinder Pr. Inc., New York.

Vazquez, A. Sanchez (1974), *Art and society*, Monthly Review.

Ian H. Birchall

Notes on further reading

While there is no substitute for wide reading of the works of Marx and Engels the compilation, *Marx, Engels on Literature and Art*, ed. Baxandall and Morawski (1974), International General, New York, is a useful introduction to some seminal passages; it also contains an extensive bibliography of Marxist writing on aesthetics. Useful commentaries are M. Lifschitz, (1973), *The Philosophy of Art of Karl Marx*, Pluto, and the rather more anecdotal P. Demetz, (1967), *Marx, Engels and the Poets*, University of Chicago. Lenin's contribution (1967) can be studied in *Lenin on Art and Literature*, Moscow and Lenin and Gorky, (1973), *Letters, Reminiscences and Articles*, Moscow; Trotsky's (1960) in L. Trotsky, *Literature and Revolution*, Ann Arbor, and (1970) *Leon Trotsky on Literature and Art*, Pathfinder.

Two useful anthologies of Marxist writing are D. Craig (ed.) (1975), *Marxists on Literature: An Anthology*, Penguin, and L. Baxandall (ed.) (1972), *Radical Perspectives in the Arts*, Pelican. The major works of Lukács, Goldmann, Benjamin and Sartre, discussed elsewhere in this volume, are all of importance. A useful introduction to Brecht's work (1965) is *The Messingkauf Dialogues* translated by John Willet, Methuen. Among a rich literature of Marxist criticism from the more recent period it is worth noting E. Fischer, (1963), *The Necessity of Art*, Penguin; A. Sanchez Vasquez (1974), *Art and Society*, Monthly Review; and P. O'Flinn, (1975), *Them and Us in Literature*, Pluto.

Georg Lukács

John Orr

Georg Lukács is one of the great literary critics of the twentieth century. He is also one of its outstanding Marxists. The result has been a Marxist aesthetic based very rigorously upon a Marxist interpretation of history. In the sphere of literature, no other Marxist critic has had Lukács's totality of vision. Though he never used the term, Lukács is the founding-father of what we now call the sociology of literature. If most of modern social theory is a debate with the ghost of Marx, most of the sociology of literature has been a debate with the ghost of Lukács. The difference is that much of this debate took place in his own lifetime. After his flight from Nazi Germany to Moscow in 1933 and particularly during the years of Stalin, he became very timid and cautious. After 1953 he was bolder and more critical, but as a member of the Hungarian Communist party there were necessarily political limits to his boldness. Despite these constraints, and despite his own ideological priorities, he has left an impressive volume of work written under hostile conditions. The irony, and tragedy, of Lukács is that some of his best literary work was written when his political behaviour was most suspect.

Georg Lukács was the son of a wealthy Jewish banking family in Budapest. He took an active part in Hungarian literary circles until moving to Germany. He settled in Heidelberg in 1913 and became a member of Max Weber's intellectual circle there. At this time politics and sociology had only peripheral interest for him. He shared with Thomas Mann a romantic inwardness and sense of alienation from bourgeois life. He detested the West without having any political formula for opposing it. By 1917 he had cured his inner despair and found a formula in Marxist world-revolution. While Mann became a democratic republican, Lukács became a Sorelian Marxist and later a fully-fleged Leninist. Despite their political differences, Lukács was always to respect and praise the writer whose creative spirit had come closest to his early criticism. Lukács's pre-war study *The Theory of the Novel* has its creative counterpart in Mann's short story *Tonio Kröger* – the cultivation of the romantic anti-bourgeois spirit bereft of political consolation. Mann's attitude towards the revolutionary critic was one of obvious fascination but ultimately less flattering: Lukács is the model for Leo Naphtha, the Jewish Jesuit in *The Magic Mountain*, a character whom Lukács later called 'a reactionary mystic'. Whether Lukács recognised this back-handed compliment and wilfully turned a blind eye we shall never know. The point was that Mann saw in him elements of both revolution and reaction which, at that historical period, were peculiarly central-European. Lukács shared Mann's conservative background and irrational romanticism before his conversion to rational Marxism. He repudiated liberalism from both standpoints, yet spent the rest of his life exorcising the traces of his previous sentiments.

One feature of this singular situation is immediately striking. His pre-Marxist criticism has had the greatest impact upon his Marxian disciples, in particular Lucien Goldmann and Michel Zéraffa. In the *Theory of the Novel* there is, as Lukács later admitted, an admixture of Hegelian and romanticist components. Here Lukács outlines his concept of the 'problematic hero' in modern literature. In this type of hero is contained the alienation of the human soul from the external world. Here Lukács rejects Hegel's Christian theology and replaces it with Nietzsche's anti-Christian activism. The world of the problematic hero has already been abandoned by God. The flawed relationship of soul to external reality has three different genres, hence three different types of problematic hero. The first is where the hero's vision is too narrow for the complexity of the world, as in Don Quixote. In nineteenth century novels the opposite is the case. The soul is wider and larger than the destinies which life has to offer it. 'Here' writes Lukács, 'the tendency is towards passivity, a tendency to avoid outside conflicts and struggles rather than to engage in them, a tendency to deal inside the soul with everything that concerns the soul.' This creates problems of form and content. It leads to 'the disappearance of epic symbolisation, the disintegration of form in a nebulous and unstructured sequence of moods and reflections about moods, the replacement of a sensuously meaningful story by psychological analysis' (Lukács 1971 : 112-3). A further and more serious consequence occurs. The external world 'must be entirely devoid of meaning'. The extreme of this type of hero that Lukács mentions is Oblomov. One that he was not to know about at the time, also comes to mind – that of Hans Castorp in *The Magic Mountain*.

The middle way between these two extremes, is exemplified by Goethe's *Wilhelm Meister*. Here a compromise is effected through the self-constraint of the hero. The theme in this case, according to Lukács, is 'the reconciliation of the problematic hero, guided by the loved experience of the ideal, with concrete social reality' (Lukács 1971 : 133). This formula is the closest of the three to Lukács's later formulation of literary realism. It is classic rather than modern and contrasts most clearly with what he considered to be the most advanced literary

Georg Lukács

tendency of the pre-war period. At the end of the book he made the notorious remark about Dostoevsky that he 'did not write novels'; that 'he belongs to the new world'. What this world was, Lukács does not say. But he hints that it goes beyond nineteenth century romanticism and beyond the bourgeois world. By 1917, he had found an altogether different type of alternative for his vision of the new world. Here there is no room whatsoever for the modernistic implications of Dostoevsky's fiction.

The reconciliation of man and the social world assumed a completely different form under Lukács's post-war Marxist aesthetics. Here its possibility is tied to the course of history, and in particular the history of class struggles. Lukács evaluates literature in accordance with the historical epoch in which it was written. At the same time he repudiated the ideological variants of a vulgar Marxism on two fronts. Firstly he criticised the assumption that all literature can be explained in terms of the social class of its author. Secondly he rejected the mechanical materialism of Plekhanov and Fritzsche. Lukács's analysis is at times excessively historicist, but it is also dialectical. The starting-point of his aesthetics is the famous letter which Engels wrote to Miss Harkness in 1888 on the subject of Balzac. Engels claimed that in writing Balzac was 'forced to act contrary to his own class sympathies and his own political biases'. His vision of the rising bourgeoisie was 'one of the great triumphs of realism'. Yet Lukács's rejection of class-sectarianism, particularly that of the *Proletkult* during the twenties, is hedged by historicist qualifications. The possibility of a writer fully transcending his class prejudices is, with one or two exceptions, only possible during the historical period of unchallenged bourgeois domination. Lukács attributes the deterioration in European literature to the growth of class-struggles in capitalist society after 1848, in other words after the first entry of the proletariat as a political force into the arena of class-struggle.

The limitations on modern writers are not directly class-based but historical. Lukács associated the deterioration in literature of the representational genre with the growing crises of capitalism. The dating of these crises is something we can return to later. A more immediate question is, what are those literary qualities which deteriorate? The first is the genre of artistic expression, the second its scope. Lukács traces a decline in realism parallel to a growing degeneration of the quest for totality. What does he mean by 'totality' in this context? The quest for totality cannot be separated from the attempt of art to mirror reality. But the artistic representation of reality is not simply a reflection of life's appearances. It goes beyond appearance to establish man's relationship to the world through representing what is typical of an epoch, a class, a group of people. This typicality is achieved by 'the sensuous generalisation of the whole man'. What is typical is grasped through the portrayal of the unique, the particular, and the sensuous. Following Hegel, Lukács sees this quest for totality operating in both science and art. It is a quest which, cognitively speaking, reaches its completion in the doctrine of Marxism. Although for political reasons Lukács has accepted that the true Marxist doctrine is superior to any form of knowledge, great literature in many ways parallels the Marxian completion of totality. Both strive for 'the whole man in the totality of his social world', against the social division of labour, against the divisions of classes, against distortion and alienation.

Totality also differs according to literary form. Lukács says that intensive totality is to be found in drama, extensive totality in the novel. Of the difference Lukács states the following:

> 'Drama deals with human destinies, indeed there is no other species of literature which deals so exclusively with the destinies of individuals, and particularly such as arise from men's antagonistic relations with one another and from these alone. But drama deliberately stresses this exclusiveness. This is why the individual destinies are conceived and represented in such a special way. They give *direct* expression to general destinies, destinies of whole nations, whole classes, indeed whole epochs' (Lukács 1969: 152).

Of the novel he writes

> 'The novel's manner of portrayal is *closer* to life, or rather to the normal appearance of life than that of drama . . . by representing a limited section of reality, it aims to evoke the totality of the process of social development.
> . . . The novel has the task of evoking the full span of life, the complexity and intricacy of its developments, the incommensurability of its detail. Hence the problem of the "totality of objects" as the representational aim of the large epic . . . should be understood in a very broad sense i.e. this whole includes not simply the dead objects through which man's social life manifests itself, but also the various habits, customs, usages etc. characteristic of a certain phase of human society and the direction it is taking. Society is the principal subject of the novel, that is, man's social life in its ceaseless interaction with surrounding nature, which forms the basis of social activity, and with the different social institutions or customs which mediate the relations between individuals in social life' (Lukács 1969: 162-3).

The drama is concentrated in its nature and immediate in its impact.

The novel is loose and extensive, mediated by the contemplation of its readers. It should be added that Lukács was at a loss to deal with non-epic poetry within this frame of reference. As epic, the poem shares elements of both intensive and extensive totality. On modern poetry, on *vers libre* and poetry as personal statement, Lukács has practically nothing to say.

We can now return to the problem of realism. Lukács's observations on novel and drama relate to a historical period of bourgeois ascendancy in western Europe, from the period of Elizabethan drama to *La Comédie Humaine*. Outside Western Europe they refer to Russian and Scandinavian literature up until 1917, and to Soviet socialist realism thereafter. Realism triumphs, totality is achieved for the most part under certain strictly delineated circumstances. The exceptions to this rule, as Lukács time and again points out, are rareties. The major exception is Thomas Mann. Lukács's stringent historicism has both conservative and revolutionary implications. It points to the fact that his personal literary preferences are for writers in the classic realist mould – Shakespeare and Goethe, Balzac and Tolstoy, and to his alienation from modern, progressive experiments in literature. It means also a repudiation of his early theory of literary forms, in particular the rejection of conceptualising literature in terms of the relationship of the soul of the problematic hero to the external world. In the Marxist writings the problematic hero disappears altogether since he lacks typicality. The attempts of René Girard and Lucien Goldmann to resuscitate him are linked to a more favourable attitude towards twentieth century literature. The revolutionary implication of Lukács's historicism is that literature will only undergo a renaissance within the context of a socialist society. The continuity of Russian and Soviet realism is possible only because of the unique economic backwardness of pre-revolutionary Russia, where there was no fully developed capitalism.

Lukács's theory creates something of a historical paradox. Russian realism is more recent than its Western European counterpart precisely because its society is more backward. Tolstoy wrote *Resurrection* at a time when the realist tradition in French literature had already gone into a decline. The significance of this can be seen in the comparison between Tolstoy and the early English novelists.

'The world depicted by Tolstoy is much less bourgeois than the world of the eighteenth century English novelists, but, – especially in *Anna Karenin* – it is a world in which the process of capitalist development is more strongly apparent than in the English novels which nearly always depict one particular aspect of it. In addition the great English novelists of the eighteenth century lived in a post-revolutionary period, and this gave their works (especially those of Goldsmith and Fielding) an atmosphere of stability and security . . .

In contrast to this Tolstoy's literary career began and ended in a period of approaching literary storms. Tolstoy is a *pre-revolutionary* writer, and precisely because the central problem in his works was the Russian peasant problem, the decisive turning-point in the history of western literature i.e. the defeat of the 1848 revolutions, left no trace upon him' (Lukács 1964: 149-150).

Lukács suggests the great advantage in living during the early tumult of capitalist expansion before its economic contradictions became manifest. At the same time Tolstoy is less bourgeois because there has not yet been a stabilisation of capitalism, and also because his concern with the peasantry places him outside the fated arena of class-struggle between bourgeoisie and proletariat. The passage in fact contains a number of contradictory ideas. Tolstoy is both 'early' in capitalist terms but thematically outside capitalism altogether. Lukács fuses historical background with thematic analysis in a rather casuistic manner. Writing during the early volatile period of a nascent capitalism, Tolstoy writes *about* the peasant problem.

Lukács's work is seriously flawed by this tendency. He transfers the limitation of historical context to the plane of the thematic analysis. For *Anna Karenin* is quite clearly a novel about the Russian ruling classes and the peasant problem is a secondary theme seen through the eyes of Constantin Levin, the landowner. Lukács clearly seeks refuge in the safest haven, the furthest spot from the class-divided mature capitalist society. Locating Tolstoy there also permits the free play of illusions on the part of the Russian novelist. While Balzac recognised and overcame his political biases through his fiction, Tolstoy's political illusions are embedded in the fiction itself and this is the source of their greatness. 'The incomparable epic greatness of Tolstoy's novels', he writes, 'is based on the illusions which caused him to believe that this was not a tragic conflict (the peasant problem) for which there was no way out for the honest representatives of his class, but a problem capable of solution, (Lukács 1964b: 150). The licence, or luxury, of political illusion is rationed out historically. While Lukács is quite right in pointing to the continuity of the Russian realist tradition, he is wrong to see transformation in the West as a function of historical necessity. While important economic and political factors have to be taken into consideration in any sociological explanation, Lukács's view is excessively fatalistic and deterministic. Historical 'necessity' explains in advance the 'failure' of the literature he seeks to disparage.

Lukács's preference for classic European fiction in many ways parallels F. R. Leavis's argument of the 'great tradition' in English literature. Unfortunately the English novel presents problems that, had he tried, Lukács would probably have failed to overcome. As his work stands, failure to look in any detail at Victorian literature is a major sin of omission. One might speculate for example about where, historically, he would locate the deterioration of a realist genre. In George Eliot's *Daniel Deronda* perhaps? How would he treat *Wuthering Heights*, commonly regarded as a romantic novel? If England was the most economically advanced capitalist society at what date does its literature deteriorate, considering that little happened there in 1848, the year of revolutions? Is literary deterioration heralded by the state of the economy or by the political consciousness of the emergent proletariat? Lukács seems happier mapping out the decline in realism in French literature where it was accompanied by more overt polemics, especially on the part of those writers, such as Flaubert, the Goncourt brothers and Zola, who were seeking out new literary forms.

These new forms were conceptualised by Lukács as 'naturalism'. The distinction between realism and naturalism which he took from Engels is the enduring polarity in his study of European literature, although in 1956 he was to change the terms to critical realism and modernism. Before discussing naturalism, we need to look at the virtues of the realist tradition in more detail. In bourgeois society, they are twofold. The first is the emergence of the historical novel perfected by Scott, Tolstoy and Manzoni. Through this fiction the bourgeoisie gain an awareness of their own pre-history, of the long transformation from feudal society into the bourgeois nation-state. Such fiction is humanist in its emphasis upon the potential self-fulfilment of the human personality. It is a fiction of optimism and hope, the aesthetic antithesis of reactionary romanticism. The extensive portrayal of war is not gratuitous, but a crucial link between the patriotism of the emergent nation-state and the process of social transformation. The second virtue of the realist tradition is its totalising perspective upon the social contradictions of an emergent capitalism. Here the contemporary novel of Balzac and Stendhal marks the departure from the historical novel. Where the latter is epic and heroic, the fiction of Balzac signifies a confrontation between literature and an exploitative capitalist world.

While the *arriviste* morality of Balzac's heroes is usually based on amoral foundations, Lukács probably exaggerates the critical element in his work. The Balzacian hero is still a hero, despite the fact that his fate is not decided by honour or principle but by material success. This certainly alters the heroic status of the contemporary realist character as opposed to the historical one. But the suggestion that because Balzac accurately portrays the corruptions of a capitalist culture he also condemns them, is tendentious to say the least. It means in addition that Lukács's account of the transition from realism to naturalism is not always based on solid foundations. *La Comédie Humaine* does not really contain the tragic vision Lukács ascribes to it. The following comparison between Balzac and Flaubert, for example, is something of a ritual ideological formula:

> 'Balzac depicted the original accumulation of capital in the ideological sphere, while his successors, even Flaubert, the greatest of them, already accepted as an accomplished fact that all human values were included in the commodity structure of capitalism. In Balzac we see the tumultuous tragedy of birth; his successors give us the lifeless fact of consummation and lyrically or ironically mourn the dead. Balzac depicts the last great struggle against the capitalist degradation of man while his successors paint an already degraded world' (Lukács 1964b: 63).

In this type of passage we see Lukács merging conscious ideology and artistic achievement. In *The Historical Novel* he derived changes in literary form and content from changes in philosophy. Naturalism is seen as a genre which mirrors the philosophical movement away from the Enlightenment and the idea of progress. On the other hand the difference between Balzac and his successors is also attributed to the commodity structure of capitalism. Lukács gives a materialist explanation of this change, but also an idealist one. Balzac and Flaubert represent in their work the social reality which conditions it. One can deduce the change in social reality by looking at the literary differences in their work, but one can also explain the literary differences in terms of the transformation of social reality. From a philosophical viewpoint the literary differences can also be deduced from conscious ideological statements about literature, these being derived in turn from the main currents of philosophical thought of that epoch. Lukács attributed a rather exaggerated importance to the polemical defence of their literature by the early naturalists. Instead of starting with the problem of comprehending the text, his analysis of Zola and Flaubert starts from isolated comments made by the authors on the practice of writing. These then provide, often wrongly, the conceptual framework for interpreting the literature as a whole. This alternating idealism and materialism at the level of generalisation often obscures the penetrating insights Lukács had into the actual changes of literary form and content which took place.

In the critical essays which he wrote in Moscow during the thirties, Lukács sees naturalism as both genre *and* ddoctrine. The same is not true of his discussion of realism. Realism is an artistic mode of expression but not a doctrine. In naturalism, on the other hand, Lukács sees evidence of two apparently contradictory philosophical trends. It mirrors the subjectivist philosophies of Schopenhauer, Nietzsche and Carlyle, especially their heroic pessimism. On the other hand it is inspired by positivistic tendencies within the social sciences, in the work of Taine and later Durkheim. Both are in opposition to the dialectical mode of analysis which Lukács uses in his own philosophy and aesthetics. It would probably be true to say however that Lukács sees evidence of these tendencies within literature itself. This polarisation is not a superimposed artefact, but something discerned within the genre which nonetheless parallels developments in philosophy. But the evidence offered is selective. In considering Flaubert and Zola, *Madame Bovary* and *Germinal* are largely ignored in favour of *Salammbô* and *Nana*. The validity of the argument is never wholly established. Nonetheless there remain invaluable insights in Lukács's argument, crucial for sociology and literary history.

These arise out of the tendencies he discerned in naturalism to abandon the quest for literary realism. There are three predominant ones – description as opposed to narration, fragmentation as opposed to totality, and the portrayal of average everyday occurrences as opposed to typical events. Lukács gives an excellent account of the first transformation when he compares the horse-race in *Nana* with that of *Anna Karenin* (Lukács 1970a: 110ff). In Zola's novel, he claims, the description of the race from the standpoint of an observer is complemented by the chance association between the winning horse and the name of the heroine. This provides a connection between a particular but important event and the main plot which is, to say the least, arbitrary. By contrast in Tolstoy's novel there is a narration of the event from the standpoint of the participant, Vronsky, as well as an account of the race as seen by its spectators. The outcome of the race has an important bearing on the affair between Anna and Vronsky. Failure for Vronsky is both symbolic and actual. The narrative provides the connection between event and plot. It also reveals the dialectic of subject and object within the text. Vronsky's aspirations come into conflict with the reality of the external world, and what results is an outcome of that conflict.

John Orr

The question of totality can also be elucidated in a comparison between Tolstoy and Zola. While Tolstoy's work displays extensive totality, Hegel's 'totality of objects', Zola hopes to create the same effect by exhaustive enumeration. In Tolstoy's novel, each set of distinct events in a distinctive setting constitute some decisive point in the evolution of one or more characters in the novel. Zola, on the contrary, describes a background of objects without intrinsic significance. His markets, stock exchanges, underworld haunts and theatres offer an excessively detailed backdrop with little dynamic relationship to the development of plot or character. To call them 'realistic' because they are authentic Parisian settings is to miss the point about realism in literature. To be real is to possess meaning in the text, not to make a documentary account of events which can be checked against them.

The third distinction Lukács makes is between the *average* and the *type*. This complements the previous distinction. Pure biographical description leads to flatness of characterisation in the novel, while emphasis on the average or the mean of social life results in banality. This distinction has its philosophical basis not merely in Lukács's repudiation of positivism but also in the influence exerted on his thinking by Max Weber and Georg Simmel. It parallels in many ways the distinction in social science methodology between Durkheim's average types and Weber's ideal types. But Lukács not only contrasts the type with the average, he also contrasts it with the *eccentric*. While the life of the average hero is everyday and banal, that of the eccentric hero is purely subjective, often solipsist. While the typical hero (who now replaces the problematic hero in Lukács's Marxist aesthetics) possesses common characteristics of his era, his class, his nation and so on, he also possesses other attributes. One of his abiding qualities is 'intellectual physiognomy' (Lukács 1970a: 149ff). Like the problematic hero, he experiences the contradiction between self and external world. But Lukács sees that contradiction in a different light. What is important is the relationship, and the contradiction, between abstract idea and personal experience. The great characters of realist literature, from Constantine Levin to Gregor Melykhov and Adrian Leverkuhn, all illuminate this important aspect of the literary type. Their intellectual concern with abstract ideas may be greater than those surrounding them, may not indeed be typical in the usual sense of the word. Nevertheless for the success of the novel it has to be explicit, not merely implied. One of the criticisms Lukács makes of some Soviet literature is that it does not possess the clear intellectual physiognomy of Maxim Gorki, a criticism he extends to eminent writers such as Fadeyev

118

and Ehrenberg.

In the successors to Flaubert and Zola, Lukács sees an accentuation of naturalist tendencies – the concern with the average in Gerhart Hauptmann, the cultivation of the eccentric in J. K. Huysmans. But he goes much further than this. He uses naturalism as a general category for all the literature of the avant-garde, all of which exhibits one or other of its polar tendencies – extreme subjectivism or extreme objectivism. He writes of twentieth century naturalism:

> 'We encounter it in symbolism's impressionist methods and its cultivation of the exotic, in the fragmentation of objective reality, in Futurism and Constructivism and the German *Neue Sachlichkeit* or again, in Surrealism's stream of consciousness' (Lukács 1963a: 34).

In all these diverse movements he claimed that purely descriptive techniques had lead to schematism and monotony. Either the flatness of the external world was described without reference to the experience of the human subject, or else the inner life of the individual consciousness was described without reference to the external world. Man's subjective world becomes static and reified while the external world becomes a historical lacking in temporal dimension. His dogmatic rejection of all forms of experiment in modern literature led to an aesthetically conservative which he upheld by his continued allegiance to revolutionary communism, The exceptions to his dogmatic viewpoint were either very personal, as in the case of Thomas Mann, or else political. In *The Historical Novel* there is direct evidence of the translation of the communist Popular Front strategy into literary criticism. Having seen in Flaubert's *Salammbô* a sharp deterioration in the realist qualities of the historical novel, Lukcs sees a renaissance of the genre in the more recent work of Heinrich Mann, Romain Rolland and Leon Feuchtwanger. He labelled their work 'democratic humanism'.

This essay is overtly polemical. Lukács is proselytising a communist audience in order to gain some recognition amongst them of the validity of contemporary western literature. Somehow, the essay does not seem central to his literary theory, however. Lukács can give no other reason for the renaissance of the historical novel except the progressive political opinions of their authors. While he shows their literature to be realist he can give no convincing explanation as to why it should occur at that particular historical period. Both their realism and his willingness to consider them as realists have the same origin – the Popular Front. Lukács's analysis is again reductionist but this time political rather than economic.

After the war, Lukács returned from Moscow to Budapest, where he wrote two important literary studies – his *Essays on Thomas Mann* and *The Meaning of Contemporary Realism*. The latter marks a significant change in his assessment of western literature. Published in 1956, it revealed that Lukács had had more time to assimilate and digest modern literary developments including post-war literature. As a result his terminology changes and his criticisms tend to be more precise. For realism he now substitutes the terms 'critical realism' and 'socialist realism'. Instead of 'naturalism' he talks of 'modernism'. The changes were a response both to changes in literature and a change in Lukács's own circumstances. He felt and made use of the greater intellectual freedom which obtained after the death of Stalin. It was no accident that one of the best essays of the Marxist period was written at the time of the Hungarian Uprising. Political caution is still evident in every paragraph, but the study lacks the vacuous eulogies and ritual homage to Stalin and Lenin so characteristic of the Moscow period.

In effect, literary modernism is naturalism in the age of imperialism and fascism. Perceptively Lukács points out the philosophical influence on modern literature, although he exaggerates this link. In this particular case, his *bête noire* is existentialism. The equation of fascist politics and existentialist philosophy is highly convenient. Both are of German origin, and like the Frankfurt School, Lukács generalises the European, and Western, experience of the time from its sinister German aberration. Perhaps he also sees in existentialism a projection of the tendencies to which he was favourable in *Theory of the Novel* but since rejected. Whatever the reason, he asserts that it provides the world-view within the context of which modern literature has developed. The modern bourgeois novel expresses an 'ontological view of the image of man' as 'solitary, asocial, unable to enter into relationships with other human beings'. Unlike Tolstoy's Ivan Ilyich or Flaubert's Frederic Moreau where solitude is a specific social fate, in the modernist novel it is a universal *condition humaine*. The universalisation of the solitary experience results in two things: the negation of character and the negation of history. 'First the hero is strictly confined within the limits of his own experience . . . Second the hero is without personal history'. Lukács draws in his portrait of the modernist hero upon the philosophy of Martin Heidegger. Heidegger describes the human predicament as "thrownness into being" (*Geworfenheit ins Dasein*). This is exactly the experience of the modernist hero. 'He is "thrown-into-the-world": meaninglessly, unfathomably. He does not develop through contact with the world; he neither forms nor is formed by it' (Lukács 1963a:

21). The result is a total retreat from realism.

To whom is Lukács referring when he speaks of modernism? There are two main periods involved here – the novel of the twenties and the novel of the post-war period. The latter he sees as by and large an outgrowth of the former. Indeed Lukács's study is notorious for its blanket condemnation of the major novelists who emerged after the First World War. Joyce, Proust, Lawrence, Kafka, Gide and Musil are all criticised in some measure within the modernist framework though, ironically, the existentialist world-view was developed in its post-theological stage at a slightly later date. In particular, Lukács regarded the stream-of-consciousness technique as a fragmentation of perspective, excluding 'the totality of objects'. Acknowledging Walter Benjamin's studies of Proust and Kafka, he does concede the remarkable eye these authors had for realistic physical and psychological detail. Unlike Benjamin, however, he did not regard this as a sufficient condition for literary greatness. Such literature still lacked typicality and a total perspective on life. A recent riposte to Lukács can be found in the studies of Michel Zéraffa who suggests the major novelists of the twenties created genuinely original forms of 'spatial retotalisation' once they had broken with traditional linear narrative. Thus the quest for totality is seen to be preserved.

Whatever the merits of the argument, it is clear that modernism represents a departure from nineteenth century naturalism, and also from those eclectic avant-garde movements which sprang up in European art before and after the First World War. By comparison with Joyce and Proust, Flaubert and Zola did at least attempt to portray reality as they saw it. Modernism marks a departure from this endeavour. It is no longer a failure but a refusal. As a result there is a change in the artistic reflection of the social reality conditioning literary production. Modernism 'has lost the capacity to depict the dynamics of life, and thus its representation of capitalist reality is inadequate, diluted and constrained'. This suggests a change of attitude on Lukács's part towards the earlier naturalists. In a sense they are realists, but not *critical* realists, because their fiction reveals an uncritical attitude towards the life they portray. While naturalism reveals the distortion of human nature under capitalism without criticising it, modernism involves a distortion of distortion. The various stylistic devices such as stream of consciousness technique, Gide's *acte gratuite* or Musil's *active passivity*, all facilitate this process. There is a total departure from realism.

John Orr

The historical legitimation of modernism derives from the fact that the distortion of human nature, the anti-artistic character of human relationships, is an inevitable product of capitalist society. Yet since modernism portrays this distortion without critical detachment, indeed devises stylistic devices which emphasise the necessity of distortion in any kind of society, it may be said to distort distortion further. By attributing distortion to reality itself, modernism dismisses the counter-forces at work as ontologically irrelevant' (Lukács 1963a: 75-6).

In the work of Camus, Sartre and Beckett he sees a gloomy prospect for the development of western literature, a further deterioration in the same direction. At a later date, no doubt, he would have added the *Nouveau Roman.*

Twentieth century critical realism is, by contrast, a heroic genre battling against this inevitable artistic degeneration. Lukács discerns critical realist tendencies in those writers whose literature has, by and large, been officially accepted in Eastern Europe as authentic bourgeois realism – in the theatre Shaw, Casey and O'Neill, in literature Romain Rolland, Upton Sinclair, Theodore Dreiser, Roger Martin du Gard and others. Lukács's major deviation from official aesthetics here is in his fulsome praise of Thomas Mann. In his eyes, Mann's work is the culminating, and final, achievement of critical realism in the twentieth century. This elevation of Mann is partly an act of nostalgia. We have already remarked upon the similarity of their early backgrounds, the mutual feeling that each could perhaps have shared the other's fate. But Lukács also discerned in Mann that unrelenting quest for totality absent from other critical realists.

Out of all of Mann's major novels, it is the last for which Lukács seems to reserve his greatest admiration – *Doktor Faustus.* In this novel he finds a genuine tragic vision of the decline of bourgeois art and the damnation of bourgeois society. What separates Mann in this respect from Kafka is the reflexive nature of his artistic achievement. Kafka creates literature symptomatic of impending doom, whereas Mann incorporates an awareness of that fate even though he is helpless before it. In *Doktor Faustus* these two different features, symptom and its recognition, are fused into a vision of the tragedy of modern art. While modernist art is distorted and often banal, the loss it represents to Western culture is fateful and tragic. The personal fate of Adrian Leverkühn, the modernist composer, exemplifies this wider tragic fate. Leverkühn's bold attempt to create modern music denying transcendence, a masterpiece of symphony to negate Beethoven's ninth, 'to take back the good and noble', ends in madness and death. While

Mann saw it as a comment on Germany, on the Faustian pact between German culture and German barbarism, from which nonetheless, a newer more enlightened Germany would emerge, Lukács regarded it as a universal *Gotterdammerung*. When the novel was published in 1948, his response to it was immediate, for in it he saw intertwined the fate of modern art, of Nazi barbarism, and of bourgeois society. Despite his immediate recognition of the novel's greatness, Lukács's political tendentiousness again intervened. In one of the most ludicrous statements he ever made in his life, he compared Mann's attitude towards modern art as being precisely that of Soviet socialist realism under the auspices of Zhdanov! In retrospect such judgments can only be treated with the contempt they deserve.

Lukács's personal hostility towards all forms of modernism does in fact seriously flaw his analysis of Mann's novel. The latter shows an intimate knowledge and empathic understanding of modern art far beyond the capability of its critical detractors. Without these qualities, it could simply not have been written. Mann's sympathy for Nietzsche whom Lukács regarded as a demonic irrationalist and forerunner of Hitler, is the essence of the novel. At a technical level, his determination to master the aesthetic understanding of Schoenberg, with the help of Theodor Adorno, was extraordinary. The remarkable artistic use to which he puts modern composition and particularly the twelve-tone scale, suggests an attachment to his subject matter not possible with an attitude of cold ideological hostility. It seems unlikely that Mann's problematic hero could have been conceived within the framework of nineteenth century realism. Both the form and the content of modernist art are integral to the novel. Unlike Lukács the critic, Mann the writer cannot stand still. The art of Leverkühn, however barbaric, however dissonant, is nonetheless authentic. It has to be in order to be tragic, in order for there to be a sense of loss in Adrian's final madness. There is, as Lukács recognises, a genuine search for community in Leverkühn, a genuine desire for reconciliation with the world. But to discern in the final demonic speech a dialectical striving for socialist community is to reduce it to a platitude. The speech is in any case a symptom of Leverkuhn's final failure, not a didactic recognition of what the future holds.

Doktor Faustus is the artistic consummation of Tonio Kröger, the creative transcendence through tragedy of the division between artist and bourgeois, art and morality, good and evil. It has a permanence of theme far beyond the historical transience which Lukács attributes to modern art. It thus belies Lukács's insistence on seeing it as relevant to a certain historical period of time and nothing more. The element of transience involved is actually incorporated reflexively within the novel. This is achieved by the narrative technique, of Serenus Zeitblom looking back on his beloved and flourishing Germany from a point in time when it is in ruins. Zeitblom's perspective on Leverkühn's life as historical document, and monument, is itself critical. In a way Lukács merely expropriates a criticism which is already embedded within the text and transforms it into a historicist convention. While Zeitblom is the retrospective voice of reason, Leverkühn's creative genius is demonic and irrational. What Lukács designates as the tragedy of modern art is the tragedy of *all* art. The stylistic device of a dual narrative, a modernist device, is essential to the structure of the novel.

When Lukács tries to minimise the implications of the experimentation with time, he therefore misses the point. He claims that 'the apparent use of a multiple time only reinforces (though in a complicated roundabout way) the "traditional" realist treatment of time as a social and historical unity (Lukács 1964a : 84). Yet it is clear that Mann's treatment of time as a social and historical unity is far removed from traditional realism. What Lukács refers to disparagingly as a 'complicated, roundabout way' is the key to the novel. He regards what is essential as merely incidental, with the result that he has no means of showing the real difference between the critical realism of Mann and the classic realism of Balzac.

The main failure of the critical realists lies in their inability to generate a fully socialist consciousness. Again the criticism is a historicist one. Once the class battle is fully joined the best that a bourgeois writer can do is adopt Thomas Mann's attitude of 'mature resignation', a description Mann himself would doubtless have repudiated. The critique of realism here has come full circle. The stoicism Lukács attributed to Mann is the very quality for which he attacked Flaubert, the quality which actually undermined classic realism. This false attribution of 'attitudes' to writers is asociological. Where does one locate it in the actual text? In *Doktor Faustus* it is a plausible attribute of Serenus Zeitblom, the narrator. But since the novel hinges upon an absolute division between narrator and hero, it links the writer's 'attitude' tendentiously to that of one character at the expense of another who in terms of the novel is the more central. Yet critical detachment, mature resignation remain the authentic modalities for writers in late-capitalist society for a very important reason. Such a posture is superior to that of the avant-garde modernists who falsely attribute their experimental work to the dialectic of history.

Lukács looked on the avant-garde as having no historical foundation outside the processes of alienation generated by capitalism. *Ipso facto* they could never be progressive in any historical sense. The critique of modernism from the standpoint of critical realism is important here. It provides a yardstick for the measure of literary deterioration in the west. Though never socialist, their literature is genuinely representational.

Critical realism, not socialist realism, is the standpoint from which Lukács criticises modernist literature. A further divergence from orthodoxy has also been noted by cultural *apparatchniki* of the Hungarian Communist party. They have accused Lukács of making 'no criticism of critical realism from the socialist point of view'. (Baxandall 1972: 240ff). This is also true. Lukács keeps the critical and socialist genres of realism pretty well apart. Yet the separation produces immense conceptual problems, not least the problem of 'socialist modernism'. Another problem arises from Lukács's conception of socialist realism. It is a literary genre possible only within a socialist society. It cannot be the basis of a critical opposition within capitalist society. Strictly this excludes not only socialist writers like Jack London and Emile Zola but also proletarian novelists like George Gissing and Upton Sinclair. Moreover it excludes a number of writers whose support provided communism with an embarrassment of riches. Former expressionists like Bertholt Brecht and Johannes Becher, former surrealists like Louis Aragon and Paul Eluard are examples of politically committed writers linked with avant-garde movements and with communism. Moreover, the Bolshevik Revolution also generated an explosion of modernist art within the Soviet Union. Most of Lukács's literary polemics in Weimar Germany were linked to these developments. In the magazine *Die Linkskurve* he engaged in debates with a number of left-wing writers, including Brecht, on the question of realism in politically committed art. The sad fact is that the ascendancy of a realist position in communist aesthetics, culminating in the official socialist realism doctrine of 1934, was accompanied by active political repression of the avant-garde. While Lukács had always been critical *qua* critic, there is no doubt that in a communist culture his dogmatic positions have reinforced literary censorship and perhaps political repression. Particularly in the Stalinist era, there was no clear dividing line between criticism and censorship and censorship and repression. All were merged into a totalitarian control of literature which made nonsense of Lukács's optimism for the future of socialist realism.

After the Nazi seizure of power, Lukács fled to Moscow where he developed some of his important writings on aesthetics. His retrospective claim to have been a politically critical critic must be regarded with scepticism. The critical content of his work consisted at best of sins of omission. He never actively supported Gorki's idea of 'revolutionary romanticism'. He never praised, and scarcely even mentioned, the 'construction' literature of the thirties. To that extent he was an ideological deviant, a reputation he maintained in his enthusiastic application of the Popular Front strategy to bourgeois literature. But since his turn to aesthetics was the bargain offered him by the party for autocriticism and a renunciation of politics, he was able to make use of a slightly greater freedom than his Soviet contemporaries who were reduced to silence.

The concept of socialist realism marks a decisive break with the epistemology of his earlier and most famous work *History and Class Consciousness*. Here bourgeois thought is challenged by proletarian consciousness within the context of a capitalist society. In his aesthetics there is no analogous role for a socialist literature. This in fact has to await the actual creation of a socialist society. It is only within a socialist society that the transformation from critical realism to socialist realism finally takes place. Thus critical realism is a nearer literary equivalent to the challenge of Marxist ideology in bourgeois society. Unlike Marxism, however, it does not really survive the demise of that society. 'As socialism develops', Lukács contends, 'critical realism as a distinct literary style will wither away.' Yet from his actual discussion of Soviet literature, it is clear that critical realism is seen as surviving well into the nineteen twenties.

In his study of Sholokhov, it is clear that Lukács saw the first great masterpiece, *The Silent Don*, as establishing the continuity of Russian realism. It contains elements of both critical and socialist realism. Lukács sees in Sholokhov something of the same critical detachment he discerned in Thomas Mann. Sholokhov actually resisted the temptation of being dogmatic and doctrinaire about the Russian civil war and managed to present the viewpoint of the communists and the Cossacks who were caught between the Red and the White armies. The Cossack hero, Gregor Meleykhov, is a tragic figure doomed in his fight for the rights of the Cossack peasantry. Lukács sees his fate as emblematical of the middle-peasantry during a period of class-polarisation in rural Russia (Lukács 1953: 395ff). The epic totality of revolutionary struggle is portrayed without the author succumbing to narrow and dogmatic partisanship. In *The Meaning of Contemporary Realism* it is probably with Sholokhov in mind that Lukács concludes: 'During the transition period (to socialism) the dividing line between critical and socialist realism may not be drawn too rigidly.' At the same time when discussing Alexei Tolstoy or Makarenko, for example, he reverts to the more orthodox theme of the pedagogical functions of the socialist writer. Here his analysis is not dialectical but utilitarian, inspired less by Hegel and Marx than by Chernyschevsky whose tendentious criticism and fiction had such a strong influence among Russian revolutionaries.

The major paradox of socialist realism is that it flowered during its period of birth and soon withered away. Although distinctly cool about Mayakovsky and the Agit-Prop movement of the early twenties, Lukács admitted that the great novels of socialist realism were all written in the twenties – during that period, in fact, when traces of critical realism were still apparent. With only a few exceptions, Lukács is silent on the literary portrayals of the 'new man' of the Stakhanovite era. His subsequent silence speaks volumes. Socialist realism was a failure. It had not fulfilled its initial promise. Lukács, however, lacked the courage to say so. His silence was itself a form of political complicity in a policy and a literature he could not accept. Given his eminent position, his dogmatic rejection of modernism contributed to the stultification of communist culture. What in his words was usually sincere criticism was in the action of party officials and *literati* a form of censorship and repression. Given the arbitrary and universal nature of censorship during the thirties, his stirring call for a new literature was hypocritical. He was asking writers to put their heads on the block when as a critic he had no intention of doing so himself.

There is a feature of his view of socialist realism which we have not mentioned and which is sometimes overlooked. While Lukács accepted the idea that socialist literature must be popular literature, he did not regard it as a participatory art form. Socialism in no way democratised literature. Lukács's hero-worship of great authors is similar to his hero-worship of political leaders like Lenin. They are the chosen few whose work is a permanent legacy to all. In socialist realism just as in bourgeois realism, great literature is the preserve of the few, a summit of achievement only rarely to be attained. Given his commitment to realist art, Lukács assumed that great literature would automatically become popular and that its popularity would in turn be a sign of its greatness. The esoteric nature of modernist art could, by contrast, by seen as a symptom of its lack of popular appeal. He was rarely in the position of Western Marxist critics or avant-garde writers of having to justify art which was not popular.

Lukács's enthusiasm for Soviet literature was only really revived with the advent of Alexander Solzhenitsyn. After the publication of *Ivan*

Denisovitch, he claimed that continuity had at last been re-established with the major Soviet writing of the twenties (Lukács 1970b: 21). Solzhenitsyn has mastered the central problem of the post-Stalin era – to come to terms critically with Stalin. Though the novella is an account of an ordinary day in a Soviet labour camp, Lukács rejects the idea that it is merely a naturalistic account of everyday existence. Camp life becomes a symbol of the ubiquitously grey life of Stalinist Russia as a whole. Later Lukács was to view the major novels *Cancer Ward* and *The First Circle* in a rather different light. *Cancer Ward*, though never published in the Soviet Union, contained socialist and anti-capitalist ideas to offset its pessimistic atmosphere. *The First Circle*, however, was a time-bomb placed at the very centre of the Soviet literary tradition.

Lukács recognised it as a masterpiece of literary realism, and compared it with *The Magic Mountain*. At the same time he knew its critical spirit contained a total rejection of Soviet society under Stalin. The novel in fact revives the genre of critical realism within a socialist society: Gleb Nerzhin is a problematic hero, an ideologically marginal man defying a hostile environment. In this respect Solzhenitsyn's critical fiction goes far beyond the faults of the Soviet Union reluctantly conceded by Lukács just before the end of his life. Then he criticised the failure to form a tradition of democratic participation, the growth of party bureaucracy and the leadership's abuse of power. These, and the interconnections between them are all convincingly displayed in *The First Circle*. But Solzhenitsyn does more than this. He completely dissolves the attempt that Lukács had made to separate critical and socialist realism. Lukács had argued that under advanced capitalism, the writer is reduced to social isolation whereas under socialism he is reunited with the community. The critical realist experiences social contradictions as purely internal; the socialist writer locates them correctly in the external world. It is clear however that through the central character of Nerzhin, Solzhenitsyn does both simultaneously. Nerzhin experiences both internal and external contraditions, precisely because his creator has *not* been reunited with the community.

Lukacs tries to circumvent these problems by classifying Solzhenitsyn as a "plebian writer". The term has echoes of earlier remarks made by Lukács about Tolstoy's attitude on the peasant problem, the desire to seek out the quintessential nature of the Russian people without reference to party or class. Instead of a requiem for the sacrificed party faithful, Solzhenitsyn produced a requiem for all Russians forced to live in 'a social system based upon lies'. Lukács sees Nerzhin's populism as an abandonment of the principle of Party supremacy which, while subjectively justified in terms of the injustices done to Nerzhin himself, is objectively sterile. Here his critique reverts from being dialectical to being tendentious, a habitual oscillation. While accepting as credible the response of Nerzhin within the context of the novel, Lukács censors it as politically incorrect within the context of Soviet society. He accuses Solzhenitsyn of creating eccentric rather than typical characters. Yet his criterion of typicality is extrinsic. It is based on a prior judgment of the role of the Party in Soviet history. Taking Lukács's criterion of the type aesthetically, the characters of *The First Circle* are genuinely typical. What has happened is that Lukács has politically vulgarised his own ideas. Artistic acceptance becomes dependent on political acceptance, not critical recognition. Lukács cannot take the heretical step of recognising Solzhenitsyn as a critical realist in Soviet fiction, even though his analysis points in this direction.

The attribution of eccentricity is a political artefact in the middle of an essay which nonetheless pays critical tribute to a great writer. In the hands of the Soviet Writers' Union it was a political weapon to prevent the publication of Solzhenitsyn's novels. It is again apparent that there is no clear dividing line between criticism and censorship. Not surprisingly the critique of socialist realism has fallen upon stony ground in the West. European Marxists, whose aesthetics have been influenced by Lukács, have had little time for it. Avid discussion of socialist realism is not to be found either in the Frankfurt School or among the genetic structuralists in Paris. By remaining loyal to the Communist Party, Lukács has clearly demonstrated his dilemma. To be autonomous without being subversive is a major task whose accomplishment demands a balancing-trick often incompatible with genuine critical analysis. At the same time Lukács is still a dissident within the Eastern European context. Works like *The Meaning of Contemporary Realism* are largely for the consumption of a Western audience. In what is a familiar pattern the party has secured the prestige of outstanding communist intellectuals while minimising their unorthodox influence. Lukács is perhaps the outstanding example of this.

During the last period of his life, Lukács spent much of his time writing the rather massive volume on aesthetics which has not to date been translated into English – *Die Eigenart des Aesthetischen* (Lukács 1963b). This work involves a systematisation and more detailed discussion of earlier concepts and their interrelation in a general theory of aesthetics. Once again, starting from Engels and Lenin, there is a discussion of the work of art as an artistic reflection of reality. Beyond

John Orr

that there is a further elucidation of the concepts of typicality and totality. Lukács makes it clear in this work that for him, all art, however mediocre,, however distorted, reflects reality in some manner. It is a copy *(Abbild)* of the real, with varying degrees of perfection. Like Erich Auerbach, Lukács uses the Greek term *mimesis* to describe this basic function of art. The deterioration in twentieth century art, as he sees it, is a deterioration in its mimetic functions. Since reality is historical, however, this deterioration has to be attributed to historical developments in modern civilisation. For the sociology of art and literature, Lukács has provided a conceptual framework of immense importance, a theoretical starting-point for further analysis. In this respect his study of literary genre, and changes in genre, is far superior to his study of individual authors. In the latter case Lukács gave too much credence to the opinions of the author and not enough attention to the analysis of the text. But in the former he has bequeathed an enduring statement of the realist functions of art, of the current dangers of naturalist writing both in its pseudo-subjective and pseudo-objective forms, and above all of the boldness of great literature in its quest to represent the totality of human life.

University of Edinburgh.

REFERENCES CITED

Lukács, G. (1953), *Der Russische Realismus in der Weltliteratur*, Aufbau-Verlag, Berlin.

Lukács, G. (1963a), *The Meaning of Contemporary Realism*, Merlin, London.

Lukács, G. (1963b), *Aesthetik, Teil 1: Die Eigenart des Aesthetischen*, 2 vols., Neuwied am Rhein, Luchterland.

Lukács, G. (1964a), *Essays on Thomas Mann*, Grosset & Dunlap, New York.

Lukács, G. (1964b), *Studies in European Realism*, Grosset & Dunlap, New York.

Lukács, G. (1969), *The Historical Novel*, Penguin, Harmondsworth.

Lukács, G. (1970a), *Writer and Critic*, Merlin, London.

Lukács, G. (1970b), *Solzhenitsyn*, Merlin, London.

Lukács, G. (1971), *The Theory of the Novel*, MIT Press, Cambridge, Massachusetts.

Cultural Theory Panel attached to the Central Committee of the Hungarian Socialist Workers' Party (1972), 'Of socialist realism', in Baxandall, L. (ed), *Radical Perspectives in the Arts*, Penguin, Harmondsworth.

Marxist approaches to the study of literature

Alan Swingewood

In his interpretation of Marx's and Engels's writings on literature Georg Lukács has argued that they form a coherent whole, 'an organic, systematic unity of thought' and like other Marxists he claims their support for both his general literary theory and the specific concepts of the typical, partisanship and realism (Lukács 1970: 61-88 and Lifshitz 1973). But this is to claim too much: Marx's and Engels's writings are far too ambiguous, contradictory, partial and nonsystematic, merely scattered insights into the relationship between literature and society to form the basis of a Marxist theory of literature.

Taking their writings as a whole the analysis of literature falls into three main categories: I. literature as ideology forming an essential component of society's 'superstructure' and reflecting significant aspects of economic, social and political structure; II. the discussions of literary realism in which a foundation is suggested for critical judgement; III. those writings which grasp literature as an historical and creative activity requiring genetic and dialectical analysis.

I. In his 1859 *Preface* to *A Contribution to the Critique of Political Economy*, Marx argued that philosophical, juridical, religious and artistic activity are reflections of social processes and specific material interests. It is in this sense that literature becomes the direct expression of class interests and the class struggle; and the task of analysis, the unmasking of what Plekhanov called the 'class equivalents' in literature itself (Plekhanov 1953). In this formulation literature is ideology and Marx analysed certain texts from this perspective; his brief discussion of the French petty bourgeois poets of 1848 whose art defended private property and the capitalist state (Marx and Engels, 1947: 54) together with his trenchant remarks on Eugène Sue's celebrated novel *Les Mystères de Paris* (Marx and Engels 1956) leave no doubt that in Marx's view when literature comes to embody and thus reflect class interests and ideology it constitutes epiphenomena useful only as a document of the times.[1] Thus while the 1859 formulation might suggest a mechanical, causal nexus of literature and society, Marx's many other writings postulate the necessity for artistic activity to be partially autonomous for when the writer directly transposes class interests into literature he transforms it into ideology and thus bad art. It is only when the writer transcends his immediate class position that a truthful depiction of society and man's historical, living relation with it becomes possible. That is, the creative writer is a critic of society precisely because art opposes ideology as a form of *free activity*.[2] Thus Balzac, while personally sympathetic to the aspirations of the French nobility transcended this narrow, ideological standpoint to express, within his fictional universe, the necessary historical triumph of the French bourgeosie. The transindividual element thus cuts across any notion of 'class equivalent.' It is this theme which Engels takes up in his letter to Minna Kautsky (November 1885) in which he argued against the view that a socialist novel must reflect in a positive manner the class struggle. A militant standpoint, he wrote, was actually harmful, for socialist literature achieves its purpose only through 'conscientiously describing the real mutual relations, breaking down conventional illusions about them' and thereby shattering 'the optimism of the bourgeois world,' inducing doubt on 'the eternal character of the existing order.' Engels thus rejects the norm of *conscious* political commitment (or political partisanship) and condemns those writers who strive to resolve social conflicts explicitly within art. 'The more the author's views are concealed the better', and a socialist novel must 'not offer any definite solution or . . . even line up openly on any particular side' (Marx and Engels 1947: 37-40). Such pronouncements clearly oppose vulgar socialist realism and Stalinist literary norms although these remarks remain ambiguous on the question of *commitment in general*. Thus Engels distinguishes tendentiousness from overt political commitment citing as exemplars of the former Aeschylus, Dante, Cervantes and 'the modern Russians and Norwegians.' It is this ambiguity which allows Marxists such as Lukács and Ernst Fischer to defend the dogmatic and historicist argument that great realist literature was at all times committed to a socially progressive force either unconsciously as with Balzac, Tolstoy, Ibsen and Mann, or openly as with Sholokhov and Makarenko.[3]

II. Engels's occasional writings on realism, the creation of 'typical characters in typical situations' have been interpreted as providing the foundation for a Marxist aesthetic. His analysis of Balzac's *Human Comedy* is built around the transformation within Balzac's art of his private and reactionary ideology, the 'triumph of realism' which corrects worldly prejudice (Marx and Engels, 1947: 37-40). But in what way does realism as defined externally from any detailed analysis of literary texts imply *only* the necessity for typical characters in typical situations? Are positive characters always essential for an artistic rendering of a 'decaying' capitalist society? Would negative, eccentric characters in 'decadent' situations perform the same social and artistic function as the typical for instilling doubt on the nature of bourgeois society? Marx's fragmentary comments on Diderot's eighteenth century novel, *Rameau's Nephew* where a more subtle, dialectical analysis is suggested, are important here. These comments, written in Marx's 'maturity' explicitly follow Hegel's philosophical interpretation of the novel in which the negative, eccentric anti-hero is described as 'the self expressing pessimism of the self-consciousness' and the text as a whole analysed as a structure of irony and pessimism in contradiction to many of the dominant tenets of bourgeois Enlightenment philosophy[4] (Marx and Engels 1947: 69-70). Marx's critical norm here was not typicality but rather a unity of contradictory elements. In short, the 'self expressing pessimism' is the alienation of self in literature, 'eccentric' rather than 'typical'.

III. For both Marx and Engels literature develops genetically, a social, collective product bearing a dialectical, contradictory relation with the individual author, ideology and social structure. Thus, writing of ancient Greek society Marx posed the question of how an economically backward society could produce great art. His answer was that art reflected the widely accepted Greek superstructure of myth, and that art was mediated through the religious system which in itself reflected the economic and social structure. Marx argued that art bears no direct relationship with the general development of society nor with its material base or the skeleton structure of its organisation. Between culture and society there exists an uneven, contradictory relation: writing of American education and culture, for example, he suggests that there is no immediate link between them and the highly developed economic structure (Marx 1971: 215). Marx's arguments here suggest a concept of society as a totality of different levels, economic, political, cultural etc., which develop unevenly and thus generate contradictions both between themselves and society as a whole. It is moreover the cultural level which enjoys the greatest autonomy: Engels argues that although the economic factor is decisive for the development of culture nevertheless within what he called 'the higher ideologies' (philosophy, theology, art) 'the interconnections between the ideas and their material condition of existence become more and more complicated, more and more obscured by intermediate links' (Marx and Engels 1961: 493-5). The further removed a level from the sphere of material interests, economics and politics, the greater its degree of independence and the more complex the mediations. The relation of literature to society must be posed *dialectically*.

Neither Marx nor Engels worked out a systematic methodology for theory of literature. A more rigorous application of Marxism to the study of literature developed slowly and unevenly in the work of such diverse Marxist theorists as Plekhanov, Lafargue, Mehring, Lunacharsky, Rosa Luxemburg, Trotsky and Alexander Voronsky.[5] However, these Marxist approaches to literature fell victim to what Rosa Luxemburg called 'the decay and stagnation' of Marxism after Marx: the period from Marx's death in 1883 to the 1917 Russian Revolution was a time when the international Marxist movement, largely dominated by the German Social Democrats, transformed Marxism from a revolutionary dialectical theory into a dogmatic, evolutionary determinism. Theorists such as Karl Kautsky and Plekhanov defined Marxism in natural scientific terms arguing that the subjective factor in human history, consciousness and praxis, was merely the reflection of irresistible economic 'iron' laws of capitalist crisis and breakdown. Contemporary Marxist literary theory echoed this historicist interpretation: literature was analysed as a somewhat passive reflection of inevitable economic processes; the dominant contradiction in society was seen as economic; and literature was reduced to a simple property of the class struggle.[6] Thus Plekhanov's discussion of eighteenth century French drama succeeds in dissolving its complex literary structures into a mechanical correlation with social classes: the supremacy of tragedy over farce merely reflected the cultural and economic domination of the French nobility – cultural history is merely the artistic embodiment of the class struggle. Writing of nineteenth century art he observed that 'as the apple tree *must* produce apples and a pear tree pears, so must the artist who adopts a bourgeois standpoint be against the working class movement. Art, in periods of decadence *must* itself be decadent. That is inevitable' (Plekhanov 1953: 223).

It was against this reduction of Marxism to 'economism' and 'mechanical materialism' that the early works of Lukács, some of Gramsci's writings and the cultural theorists of the Frankfurt School (Adorno, Horkheimer, Benjamin) and the more recent work of Lucien Goldmann were directed.[7] These Marxists emphasised dialectics and praxis and a grasp of culture as a totality irreducible to economic forces. But with the triumph of Stalinism and the conservative, nationalist programme of 'socialism in one country' in the Soviet Union during the late 1920s, together with the defeat of the Trotskyist Left Opposition, Marxism once more turned towards dogma, and literary theory towards economism and historicism. The work of Lukács illustrates both these trends.

Lukács came to Marxism during the First World War. His early pre-Marxist works, *Soul and Form*, *The Theory of the Novel* were strongly influenced by neo-Kantianism and nourished by an idealist mode of thought which situated *form* ahistorically: the young Lukács's essays on tragedy and the novel form grasp literary structures as timeless essences (Goldmann 1963). Breaking with this tradition of thought Lukács participated in the ill-fated Hungarian Revolution of 1919, and wrote the essays which, collected in book form and published as *History and Class Consciousness* in 1923, broke away from mechanical materialist Marxism by making the concept of totality the central element in Marxist thought and seeing culture as a determinate structure in its own right. Equally important, Lukács showed the significance of the concepts of alienation and reification for Marxism and, from a methodological standpoint, the dialectical relation of parts to whole. In *History and Class Consciousness* (Lukács 1971) the elements of totality are not defined as uniform and identical, as was the case with 'vulgar Marxism', but form a dialectical and contradictory relation with one another, as a unity of oppositions: there is no mutual influence or reciprocal interaction of 'otherwise unchangeable objects' and the complex unity of any totality (whether economic, political, cultural etc.) is not dependent on one single contradiction.[8]

Lukács was quickly damned by the orthodox critics of the Communist International. *History and Class Consciousness*, rejected as a bourgeois deviation in Marxism, was eventually disowned by its author. Yet in 1967 he wrote: 'I agreed with Stalin about the necessity for socialism in one country and this shows very clearly the start of a new epoch in my thought' (Lukács 1971: xxviii). This new beginning was to culminate in the development of a literary theory widely regarded today as the most impressive contribution to Marxist aesthetics but one in which the concepts of totality, dialectics and reification as defined in *History and Class Consciousness* disappear either by a change in the definition or through simple exclusion. This is especially brought out in the function of the dichotomy reason/unreason in his thought.

In many of his literary studies Lukács argues that the irrationalism which threatens mankind under the capitalist system must be challenged by the reason itself. This is why *ethics* plays such an important role in his work, the ethical principle being embodied both in the Party and in the great realist writer. Discussing Sholokhov's novel, *Virgin Soil Upturned* Lukács justifies the moral role of the Communist Party through an entirely ideological reading of this exemplary socialist realist text: Sholokhov's fiction demonstrates the necessity to educate the people in socialist ethics *from above* (Lukács 1964a: 501). For Lukács the role of the Party in political and social questions and the function of intellectuals in intellectual matters (arts and literature etc.) is to educate the uneducated masses. Thus the great realists are to be read as examples, their work acknowledged for their moral power over readers. Lukács interprets Tolstoy's fiction as a 'means' of communicating a certain content, a 'sermon' to mankind aiming at its renewal (Lukács 1972: 193). In a similar way Thomas Mann becomes 'the educator of his people' (Lukács 1964b: 32).

Lukács thus sees society as a struggle between reason and unreason, creating contradictions that can be overcome only through the dominance of rationalism, that is, a socialist humanism. Literature is therefore important for pointing the way ahead, for overcoming the bad sides of Stalinist socialist realism and decadent bourgeois modernism. Lukács thus advises contemporary writers to follow 'the command of Hamlet, to present a mirror to the world and help humanity progress by means of such a reflected image' (Lukács 1972: 13).

Lukács's literary theory, therefore, is less concerned with the 'literary' character of literature than with its social function in society or its value for education. It is this aspect of his thought which links him with Plekhanov and the English Marxist writer Christopher Caudwell. The aesthetic element in Marxism has been developed into a frankly utilitarian aesthetic.[9] Literature becomes a document, useful or harmful in developing or impeding the growth of a 'correct' social consciousness: if life is truthfully portrayed in literature then fiction becomes 'the most effective means of throwing light on the problems of social life and an excellent weapon in the ideological preparation of the democratic revolution . . .' (ibid: 107). From such a utilitarian standpoint Lukács can only formally appreciate the totality of a literary text in favour of its future-oriented, positive educative impact, characteristics embodied in his concept of the typical. For the type is the mediation of what *is* and what *ought* to be, and the most important aesthetic category – realism – valuable precisely because it presents a true reflection of historical change through the unity, in the typical, of the specific and the particular features of an epoch. Lukács's rationalism, his emphasis on ethics and his overall utilitarian approach imply a literary theory both eclectic and arbitrary which, in the concrete analysis of texts, comes to mean the total domination of content over form, society over literature.

Thus in his extensive analyses of European realism Lukács argues that the great realist writers reflected the objective momentum of capitalist economic and social development. For Lukács the most significant contradiction for understanding cultural change and forms is the economic: literature expresses this contradiction in both its form and content. Bourgeois critical realism with its typical characters reflects the progressive, historically inevitable progress of the bourgeois class and capitalist society while modernism, with its morbid, pathological and eccentric characters, is the literary expression of declining capitalism. The thrust of Lukács's general theory is that bourgeois society in its development necessarily alienates creative writers:

> The really honest and gifted bourgeois writers who lived and wrote in the period following . . . 1848 naturally could not experience and share the development of their class with the same true devotion and intensity of feeling as their predecessors . . . . And because in the society of their time they found nothing they could support wholeheartedly . . . they remained mere spectators of the social process (Lukács 1972: 141).

The writer becomes an onlooker, an impartial judge of socio-economic change; realism is thus the reproduction of progressive historical forces. But Lukács goes further than this historicist reductionism by suggesting that a true objectivity in part depends on the attitude of the writer himself through his right choice of material to transform into the typical. And this is possible if he lives in a society characterised by historically progressive economic trends and absorbs them (Goethe, Balzac, Tolstoy) or, living at a time of capitalist decline he fights against political reaction, unreason and decadence (Keller, Mann). The result is a Marxist theory in which the writer does not transpose the world view of a class or group on a literary level but simply reproduces progressive social trends in the form of fiction always providing he enjoys the right moral constitution or the luck to live at the opportune literary moment. Literature reflects society *as a whole:* Lukács has eliminated the highly complex social structure of nineteenth and twentieth century European capitalism and it thus becomes impossible for him to distinguish the significant differences which exist between contemporary realist writers (i.e. Turgenev, Dostoevsky, Tolstoy). Lukács is thus forced to distinguish such writers in terms of their *personal* ideologies. To reduce literature to one basic contradiction – the economic – and to assimilate all literary products to one dominant structure effectively eliminates the highly complex, specific determinations of literary activity and the mediations between literary products and society.

Thus in his analysis of nineteenth century Russian realism Lukács claims Tolstoy and Dostoevsky as realists of the same school arguing that the differences between them are less important then their commitment to progressive historical change. Dostoevsky's fiction, with its emphasis on the urban misery and city culture, expresses the late development of Russian capitalism, while in contrast Tolstoy depicts this economic structure through the dissolution of 'old' Russia and the birth of the 'new' seen from the standpoint of the peasantry. Lukács conceives the concept of totality, therefore, in terms of the 'correct' reflection within the literary text of external socio-historical changes. Tolstoy's *War and Peace* and *Anna Karenina* are used explicitly in this way: Lukács discusses the main characters only in relation to their opinions on such things as peasant-gentry relations and the fact that they have opinions on these matters classifies them, and Tolstoy, as 'progressive' (Lukács 1972: ch. 6). Similarly in Lukács's analysis of Balzac and Stendhal both writers are classified as realists 'conscientiously uncovering the true driving forces of the social process, to present to the reader the most typical and essential traits in every social phenomenon' (ibid: 70). Indeed, the lack of mediations within Lukács's broad historicist framework is nowhere better illustrated than in his discussion of these two contemporary but very different authors. For Lukács the differences between Balzac's and Stendhal's fiction are idiosyncratic. His evidence is drawn from their assessment of their own work. Lukács takes Balzac's view of literature as he described it in his review of Stendhal's *La Chartreuse de Parma* (1840) where he defines Stendhal's fiction as belonging to the "Literature of ideas" that is to rationalism, and not as with his own to a synthesis of the 'literature of images' and 'ideas', that is romanticism. Stendhal's personal tastes inclined to the Enlightenment while Balzac's to post-revolutionary romanticism. How, then, was Balzac a greater realist than Stendhal, although both are realists? Lukács writes:

> Balzac may be counted among the writers who while accepting romanticism, at the same time consciously . . . strove to overcome it. Stendhal's attitude to romanticism is on the contrary a complete rejection (Lukács 1972: 68).

Thus Balzac, although personally accepting romanticism surmounts it artistically by depicting the capitalist transformation of French society:

> The deepest disagreement between Balzac and Stendhal rests on the fact that Balzac's world view was essentially influenced by all these newer trends, while Stendhal's world view was at bottom an interesting . . . extension of the ideology of pre-revolutionary Enlightenment (ibid: 77).

So Balzac, with 'a confused and often reactionary world view, mirrored the period between 1789 and 1848 more completely and profoundly than the more progressive Stendhal. Balzac could thus create the new capitalist class while Stendhal created but one capitalist figure, Leuwen, who, in contrast to Balzac's creations is 'less profound and comprehensive' appearing as 'a very lifelike transposition of the pre-revolutionary traits of the Enlightenment into the world of the July monarchy' (ibid: 77-78).

The point here is that Lukács's analysis is made without either any reference to the specific literary contexts or any grasp of the text as a whole. Characters in Balzac's and Stendhal's novels are simply compared with the 'real' world and the way they reflect the historical inevitability of capitalist social change. The text is thus 'sliced up' into separate parts and can never constitute a complex totality, a structure of levels integrated into an aesthetic whole: Lukács's theory of reflection must destroy any potential unity within a text in favour of an arbitrary, eclectic reductionism. Lukács's failure to analyse literature as part of the dialectical totality clearly stems from his omission of mediating elements in the nexus of writer and society. To understand the different structures within the fiction of Balzac and Stendhal, Dostoevsky, Tolstoy and Turgenev it is essential to establish the class/group relation: to say that literature reflects society as a whole is to negate any dialectical conception of totality for Lukács's method is not designed to explain *specific* connections and, like the nineteenth century positivist, Taine, he ends with a system of rigid, deterministic relations.

Lukács's historicism, and his non-dialectical concept of reflection lie at the heart of his rejection of 'modernism' and defence of the 'type'. Modernism (Joyce, Beckett, Musil, Kafka) is a literature which no longer portrays social progress because it lacks the historical perspective characteristic of bourgeois and socialist realism. Instead of types, modernism portrays the average, the eccentric, or the surface phenomena rather then the immanent tendencies of capitalism. For Lukács the importance of types is that they are confirmed by future social development:

A writer may grasp the authentic human problem . . . without consciously anticipating subsequent political and social developments. Here again the question of perspective is relevant. For a typology can only be of lasting significance if the writer has depicted the central or peripheral significance, the comic or tragic characteristics of his types, in such a way that subsequent developments confirm the portrait of the age (Lukács 1963: 57).

In short the writer must reflect, through art, historically progressive social forces. Engels's vague remarks on the type and on commitment have been extended to an inviolable dogma.

Three questions may be asked of Lukács's concept of the type:
1. Do the types found in Balzac, Stendhal and Mann who do not point the way to the future lose their value?
2. Once the types have been confirmed by historical development do they lose their *literary* significance? Or is their significance purely historical?
3. If the literary value of a text is completely related to the social progressiveness of its content does this not destroy its inner coherence as a work of art?

Many commentators on Lukács have rightly linked his literary theory with the theory and practice of Stalinism.[10] Lukács's highly conservative aesthetic, his defence of realism against all forms of modernism are clearly related to the political exigencies of the Popular Front period during the 1930s when the European Communist parties sought out allies in the 'progressive' bourgeoisie. There is no other explanation for Lukács's astonishing claim that while Thomas Mann 'symbolises all that is best in the German bourgeoisie' he nonetheless 'prescribed socialism as the future task of the bourgeoisie' and consistently sought 'to link arms with the workers' and thus generate a revitalised 'German life and culture' (Lukács 1964b: 105). Lukács's utilitarian approach to the study of literature and his reduction of the specifically literary to the economic form part of this conservative structure. Echoes of it can be found in England during the 1930s when a Marxist literary theory emerged for the first time in the work of Caudwell, Ralph Fox, Alick West and a number of other writers grouped around the magazine *Left Review.*

The dominant theme in this first school of English literary Marxism was that literature reflected the dynamics of the class struggle through embodying ideological elements. Literature was explained by both a 'vulgar' theory of inevitable social change and a mechanistic concept of 'base' and 'superstructure'. Class was the key to literary value: the complex mediations between a literary work and the social structure disappeared as literature was analysed solely as a medium through which a 'rising' or dominant social class expresses itself ideologically. Thus the rise of capitalism is coeval with progressive bourgeois ideology and realism; but with the decline of capitalism and its 'final crisis' literature increasingly reflects a pessimistic and subjective ideology. Political commitment through the Communist party becomes the only way of solving the artistic crisis.

In the pages of *Left Review* the thesis of art as weapon in the class struggle was developed.[11] For Edgell Rickwood 'the work of literature will reflect the stage the class struggle has reached . . .' (*Left Review*, 1935) while for Christopher Caudwell, in his *Illusion and Reality* (1937: 203-4) a class society must necessarily produce class art. Caudwell's work has been highly praised as the only significant English Marxist work to come out of the 1930s but a close examination of its central ideas situates it firmly with the historicist school of Lukács. A direct correspondence between poetry and economic structure is asserted and the complex history of English poetry reduced to the waxing and waning of the class struggle. Caudwell's main point is that poetry reflects bourgeois ideology, the bourgeois 'illusion' of a concept of freedom external to the practice of the class struggle. Bourgeois poetry cannot reflect an active struggle against capitalist social relations because literature is causally bound to the dominant class: during the eighteenth century 'bourgeois poetry expresses the spirit of manufacture, of the petty manufacturing bourgeoisie'. As for the nineteenth century poets they become, like Byron, 'conscious of the . . . necessity to go over to the bourgeoisie' and, like Shelley, speak 'for the bourgeoisie'. Or they revolt and seek a return to nature, itself part of the bourgeois illusion of freedom, and like Wordsworth may exist in 'austere idleness in Cumberland' precisely because the capitalist division of labour creates a sufficient economic surplus to maintain withdrawn bourgeois creative activity. Finally the revolutions of 1848 and 1871 sound the 'doom' of bourgeois poetry which becomes a flight from reality (ibid: 75-98).

Characteristic of this form of historicist reductionism is an emphasis on the social function of literature. If social class and ideology relate immediately to literary products it is but one short step to the proposition that in the epoch of capitalist 'decline' only a politically committed literature can correspond to the new stage of the class struggle. In Alick West's *Crisis and Criticism* (1937) the 'good' writer is defined as one who 'actively feels the productive energy of society and identifies himself with it' thereby expressing 'the conflicting phases of its organisation'. Literature expresses the 'actual' and the 'desirable', thereby 'exciting' and 'directing' man's social energy to definite social goals. Literature 'awakens the fundamental experience that continual energy is required in the endless war against the forces of disintegration' (West 1974: 113-9). In these formulations art and literature become modes of cognition, a means for understanding and mastering the social world and it is this utilitarian concept of literature which lies at the heart of Caudwell's Marxism. Like science, art and literature are guides to action, weapons in the class struggle, and it therefore becomes essential to organise them on this basis. There is a close connection here between Caudwell and West and the Proletkult theories of literature developed in the Soviet Union during the 1920s, which formed the basis for Stalinist Socialist Realism.[12]

Thus for Caudwell art reveals 'the various ways' in which man adapts himself to experience making possible 'new levels of conscious sympathy, understanding and affection between men, matching the new levels of material organisation achieved by economic production' (Caudwell 1974: 154-5). Poetry is 'an adaption to external reality' (ibid: 214) a mode of changing men's minds for beauty itself is a guide to action (ibid: 155-6). Caudwell's conclusion that art 'is all active cognition' while 'art in contemplation is all active organisation of the subject of cognition' and therefore an 'affective experimenting with selected pieces of external reality' corresponding to a scientific experiment (ibid: 262-3; 265-7) can be judged only as a form of crude materialism. To define the relation of literature to society in terms of a simplistic correlation between class and economy and to analyse the complex structure of literary forms solely in terms of their class, ideological content necessarily leads to a strictly utilitarian aesthetic. It is probably true that in the 1930s only L. C. Knights in his *Drama and Society in the Age of Jonson* (1937) grasped the Marxist notion of dialectical mediation in his attempt to relate the specific ethical, political and social content of Jonson's writings not to an abstraction such as the mode of production but both to social groups within the mode of production and the partially autonomous cultural superstructure, and thus grasp the literary product as a structure of developing capitalist and pre-capitalist elements.[13]

Given the utilitarian and historicist assumptions of the English Marxists it is not surprising to find little actual textual analysis. Their comments on specific literary works are in general banal and uninteresting. In contrast the Marxists writers of the Frankfurt School, while still spending little time on actual analysis, developed a sophisticated theoretical position better able to point the way to textual analysis. Their work combined a deep sympathy with the concepts of totality and mediation as developed by Lukács's *History and Class Consciousness* with a rejection of Stalinism. For Adorno, Horkheimer, Marcuse, Benjamin and Sigfried Kracauer, capitalism, far from being in its final crisis, was resiliently shoring up its defences against the proletariat by a new form of cultural domination. Placing great emphasis on the autonomy of the 'superstructure' the Frankfurt theorists pointed to the emergence of a totalitarian culture in which art and literature become mere commodities. Modern capitalism is a culture dominated by alienation, reification, collectivism and the virtual eclipse of the autonomous individual. A contrast is thus drawn between the manipulative mass media and mass culture which seeks to reconcile all contradictions and affirm the inevitability of capitalism, and the transcendent, critical structure of genuine art and literature. 'A successful work,' writes Adorno, '. . . is not one which resolves objective contradictions in a spurious harmony, but one which expresses the idea of harmony negatively by embodying the contradictions pure and uncompromised in its innermost structure' (Jay 1973: 179). Unlike Lukács, Caudwell and other contemporary Marxists the Frankfurt theorists saw in modernism a genuine, artistic challenge to the alienation and reifying trends of a collectivist capitalism; nineteenth century realism was no longer capable of expressing the deep crisis of modern, regulated mass society. The study of literature, therefore, becomes a necessary component of 'Critical Theory', a means of forging a critical consciousness and humane resistence to totalitarianism. In his essay, 'Art and Mass Culture' Horkheimer developed this theory, arguing that genuine art ('high culture') had always resisted the dominant values of society: 'Art, since it became autonomous, has preserved the utopia that evaporated from religion.' The products of 'the culture industry', because they appeal to a vast, necessarily homogeneous public, allow no scope for the imagination, constituting an 'impoverishment of aesthetic matter, which, far from involving the reader in a genuine dialectic, conceives him as a passive object to be manipulated and controlled. In the world of the 'culture industry' 'a blind wallowing in wish fantasies' frustrates 'normal emotional life' and educates man into obedience (Horkheimer 1972: 273-90).

However, not all members of the Frankfurt School 'wrote off' modern 'mass society'. Both Walter Benjamin and Bertolt Brecht argued, like Adorno, for literature as a *praxis*, a critical consciousness, but *only* if the author is producing directly for the proletariat within new forms of communication. The old bourgeois art forms were dead and its apparatus of production and publication must be rejected since it 'can assimilate an astonishing number of revolutionary themes, and can even propagate them without seriously placing its own existence or the existence of the class that possesses them into question (Benjamin 1973;

Brecht 1974). For Brecht and Benjamin it was necessary to develop against Lukács's 'contemplative aesthetic' a 'production aesthetic' – literature as a transforming praxis and not the mimesis of class struggle.

The basis for these arguments was Benjamin's attempt to expand Marx's theory of economic production to artistic and literary production through a recognition of the technical and mechanical roots of cultural reproduction. He argued that the development of technology in printing, radio, films and photography have had a decisive effect on both the art forms themselves and the social position of the author. He notes, for example, that the art of caricature was unknown in Antiquity, as the only cheap means of reproduction was the minting of coins and there was no mass distribution of products (Benjamin 1975: 57). In a similar way Benjamin proposed a new theory of the novel. He argued that the novel form develops out of storytelling and different forms of social organisation. The story is an 'artisan form of communication' with its origins in oral tradition and the pre-industrial societies of artisans, peasants and traders. Handed down from generation to generation the story becomes the collective expression of an organic community. In contrast, the novel is an epic genre striving to depict the whole, not a segment of society. Its world is industrial and bourgeois and its reader individualistic and privatised. The novel's technical basis, essential for its development was mass reproduction through innovations in printing and mass distribution through bookshops and libraries. In this way the novel is passed on through social institutions. But with the development of modern capitalism a new form of communication emerges: information. Benjamin, unlike other members of the Frankfurt School, saw in modern collectivist society a new collectivist art very different from the mass art and culture which Adorno and Horkheimer identified as the dominant characteristic of contemporary capitalism. He argued that it was no longer possible to write for a distinctive middle class public since changes in the means of artistic production must necessitate changes in the 'social relations of artistic production' (social position of writers, the nature of their products, etc). In this situation a writer ceases to be an artist but becomes a *producer*. His creative activity is linked to the transformation of capitalist artistic and literary production from an individualistic to collectivist basis. All men are now producers, for the development of newspapers, magazines and other agencies of information breaks down the old distinction between author and public. Individuals can now write letters to newspapers and, drawing on experiments in the Soviet Union during the late 1920s, Benjamin suggests that a collectivist literary enterprise such as Gorky's projected History of Russian Factories written by the factory workers themselves is possible (Benjamin 1973).

The weakness of the Brecht/Benjamin argument lies in the explicit identification of literature with social class and its reduction to one political structure. To suggest as Benjamin does that the 'correct' political tendency is always correlated with the 'correct' literary tendency is to assimilate politics non-dialectically to literature and all art to the political class struggle. Nonetheless, Benjamin's insight into the material basis of literary forms is important and represents a clear alternative to Lukács's formalistic and historicist concept of realism.[14]

Like Lukács, Adorno and Benjamin, L. Trotsky's approach to the study of literature was broadly humanistic; but it was neither historicist nor reductionist. In *Literature and Revolution*, as well as in his shorter writings on Jack London, Celine and Malraux, Trotsky advanced the argument that literary value does not hinge on the class or political ideology of the author. Of course class is important for any Marxist analysis of literature 'but this class criterion must be refracted artistically' and thus conform with immanent literary necessity: literature must be grasped as literature, a qualitatively different practice from politics with its own specific laws. *Literature and Revolution* was written largely as an attack on the crude utilitarian literary theories of left groups such as LEF and the Proletkult during the early 1920s which identified literary quality exclusively with class and left politics. But Trotsky's analysis can be read as a counter both to the approaches of Benjamin and Brecht and of vulgar materialists such as Caudwell and Alick West:

> The heart of the matter is that artistic creativity, by its very nature, lags behind the other modes of expression of a man's spirit, and still more of the spirit of a class . . . The political writing of a class hastens ahead on stilts, while its artistic creativity hobbles along behind on crutches (Trotsky 1970: 66).

This dialectical grasp is the hub of Trotsky's sympathetic although critical analysis of literary 'fellow-travellers' such as Boris Pilnyak who, while hostile to Bolshevism nevertheless accepted the revolution. Thus discussing Pilnyak's novels Trotsky shows both the relation of form and content with Pilnyak's *contradictory* understanding of the revolution. That is, Pilnyak accepts and even 'praises' the October revolution but 'he cannot acquit it artistically because he cannot grasp it intellectually'. He lacks a world view, Trotsky argues, a coherent understanding of the revolutionary epoch and thus he depicts post-revolutionary Russia not as an integrated whole but 'episodically' and 'partially' (Trotsky 1957: 80-82). Similarly, in discussing Blok's great poem. *The Twelve*, Trotsky says it represents both 'a cry of despair for the dying past, and yet a cry of despair which rises in a hope for the future.' Blok's poem is an individualistic rendering of an immense collective act the 'inner meaning' of which 'remains somewhere outside the poem' (ibid: 119-121). So it is with Malraux's novels of the Chinese Revolution: affirming revolution they are nonetheless 'corroded' by 'the excesses of individualism' and fail as a unified artistic depiction of revolutionary practice because Malraux has no integrated world view (Trotsky 1970).

Trotsky's concepts and analyses are superficially similar to those of Lucien Goldmann especially the argument that artistic coherence must ultimately relate both to extrinsic social factors and the demands of literary form. Goldmann's 'genetic structuralism' is one recent attempt, working within a broad Marxist framework, to grasp literature as a partly autonomous whole irreducible to economic structure: 'A literary work is not the simple reflection of a real and actual collective consciousness, but the outcome, at the level of a highly developed coherence, of the tendencies proper to the consciousness of this or that group, a consciousness which must be conceived as a dynamic reality . . .' (Goldmann 1975). Arguing that a 'significant literary form' (novel, poem etc.) depends on aesthetic coherence Goldmann suggests the concept of 'world vision' and advocates the methodology of the young Lukács, namely that analysis of literary texts must consist in a constant dialectic between the parts and the whole. The positive side of Goldmann's work is the emphasis on totality and mediation as exemplified in his analysis of the tragic vision in the philosophy of Pascal and drama of Racine (Goldmann 1964). His weakness is a tendency to reductionism and historicism as, for example, in his study of the modern novel, he attributes its form and content non-dialectically to the capitalist mode of production: the decline of the hero in modern fiction is linked mechanically with the development of 'organised capitalism' (Goldmann 1975). Paradoxically Goldmann's sociological theory of the novel embraces the very position his method had set out to attack. On the one hand he advocates the dialectical analysis of a text in terms of praxis and world vision, yet on the other employs a mechanical correlation between literary form and changes in capitalist economic organisation.

When one surveys the many approaches to the Marxist study of literature one conclusion is surely inescapable. To analyse literature in terms of its social context and relation to social classes is not necessarily a Marxist perspective for Marx himself emphasised that the class struggle and the social determination of ideas were concepts first discovered by bourgeois historians and philosophers. Yet the dominant trend of Marxist literary theory has been to reduce the complex inner structure of art products to a crude theory of reflection and to minimise what must surely be the hallmark of a Marxist theory, dialectical unity and contradiction. But there is something else: literature is a humanism, a grappling with the unresolved complexities of human experience within a definite historical context, a means whereby man affirms his autonomy and freedom to transform the social world through his purposes and practices. It is in this sense that a Marxist analysis of literature must bring that literature closer to readers and criticsm itself become a creative practice.

London School of Economics and Political Science.

FOOTNOTES

1. Engels occasionally lapses into a crude mechanical approach as when he uses Homer's *Iliad* as a reflection of population increase, the expansion of agriculture, shipbuilding and metalworking (Engels 1961).

2. See for example Marx's comment that a writer must 'make a living in order to exist and write, but he must not exist and write in order to make a living. The writer in no way regards his work as a means. They are ends in themselves' (Marx and Engels 1974: 55).

3. Thus Ernst Fischer writes that to attain genuine objectivity modern writers must take 'sides with the working class' and adopt 'the viewpoint of an undogmatic Marxist' (Fischer 1963: 111).

4. Hegel discusses Diderot's novel in the section 'Spirit in self-estrangement' in his *Phenomenology* (1807).

5. I have discussed Trotsky and Voronsky in *the Novel and Revolution* (Swingewood 1975a: 90-98).

6. Historicist theories necessarily conflate the specific and general determinations of phenomena reducing them to one contradiction or one structure and by doing so eliminate the dialectical element. Althusser (1969) and Poulantzas (1973) are right to criticise Lukács in this way and their critique of historicist totalities would apply to many other Marxists. Nonetheless, in combatting one form of determinism they embrace another, structural pluralism, which leaves little scope for human activity.

7. On the Frankfurt School see Jay 1973, and from a more critical standpoint Schroyer 1974, and Swingewood (1977).

8. In his later writings Lukács rejects this notion of complex contradiction in favour of an historicist conception, although it should be noted that *History and Class Consciousness* develops an immanent historicism. See my *Marx and Modern Social Theory* for a critique of Lukács's text (Swingewood 1975b).

9. Strongly utilitarian conceptions of art and literature are normally characteristic of:
   i. pre-revolutionary societies such as France during the Enlightenment period, where literature and art were classified below philosophy as additional forces in the struggle of Reason against feudal superstition and traditionalism; and in Russia during the nineteenth century where Belinsky, Chernyshersky and Dobrolyubov and Pisarev defined the value of literature almost exclusively in terms of education: and
   ii. societies maintained through dictatorships such as Nazi Germany and Soviet Russia where the principles of literature are laid down by the state.

10. See especially I. Deutscher's (1973) 'Georg Lukács and Critical Realism', and M. Lowy's (1975) 'Lukács and Stalinism'.

11. *Left Review* was published between 1934 and 1938 and in general reflected the Communist Party line although it was never a C.P. journal. For example, in volume 1 (February 1935) Stephen Spender voiced considerable unease over the suppression of the Proletarian Writers Organisation (RAPP) in Russia, but T. H. Wintringham, a party hack, reviewing like Spender Max Eastman's critical study of Stalinist literary practices, *Artists in Uniform*, described it as 'rather ludicrous' and anti-Marxist since it denied that 'art is a class weapon'. In contrast, the Scottish novelist, Lewis Grassic Gibbon, could write that capitalist literature was not in decay although capitalist economies were, and – in complete opposition to the current dogma – assert that in periods of decay art and literature reached their efflorescence.

12. See my discussion in *The Novel and Revolution* (Swingewood 1975a).

13. Alick West's review of Knights's book in *Left Review* (September 1937) and Knights's reply throw into sharp relief the differences between the crude Marxists and the rival *Scrutiny* school. Whereas Knights sought out the contradictory elements in Jonson – that he combined the qualities of emerging capitalist humanism with a 'sturdy feeling for traditional values' – West simply made Jonson a mirror of inevitable large scale economic change. For West the mode of production was simply an undifferentiated structure with all literature linked causally and mechanically to it. For Knights the whole point of analysis lay in disclosing the specific groups within the mode of production.

14. Benjamin's main argument was that with new techniques of reproduction and the changing social relations of reproduction, the novel is fundamentally affected by the trend towards a collectivist society and the new modes of communication. Realism in Lukács's sense is no longer apposite. See Benjamin's 'The Storyteller' in *Illuminations* (1970).

REFERENCES CITED

Althusser, Louis, (1969), *For Marx*, Allen, London.

Benjamin, Walter (1970), *Illuminations*, Cape, London.

Benjamin, Walter (1973), *Understanding Brecht*, New Left Books, London.

Benjamin, Walter (1975), 'Edward Fuchs: Collector and Historian' *New German Critique*, No. 5.

Brecht, Bertolt (1974), 'Against Georg Lukàs', *New Left Review*, 84, 39-53.

Caudwell, Christopher (1974), *Illusion and Reality*, Lawrence and Wishart, London.

Deutscher, Isaac (1973), 'Georg Lukács and Critical Realism', *Marxism in Our Time*, Cape, London.

Fischer, Ernest (1963), *The Necessity of Art*, Penguin, London.

Marxist approaches to the Study of Literature

Goldmann, Lucien (1963), 'Introduction aux Premiers Ecrits de Lukàcs' in G. Lukàcs, *La Theorie du Roman*, Gonthier, Paris.

Goldmann, Lucien (1964), *The Hidden God*, Routledge, London.

Goldmann, Lucien (1975), *Towards a Sociology of the Novel*, Tavistock, London,

Horkheimer, Max (1972), *Critical Theory*, Herder, New York.

Jay, Martin (1973), *The Dialectical Imagination*, Heinemann, London.

Lifshitz, Mikhail (1973), *The Philosophy of Art of Karl Marx*, Pluto Press, London.

Löwy, M. (1975), 'Lukàcs and Stalinism' in *New Left Review*, May/June.

Lukàcs, Georg (1963), *The Meaning of Contemporary Realism*, Merlin, London.

Lukàcs, Georg (1964a), 'Neuland Unterm Pflug', *Werke*, Band 5, Neuwied.

Lukàcs, Georg (1964b), *Essays on Thomas Mann*, Merlin, London.

Lukàcs, Georg (1970), *Writer and Critic*, Merlin, London.

Lukàcs, Georg (1971), *History and Class Consciousness*, Merlin, London.

Lukàcs, Georg (1972), *Studies in European Realism*, Merlin, London.

Marx Karl (1971), *Introduction to a Critique of Political Economy*, Lawrence and Wishart, London.

Marx, K, and Engels F. (1947), *Literature and Art*, International Publishers, New York.

Marx, K, and Engels F. (1961), *Selected Works*, Vol. 2, Lawrence and Wishart, London.

Plekhanov, Georgi (1953), *Art and Social Life*, Lawrence and Wishart, London.

Poulantzas, Nicos (1973), *Political Power and Social Classes*, New Left Books, London.

Schroyer, Trent (1974), *The Critique of Domination*, Brazillier, New York.

Swingewood, Alan (1975a), *The Novel and Revolution*, Macmillan, London.

Swingewood, Alan (1975b), *Marx and Modern Social Theory*, Macmillan, London.

Swingewood, Alan (1977), *The Myth of Mass Culture*, Macmillan, London.

Trotsky, Leon (1957), *Literature and Revolution*, Russell and Russell, New York.

Trotsky, Leon (1970), *On Literature and Art*, edited by P. N. Siegal, Pathfiner, New York.

West, Alick (1974), *Crisis and Criticism*, Lawrence and Wishart, London.

A reputation made: Lucien Goldmann

Jane Routh

Few major reputations can have been sealed so decisively by obituaries as was Lucien Goldmann's. The front page headline in the *Times Literary Supplement* of 26 November 1971 marked his death by coining a phrase so nice, so succinct that it is used again and again as the measure of the limits of Goldmann's achievement: 'Portrait of the artist as midwife'.

Of course there are many aspects of this article, and of other similarly harsh commentaries, which present a perfectly reasonable assessment of Goldmann's work. Ultimately we may want to concede that Goldmann 'leaves the vast majority of mortals in a kind of sleepwalking condition (including the artist himself), while arrogating to the sociologist of literature a position so privileged as to be almost godlike' (Caute 1971: 1466). Yet such roundly echoed criticisms firmly established so early after Goldmann's death may have been in their unlooked-for, long-term influence decidedly unfair. Opinion about his work has ossified, his reputation has been settled, the limitations of his work agreed before his work has had the full impact which it might have had – particularly in this country. A feeling that the dust has settled has been increased by the unavailability in English of some of Goldmann's later work – particularly that on 'microstructures'. (The publication in 1975 of the English edition of *Towards a sociology of the novel* did nothing to change this, for it was a book published eleven years previously in France, and has been the focus for the greater part of the negative reception of his work).

Many critics mention Goldmann's tendency to state and re-state his points rather than argue them.[1] While Caute thinks that much of Goldmann's work serves only to demonstrate a belief that 'a sound doctrine was worth reiterating' (1971: 1465), Williams is prepared to find in the restatements that 'he produced refinements and further definitions, in so complex a field, from which we can all learn' (1971: 17). Yet already in 1956, Goldmann could refine the essence of his theory of genetic structuralism as:

> . . . any great literary or artistic work is the expression of a world vision. This vision is the product of a collective group consciousness which reaches its highest expression in the mind of a poet or thinker (Goldmann 1964).

Behind the few words 'great literary or artistic work is the expression of a world view' is a profound and careful attempt to articulate the nature of the relationship between literature and society, recognised by Marcuse as a deep concern to *protect* literature (Marcuse 1974). The main theoretical problem at the centre of the sociology of literature is at the heart of Goldmann's work.

The social genesis of literature

Goldmann's work is located firmly within the third conception of the relationship between literature and society described in the introduction as the question of how literature arises in society. But unlike some other writers who are content to characterise this relationship as 'reflection', Goldmann articulated the social genesis of literature through structural concepts.

He gave many accounts of this relationship, describing its main features as follows: the essential relation between art and social life does not reside in the content of a work of art offering a description of the events and characteristics of that life. Rather, the relationship rests in the categories which organise both the day to day consciousness of a social group and the imaginary universe created by the writer. The action of any social group will be significative, attempting to transform reality in a direction more favourable to its own needs and the praxis of such a group will engender within the consciousness of its members *mental structures* which will govern the individual's activity independently of the problems by which they were generated. No single individual will himself have an experience sufficiently rich to create such complex structures: the mental structures are not individual, but social phenomena. And since these structures have their genesis in social action, they are located not in individual consciousness, but in what Goldmann calls the transindividual subject. Every individual will be involved in a number of social actions, and participates in a number of transindividual subjects.

Goldmann did not claim that this transindividual subject has any reality of its own, but asserted only that it is present in the mental structures of those who participate in it. These structures he located in a special level of consciousness, the 'non-conscious', which he likened to nervous or muscular response to distinguish it from the unconscious (the repressed libidinal level of consciousness) and the conscious (of which we are aware). It is these non-conscious structures (rather than content) which Goldmann thought were transposed by an artist into his art, by a philosopher into his philosophy and so on, for the organisation of an artist's work and the day-to-day consciousness of a social group are bound by a 'more or less rigorous homology' (Goldmann 1973: 10).[2]

Although individual consciousness will partake of several transindividual subjects, Goldmann maintained that the structure of the writing, painting, conceptual thought and so on of certain exceptional individuals might coincide with the mental structures corresponding to *one* of the transindividual subjects to whom they are linked (Goldmann 1967: 904).

Leaving aside for a while the question of 'certain exceptional individuals', it can be seen that the relationship between literature and society hinges on the notion of structural homology. Glucksmann is unhappy with this limited articulation of the relationship between structures, pointing out that Lévi-Strauss has identified many possible relationships (inversion, contradiction) *other* than that of crude parallel necessitated by Goldmann's insistence on homology (Glucksmann 1969).

The idea of structuration is perhaps most usefully likened to Saussure's distinction between *langue*, which is supra-individual which structures and limits *parole*, yet is not conscious. In the same way that no one individual will speak a *langue* exactly, so individual expressions will not exactly correspond to the mental structures of the transindividual subject. By conceptualising the link between literature and society through a homology of structures between individual thought and collective consciousness in this way, Goldmann is able to trace a link between even a fairy tale and the group which produced it – that is, between *contents* which may be widely different.

Although acknowledging the variety of transindividual subjects in which any one individual may be involved, Goldmann asserted that from the point of view of intellectual and artistic creation, the most important group to which an individual belongs is that of class:

> Every time it was a question of finding the infrastructure of a
> philosophy, a literary or artistic current, ultimately we have been
> forced to consider, not a generation, nation or church, not a profession
> or any other social grouping, but a social class and its relations to
> society (Goldmann 1969: 102).

Goldmann saw classes as the important groups simply 'because our own researches . . . have almost always shown us the outstanding importance of this social group in comparison with all others' (ibid: 101-2). He sketched a privileged position in the life of man for economic factors based on biological need (ibid: 87), but for the most part was content to assert that

> The totality of relations between individuals and the rest of social reality is such as to give rise to the continual formation of a certain psychic structure which is common to a very great extent to the individuals who form one and the same social class (ibid: 127),

and that

> there are certain social groups (and empirical research has shown that during the course of history, these groups have most often been social classes) whose aspirations and needs correspond either to the total structuring of all inter-human relations or to relations between man and nature (1967: 904)

This 'total structuring' of a privileged group is the main characteristic that Goldmann attributed to a world view. Furthermore, he argued that a *coherent* world view could only be formed on the basis of the maximum potential consciousness of one of those groups. This 'coherence' is one of the most important terms in Goldmann's theory, for it is this which lends 'greatness' to a work of art. The unity and coherent structure of a work of art is, according to Goldmann, informed by the world view. Thus, he could argue that great representative writers are those able to express the maximum potential consciousness of their class (as distinct from the less coherent, less total, *real* consciousness of a group limited by other groups and natural forces).

Goldmann's propensity to assert, rather than argue through, leaves us with his insistence that total structuring in a coherent world view can only be found in the maximum of potential consciousness of a class grouping, although the privileged position he gave to class in this context depends on our acceptance of his assurances that in all empirical work he had found it to be of greatest importance. He thus ruled out the possibility of an overriding structure being located in some instances in, say, a feminist community, or the family.[3] (It is useful to compare the way in which Sartre's analysis of Flaubert brings to the fore the role of the family in shaping Flaubert's imaginary worlds).

His belief that world views are few in number – fewer than the number of classes found in history, explained for Goldmann why certain *types* of world view, such as the one he entitled 'the tragic vision' recur. This led him to suggest that an eventual typology of world views may be possible. He acknowledged that numerous structurings of consciousness could be identified, but thought that these would not be *total* like the world view. Partial structurings he termed ideologies. The total quality of a world view will render the world intelligible, although it be of only temporary value for groups in a concrete historical situation. Thus, he thought that as social reality shifts, an unchanged world view becomes dogma.

In *The hidden god* Goldmann demonstrated how the social consciousness of Jansenism had its genesis in the social displacement of the *noblesse de robe*. This class of court officials was dependent economically on the crown, yet increasingly powerless. The contradiction thus engendered in their world vision of denial of the world and reluctance to initiate change is expressed in the work of Racine, as a world vision of protesting against the world yet accepting it as the only world there is. Goldmann also uncovered these straightforward homologies between social class/consciousness/literature in Genet's plays. He identified the universe of all Genet's plays as structured by an all-powerful group of rulers dominating a group that both loves and hates them. An inadequate reality turns participants to fantasy and ritual, in which the ruled can identify with the rulers and overcome them. Goldmann related this fascination for hatred of power to the experience of a small class of militant workers and left wing intellectuals. Their concern, he suggested, is to establish a non-capitalist social order, but one which, unlike Stalinism, will preserve individual liberties. The world vision of this group is thus one of rejection of capitalism, while knowing the incomparably serious risks that this rejection entails.

Even this articulation of the relationship between literature and society is for Eagleton 'too trimly symmetrical, unable to accommodate the dialectical conflicts and complexities, the unevenness and discontinuity, which characterise literature's relation to society' (1976: 34). Yet the concept of world vision in these analyses gives Goldmann a fairly sensitive level of mediation between social life and literature – a level which he abandoned when he turned to an analysis of the modern novel.

The most hostile criticism has rightly attacked the change in direction Goldmann took in *Towards a Sociology of the Novel*. Here the work of art was no longer seen as the imaginary transposition of a group's structures of consciousness, so much as a *direct* transposition of economic life into creative life without any intervening level. Goldmann's assessment of market societies was that this level of consciousness ceases to exist:

> the collective consciousness gradually loses all active reality and tends to become a mere reflection of the economic life and, ultimately, to disappear (1975: 11).

He saw the reification and increasing fetishisation of merchandise in the market economy taking away any appreciation of the real use-value of goods. With the whole of social life dominated by exchange values, Goldmann assumed a widespread dissatisfaction, so that the modern novel embodies 'a search for values . . . which economic life tends to make implicit in *all* members of the society' (Goldmann 1975: 10). Yet in a society where exchange value has become an end in itself, only a few 'problematic' individuals will embody qualitative values – the creators who can still regard their own work for its quality in spite of its rapid takeover by the market economy. Goldmann claimed that the novel genre, expressing discontent with exchange values, must embody a widespread discontent that has developed throughout society (since no work is the expression of purely individual experience) although this discontent is '*non-conceptualised*'. In addition, the widespread competitive market value of liberal individualism has spread throughout society. On this basis, he could identify the problematic individual, who is the centre of the novel form experiencing quality values and the constraints of society upon individualism. On the evidence of a rather small number of French writers, Goldmann traced two subsequent shifts in the novel form, which he related to the shift in the market economy by which competition is replaced by monopoly.

We are still speaking of a relationship between literature and society that is couched in terms of structure, but now the analogous structure at the level of collective consciousness has gone:

> The two structures, that of an important fictional genre and that of exchange proved to be strictly homologous, to the point at which one might speak of one and the same structure manifesting itself on two different planes (ibid: 8).

Goldmann's critics are agreed as to the status of this attempt to conceive the social genesis of literature *without* the mediating concept of world view. He does not give sufficiently detailed attention to the changes in capitalist economy, or in the novel genre. There is no room for any relative autonomy in creative activity. We have only 'a crude and mechanistic homology' (Mellor 1973: 102), 'an essentially mechanistic version of the base-superstructure relationship' (Eagleton 1976: 34), 'economic determinism' (Glucksmann 1969: 59).

We should not be surprised that Goldmann insisted on the primacy of economic factors in this way: he attributed to them overriding importance in *The human sciences and philosophy* (1969). What *is* surprising is that he chose to abandon the concept of world view when faced with the modern novel. He had written earlier that he could see Malraux's early novels, Robbe-Grillet's fiction and films (all the subject of analysis in *Towards a sociology of the novel*), Beckett's writings, as well as Genet's theatre as the literary transposition *of the world vision* of a group which he characterised as 'a small number of workers and creative intellectuals and a fairly large number of educated people who refuse to accede to modern capitalism' (1973: 12). Why this earlier established analysis resting on a world view should be the right method of approach for Genet's theatre, but the wrong method for Malraux's novels is not clear, but his work on Genet fits the pattern established and well-received in *The hidden god*.

The artist and his work

It can be seen that since only a social group can elaborate the structure of a world view, the coherent structure generated by the world view and transposed into a work of art is not an individual but a social creation. It is this designation of the creative subject as social rather than individual that has aroused most criticism of Goldmann's work, since it appears to devalue the special place usually accorded to artistic genius, which is now demoted to a midwife in the delivery of world views.

The problem of what constitutes 'great' art is a block which sociologists carefully skirt, or over which they stumble as evaluation and analysis become confounded. Goldmann did not negotiate this difficult terrain unscathed, but we must recognise the care with which he attempted to establish an analytic basis for aesthetic value.

'Great philosophical and artistic works represent the coherent and adequate expressions of. . . world views' (Goldmann 1969: 129). This world view is the maximum of possible consciousness of a class, and the very essence of literary creation rests, according to Goldmann, on the possible. (In 'Criticism and dogmatism in literature' he argues that the impoverishment of contemporary literary cultural creation stems from the disappearance of the possible from men's consciousness). It is the structures of the world view which gives a work of art 'its unity, its specifically aesthetic character and its own literary quality' (Goldmann 1973: 11). This view of literary greatness has obvious problems and was immediately challenged. In the first place, to look only at the overall structural unity of a text may seriously misrepresent the contradictions and complexities which it will necessarily contain. In the second place, when literature becomes only an expression of a world view, it is truncated in two ways: it has neither autonomy to develop its own formal traditions and inheritance, nor autonomy to speak in disputation with a world view.

Goldmann was quick to respond to criticisms, and went to some lengths to emphasise that the stress he put on unity in a work of art was necessary in the context of French literary scholarship; in no way was it intended to deny the richness of a work of art:

> in consecrating most of our efforts to the unity of a work of art and to the relation between this unity and the consciousness of certain social groups, we neglected in effect the richness and complexity of the world of a work of art, even if we never ceased to recognise its importance (yet) it appeared to be both the most urgent and the most difficult task, given that erudite university criticism . . . entirely neglected . . . the wholeness of the text (Goldmann 1968: 143-144).

Goldmann restored richness to literature in two ways. Firstly, basing his understanding of the richness of literature on Kant, he defined a work of art as a transcendence of the complexity of an imaginary universe and the unity and rigour of creation. On the epistemological level, he identified dogmatism as the necessary ordering of the world in order that men may live and act efficaciously. Opposed to this is criticism – the critical spirit applied to dogma to check when the social and individual sacrifices demanded by dogmatism become superfluous and ready to be overthrown. He argued that the unity of creation parallels dogmatism on the aesthetic level; the complexity of an imaginary universe parallels criticism. This allowed him to look at a work of art and find there not just unity but also contradictory elements, which are 'sacrificed' to the overarching unity. He suggested that these contradictory elements will be

   (i)   the values which have been *rejected* in favour of those of the world vision,

   (ii) the necessity for a world vision to come to terms with death,

   (iii) individual *libido* militating against the structural unity.

This was to attempt to restore richness at the level of structure. Secondly, however, Goldmann acknowledged that he had not paid sufficient attention to the specifically literary richness of the text. He endeavoured to demonstrate how this could be redressed by suggesting that literary form was itself a structured phenomenon, consisting of semantic, semiological and phonological microstructures in homologous relationship to the global structure of the text. This would give us three levels of structure:

   (i)   the world view,

   (ii) its transposition in a coherent, imaginary universe of characters and situations,

(iii) its expression in language related to the global structure of the
text.

In an analysis of Genet's *The Blacks*, Goldmann showed how the
overall structure of the text still has primacy over partial structures,
stage directions, language and so on. He identified a common structure
of conflict between rulers and ruled in *The maids*, *The balcony*, *The Blacks*
and *The screens*. *The Blacks* moves on from the two earlier plays in
offering some element of hope to the oppressed group towards the end.
Goldmann characterised the structure of this play as a whole in
simplified form as: a ritual movement of the Blacks' aggression against
Whites, aggression which the Whites try to interrupt or prevent by their
own opposing aggression, and the conflict of these two forces ending in
the defeat of the Whites and a break with African ties. Behind this
conflict on stage, a 'real' struggle is set off-stage which gives the Blacks
aspirations of victory.

Analysing in detail the first twenty-five speeches of the play itself,
Goldmann found reduced models of this overall structure occurring
repeatedly. For example, in the opening mime of the play, he noted that
the stage directions indicate that the Blacks dance a *minuet*, break off
and bow ceremoniously to the Court (Whites) and audience (also
Whites).[4] One of them begins a formal address with 'Ladies and
Gentlemen', to which the Court responds with

> very shrill but very well-orchestrated laughter. It is not free and easy
> laughter. This laughter is echoed by the same but even shriller
> laughter of the Blacks who are standing round Archibald (Genet 1960:
> 10).

Goldmann interpreted the mime of the minuet and the adoption of
'Whitese' in 'Ladies and Gentlemen' as aggression from the Blacks.
White aggression in the Court's shrill laughter interrupts this, to be
overcome by 'even shriller' laughter – Black aggression. In other words,
this gives us a reduced model of the global structure of the whole play.
Reduced models, or microstructures, can be found in every speech, in
every stage direction, even in a single word. It is at this point that Caute
dismisses the work on microstructures:

> The limits of scientific seriousness are surely reached when the third
> speech of the play, the single word 'Hallelujah!', is accorded eight
> lines of solemn commentary (Caute 1971: 1465).

Yet many single words have been accorded commentary of similar
status, and Goldmann must be given credit for the care with which at

the level of microstructure as well as at the level of structure he married his theory and his empirical studies.

Although Goldmann gave these answers to the charges of over-simplified analysis, questions raised about the relative autonomy of literature seem to have found no satisfactory answers: 'There is no concept of the relative autonomy of art, . . . or of formal traditions' (Glucksmann 1969: 57). Yet while Goldmann conceded no place in his analyses to formal literary traditions, he was not unaware that questions could be raised about the influences on a writer and his work. However, he insisted that this question of *influences* was not the issue, for '*influences* of any sort explain little' (Goldmann 1969: 92). For Goldmann, influences were not worth studying for themselves; the real question which they pose is rather why particular writers, philosophers and so on 'sustained precisely this influence in this particular period of their history or their life' (ibid). And why certain literary or philosophical influences were sustained by a particular writer can only, once again, be explained by reference to the social and economic factors shaping the consciousness of the group to which he belonged.

The distinctions described in 'Criticism and dogmatism in literature' would place an art form developing its autonomy without reference to present social conditions on the level of dogma. Moreover, *The human sciences and philosophy* does grant a certain measure of relative autonomy to law, art, religion and so on. While Goldmann insisted that the fundamental elements of a world vision will have their genesis only in social action, he recognised that coherent expressions will contribute to their own further development and expression as 'artists of the period will tend to develop them more and more in all their consequences' (ibid: 96). This assertion is unfortunately hurriedly glossed over with an exhortation to distinguish between the fundamental elements of a world vision and details not directly related to infrastructures *in individual cases* – a distinction 'which does not admit of any general rule' (ibid: 96). Empirical study is thus once again recommended when a problem on the borders of Goldmann's theory remains unresolved.

But where is the artist? If Goldmann *did* relegate him to the role of midwife, it was not in order to deny *special* qualities to the artist. He reiterated that only an *exceptional* individual will be able to bring world view into expression. These individuals may be exceptional because of their marginality and independence of society:

> the freedom of the thinker and writer differs greatly from that of other persons; their ties with the life of society are diversely complex and medialised in different ways (ibid: 59).

In *Towards a sociology of the novel*, this exceptional individual can be characterised by his adherence to use value in a society where people are almost exclusively oriented to exchange value. His creative activity is perceived by the artist initially for its intrinsic quality, even if it is immediately given a price label in a market economy. The very nature of his activity makes the artist marginal.

Goldmann did not deny that a work of art expresses an individual's thought and feelings, but took any analysis that rests at this level as inadequate. An individual's thoughts and feelings can only be understood in terms of the inter-subjective reality of which they are a part. No work of art can be explained, he thought, by reference to individual feelings, only by reference to the structures of collective consciousness.

If we go on to ask *how* any one individual from a wider social grouping is able to typify the world view of that group, we find no answer in Goldmann's work other than the suggestion of the central importance of marginality. Sartre's crystallisation of the problem of individual participation in a world view, encapsulated in:

> Valéry is a petit bourgeois individual, no doubt about it. But not
> every petit bourgeois individual is Valéry (Sartre 1963: 56),

receives no attention from Goldmann. Eagleton locates the particularity of the Brontës' work in the overdetermination of their social position (1975). Sartre finds the particularity of Flaubert in his response to his family situation (1972). And again in his study of Genet's work, it is the family situation of orphanage/adoption which Sartre finds at the root of Genet's response to the social world (1952). The contrast in Sartre's and Goldmann's analyses of Genet's works is instructive: Sartre reconstructs Genet's biography as a way of living contradictions in the social world; Goldmann saw Genet as a representative only of a left-wing intellectual group which experiences contradictions in the social world *as a group*. Sartre explains Genet's writing as a personal *project*, a way of resolving the stress to which society subjected him and of revenging himself on it. Individual projects, whether at a social level or at a literary level, do not exist in Goldmann's work: Genet's work was discussed neither as an attempt to resolve *individual* social contradictions, nor as an attempt to break, change or develop existing dramatic and literary conventions. Sartre shows Genet using writing to change his own social position and to change his audiences' perceptions of social reality. Goldmann (returning to the earlier discussion of lack of aesthetic autonomy) only demonstrated that the plays are structured by the consciousness of the group to which Genet belongs.[5] Yet to have said to Goldmann 'Genet is a French left-wing intellectual, no doubt about it. But not every French left-wing intellectual is Genet' would surely only have evoked the response that that is beside the point:

> In so far as *the tendency to coherence that constitutes the essence of the work is situated not only at the level of the individual creator, but already at that of the group*, the approach by which this group is seen as the true subject of creation may account for the role of the writer and integrate him in its analysis, *whereas the reverse does not appear to be the case* (1975: ix).

A certain *comprehension* can be gained by understanding Genet's childhood, but a great comprehension of the whole of his texts can be found in their structures. But above all, Goldmann would have argued that we only have *explanation* when the relation between the meaning of the text and the behaviour of a collective subject is demonstrated, for the ultimate focus of sociological work is not to explain the individual but the social whole.

Goldmann's own assessment of his work in comparison with other approaches to literature was that studies of language, of biography, of literary complexity and so on were not necessarily precluded by his work, although the most comprehensive level of analysis was that of the world view. (Conversely, studies of language would of course preclude explanation in terms of world view). His critics have concentrated on the limits which his work could be seen to set rather than take up the challenge he offered to test his ideas on empirical work. For is there yet, after all, any more satisfactory account of individuals' participation in wider social groupings which avoids the fluidity and biographical fantasy of Sartre, or any more precise accord of status and value to literary works, which is felt but not explained by so many sociologists?

University of Lancaster.

FOOTNOTES

1. See for example David Caute (1971) or Miriam Glucksmann (1969).

2. Unattributed translations from the French are my own.

3. In 'The Genetic-Structuralist method' in *Towards a sociology of the novel* Goldmann gives a slight indication that he would be prepared to move a little from the strict advocacy of class as the only group whose consciousness tends to an overall vision of man. However, he says that this can only be settled by positive empirical research.

4. This play . . . is intended for a white audience, but if, which is unlikely, it is ever performed before a black audience, then a white person, male or female, should be invited every evening . . . The actors will play for him . . . (Genet 1960:6).

5. Admittedly, the structures of the plays are seen as *changing*, but Goldmann does not speculate as to how the earlier plays themselves might have contributed either to the group's world view, or to the more hopeful structures of the later plays.

REFERENCES CITED

Caute, David, (1971), 'Portrait of the artist as midwife', in *Times Literary Supplement*, 26 November, no. 3639, 1465-1466.

Eagleton, Terry, (1975), *The myths of power*, Macmillan, London.

Eagleton, Terry, (1976), *Marxism and literary criticism*, Methuen, London.

Genet, Jean, (1960), *The Blacks*, Faber, London.

Glucksmann, Miriam, (Jul/Aug 1969), 'Lucien Goldmann: Humanist or Marxist?' in *New Left Review*, 56 49-62.

Goldmann, Lucien, (1964), *The hidden god*, Routledge & Kegan Paul, London, the English edition of *Le dieu cache*, (1956), Gallimard, Paris.

Goldmann, Lucien, (28 September 1967), 'Ideology and Writing' in *Times Literary Supplement*, 903-905.

Goldmann, Lucien, (1968), 'Criticism and dogmatism in literature' in David Cooper (ed.), *The dialectics of liberation*, Penguin, Harmondsworth.

Goldmann, Lucien, (1969), *The human sciences and philosophy*, Cape, London.

Goldmann, Lucien, (1973), 'Le théâtre de Genet' in *Sociologie de la Littérature*, Editions de l'Université de Bruxelles, 9-34 (2me ed.).

Goldmann, Lucien, (1975), *Towards a Sociology of the Novel*, Tavistock, London.

Marcuse, Herbert, (1974), 'Some general remarks on Lucien Goldmann' in *Lucien Goldmann et la sociologie de la littérature*, Editions de l'Université de Bruxelles, 51-52.

Mellor, Adrian, (1973), 'The Hidden Method', in *Working Papers in Cultural Studies*, 4, 86-103.

Sartre, Jean Paul, (1952), *Saint Genet*, Gallimard, Paris.

Sartre, Jean Paul, (1963), *The problem of method*, Methuen, London.

Sartre, Jean Paul, (1972), *L'idiot de la famille*, Gallimard, Paris.

Williams, Raymond, (May/June 1971), 'Literature and Sociology: in memory of Lucien Goldmann', in *New Left Review*, 67, 3-18.

The literary sociology of Sartre

Jim McGuigan

Introduction

Sartre's intellectual biography may be divided into two periods: the early existentialism and the later Marxism. Such a division superficially implies a theoretical rupture occurring between an individualist and a collectivist conception of the world. However, it is very difficult to identify a straightforward break in Sartre's thought. In my view, his work is best understood as an evolving unity rather than a direct passage from one philosophy to another. Sartre has consistently retained a characteristically existentialist emphasis on lived experience, an emphasis which is at the core of his latterday criticisms of orthodox Marxism and both Marxist and non-Marxist structuralism. During the late fifties Sartre argued that existentialism, although a 'parasitical' ideology, could be used to regenerate Marxism, the most profound philosophy of our time. According to Sartre, existentialism might serve to revive the humanism of Marx, following the period in which Marxism had been reduced by communist ideologues to a mechanically deterministic materialism. For Sartre, history is the product of human agency albeit constrained by alienating barriers, and not reducible to determining structures. The centrality of human agency is the unifying thread of Sartre's whole work, represented in the existentialist concept of being-for-itself and latterly in the Marxist notion of praxis. A fundamental problem in Sartre's recent work is the relationship between individual project and class praxis. One way of understanding this problem is in the context of literary sociology, on the question of the relationship between writing and class structure. Specifically, how does the nexus of writer and class structure condition the meaning of the text?

It should be underlined that Sartre's thought applied to literature in comparison with other Marxist and Marxissant theories, for instance the notable example of Goldmann's genetic structuralism, is radically individualist. Goldmann's basic thesis is that a structural homology may be adduced between the universe of certain great literary works and the underlying morphology of socio-historical reality. Because structure is located below consciousness Goldmann denies sociological relevance to the writer's reflexivity, a viewpoint which originates with Engels. Sartre on the other hand, places considerable stress on the writer's self-awareness and social experience. There are two broad moments to a Sartrean approach to literature: firstly, psychoanalytic interpretation of the writer's internal experience and secondly sociological analysis of the historical conditioning of literary meaning. The two moments of analysis interact dialectically with one another. Specific mediations (e.g. family, community and work relations) linking the writer's experience and the class structure are explored in detail.

In an essay of this nature it would be futile to attempt a full account of Sartrean philosophy. However, it is vitally important to have some grasp of Sartre's general philosophical concepts to understand the relevance of his work for literary sociology. Therefore, a brief description of Sartre's most distinctive ideas and the context of their production is apposite. The continuing stress on intentionality and experience derives from an early imbibed existential phenomenology. During the early thirties Sartre spent a year in Germany studying the philosophies of Husserl and Heidegger, whose influence is very evident in his first great treatise, *Being and Nothingness*, written in France during the Second World War.

The rapid and wide dissemination of Sartre's thought in the forties and fifties is largely attributable to his literary skills embodied in a series of novels, short stories and plays. Also, Sartre's popularity was associated with the rediscovery of the nineteenth century originator of existentialism, Soren Kierkegaard, and the contemporary vogue for various kinds of romantic individualism. Sartre's imaginative writing does not simply, as has often been suggested, illustrate his philosophy but is implicitly connected with the distinctively concrete articulation of ideas which is the mark of existentialist thought. The novel *Nausea* published in 1938 had an extraordinary impact on French intellectual life. Roquentin, the hero, has the sudden revelation that his own being is gratuitous in a brutally indifferent world. Generalising from this personal experience Roquentin comes to the conclusion that human existence is contingent, that there is no determinate reason for living. Sartre has said that he was himself Roquentin. So, it seems legitimate to interpret Roquentin's experience as Sartre's at a particular point in time. Contingency becomes manifest in Roquentin's reflections on language. Sartre holds that human beings are signifying agents. Language is the social form of man's retrieval of the world. Roquentin, while sitting in a bus, makes the unnerving discovery that there is a disjunction between the sign and the signified. For instance, the word 'seat' no longer sticks to the object it names. Roquentin becomes aware that linguistic signification and consequently intellectual categorisation are totally capricious enterprises. Words, the constructs of consciousness, apparently have no necessary connection with the material world.

> Things have broken free from their names. They are there, grotesque, stubborn, gigantic, and it seems ridiculous to call them seats or say anything at all about them: I am in the midst of things which cannot be given names (1970: 180).

Reason itself, the elaboration of coherent relationships and identification of stable phenomena is left without firm grounding. Roquentin's metaphysical unease is reminiscent of David Hume. Hume, long before Sartre, sought to show the probabilistic rather than necessary character of reason when he argued that the principle of causality could not be established *a priori*. There is, however, a more stark and evocative similarity between the young Sartre and the eighteenth century British philosopher, in the way they deal with questions relating to the self and moral action. Hume was prone to deep fits of melancholy brought on by his failure to establish the presence of a soul, a human essence, which led him towards atheism. The formulation of epistemological and moral problems as a response to the demise of God unifies various strains in philosophy, Sartrean existentialism being only one. Sartre's elliptical statement, *'existence comes before essence'* (1948: 26) has become something of a catch phrase. At the same time as making this statement (in 1946) Sartre claimed that because there is no absolute justification for human existence man is condemned to be free. Like Kant, he holds that formal reasoning provides no guidance for moral choice. Whether they like it or not men are the inventors of morality. According to Sartre, people tend to deny freedom through various strategies of bad faith (the denial of freedom by self-deception, for instance blaming others for one's own failure to act authentically). This conception of moral freedom appears at first sight to be anarchic. However, Sartre does offer some basis for choice, the good of the human community, which again echoes Kant. In choosing, the individual affirms the value of his choice for everyone. This virtual restatement of the categorical imperative places responsibility with the human agent.

There are considerable difficulties in interpreting Sartre's work as a whole. Hazel Barnes has argued persuasively that those who support a 'break' thesis have little understanding either of Sartre's early existentialism or of his later Marxism (Barnes 1974: 14). Quite clearly it is impossible to describe Sartre's Marxism without reference to existential phenomenology. However, in my view it is also impossible to do the reverse. When we look at Sartre's existentialism we are not ignorant of his Marxism. The frame of the present controls our interpretation of the past. It is sometimes suggested, justifiably, that an individualist ontology cannot provide the basis for a social theory. The problem is right at the core of Sartre's work, and can be traced back through *What is Literature?* (1947) and its dual concern for individual freedom and revolutionary social change to *The Transcendence of the Ego* (1936), Sartre's critique of Husserl, in which he says:

> The phenomenologists have plunged men back into the world: they have given full measure to man's agonies and sufferings, and also to his rebellions. Unfortunately as long as the *I* remains a structure of absolute consciousness, one will still be able to reproach phenomenology for being an escapist doctrine, for again pulling a part of man out of the world and, in that way, turning our attention from the real problems. It seems to us that this reproach no longer has any justification if one makes the *me* an existent, strictly contemporaneous with the world, whose existence has the same essential characteristics as the world. It has always seemed to me that a working hypothesis as fruitful as historical materialism never needed for a foundation the absurdity which is metaphysical materialism (Sartre 1972b: 105).

Sartre was never prepared to accept Husserlian idealism or alternatively a vulgar reduction of mind to matter. He has sought a middle way, or more precisely a dialectical method. His work has developed as a complex series of modifications in response to specific experiences generated by certain historical conjunctures. For instance, the limits to individual freedom became evident during the occupation of France and the deficiencies of both scholastic and practical Marxism were shown up by the Soviet suppression of the Hungarian rebellion in 1956. The latter experience is deeply wrought into the argument of *Search for a Method* (1958) in which Sartre discusses the relationship between existentialism and Marxism. *Search for a Method* serves as an introduction to the *Critique de la Raison Dialectique* (1960), Sartre's second large-scale philosophical work. One of the central elements of the *Critique* is Sartre's attempt to analyse how the series becomes the group-in-fusion, that is how a string of alienated individuals, captured by the striking image of the bus queue, develop into a collective agency. This analysis parallels the traditional Marxist problem of class-in-itself and class-for-itself.

Sartre's own concept of totalisation provides an instrument for understanding the unity of his work. In the *Critique*, totalisation is virtually synonymous with the dialectical concept of praxis, the practicality of thought and the thoughtfulness of practice. Fredric Jameson observes that there are three ways in which Sartre uses totalisation: at the level of history, individual action and as a kind of thinking (Jameson 1974: 230). At the level of individual action totalisation corresponds to the earlier existentialist concept of project. For Sartre the individual defines himself by his project. He is not a static entity, a fixed thing like a tree, but a willing and creative agent. The individual projects towards an indeterminate future, and thus takes responsibility for choosing himself. Through time human projects ossify and ultimately become barriers to freedom. At the level of history we have the example of the revolutionary party degenerating into a rigid bureaucracy. In Sartre's own project the existential phenomenology of *Being and Nothingness* becomes a dead object, by virtue of which others seek to deny the freedom of the living writer. Encountering barriers to freedom – the look of the other, war, the class structure – Sartre gained awareness of the determinate moment of history and reconstituted his project accordingly. Istvan Meszaros has a deep understanding of Sartre's work:

> The great variety and mass of Sartre's particular projects readily combines into a coherent whole. The extraordinary coherence of his life work is not preconceived. It is not the result of an original blueprint which is imposed on every detail as time goes by: that would be an artificial external unity. Here we have to do with the contrary, with an inner unity that prevails through the most varied manifestations of formal divergence. This is an *evolving* unity that *emerges* through the more or less spontaneous *exploration* of the 'roads to freedom' – or, for that matter, of the manifold obstacles to freedom – whatever they may happen to be. The unity is, therefore *structural* and not *thematic*, the latter would be far too restrictive for a life-work. (Some of Sartre's works are though, characterised by an attempt to achieve a thematic unity, and by no means always with a happy result, most notably his novel cycle. But this is another matter). Thus Sartre is right in rejecting suggestions that his concept of commitment in literature leads to a thematic restriction of political illustration as well as to a paralysis of artistic spontaneity (Meszaros 1975: 11).

Existentialism and Marxism

Central to Sartrean thought is a dichotomy, the radical split between culture and nature. For Sartre, the method of cultural analysis must be dialectical. On the question of the application of dialectics to nature Sartre is sceptical, sometimes firmly denying the possibility of such an enterprise while at other times preferring to take up an agnostic position. Commitment to dialectical thought is embryonic rather than overt in his early writings. The dialectic between being-for-itself and being-in-itself lacks a materialist underpinning. In this sense it is Hegelian rather than Marxist. The later concepts of praxis and practico-inert are less questionable on these grounds. At this point some definitions of Sartre's basic categories are required. Being-for-itself, according to Sartre, is the self-reflexivity of human consciousness. Being-in-itself is non-conscious facticity, the world out there. Sartre argues that all human activity is being-for-itself, which entails the appropriation of the in-itself. Consciousness introduces nothingness into being. Sartre's original term for this process is 'neantisation', usually translated as nihilation. The free human project strikes out into the world of objects. In confronting being-in-itself consciousness presents a negative moment. The world is changed and reshaped through the negation invoked by conscious activity. As Sartre says 'Human reality is its own surpassing towards what it lacks; it surpasses itself towards the particular being it would be if it were not what it is' (Sartre 1972a: 89). Sartre uses paradox to express the way freedom transcends the opposition between subject and object. At the heart of being there is a contradiction. Consciousness introduces the opposite of being – nothingness. The external world is negated. Thus human reality transcends itself with each act. Through the dialectic of being and nothingness new modes of existence emerge.

Although the reasoning in *Being and Nothingness* is dialectical, it is certainly not Marxist. An apparently non-historical relationship between consciousness and the material world is posited. Sartre moves towards a more sociological conception of reality with the category of being-for-others. Curiously enough this also falls into a kind of ahistorical essentialism. A vision of the inevitable doom of human relationships is presented. The look of the other destroys freedom, reducing being-for-itself to being-in-itself. Sartre gives the example of the voyeur peeping through a keyhole. When he realises that he is being observed by another in the passageway his spontaneous subjectivity is transfixed into a state of shame. Such an incident serves as a metaphor for social life in general. In his early work Sartre mistakenly suggests that alienation derives from the basic structures of interpersonal experience. But even at this point Sartre was moving beyond by confronting the individual with the socially liberating possibility of regarding others as beings-for-themselves.

Again the fundamental dualism is present in Sartre's later distinction of praxis and practico-inert. Praxis as we have seen is equivalent to totalisation. It is the essential principle of dialectical reasoning, as Sartre sees it, an instrument for studying individual choice and action as well as historical movement. During the fifties Sartre identified a 'sclerosis' in contemporary Marxism, the 'dialectic without men' of Stalinism. Sartre proceeded to attempt a resuscitation of heuristic Marxism assisted by the existentialist 'ideology'. Thus he sought to do for dialectical reason with the aid of existentialism what Kant did for pure reason with the aid of Humean scepticism. Sartre suggests that there are three ways of using dialectical materialism:

(1) Reduce dialectics to *identity* and thus transform dialectical materialism into mechanical materialism,

(2) Raise dialectics to *celestial law* and thus restate Hegelian metaphysics, or

(3) – the one Sartre prefers – Credit the individual with the ability to depass his situation through work and action. (Laing & Cooper 1971: 55).

This third approach brings the concept of praxis to the centre of dialectical reasoning. (Sartre subsumes under praxis his earlier concept, being-for-itself). At this point human desire is replaced by the more materialist emphasis on need. Action occurs within conditions of scarcity. The projecting individual of existentialism becomes the worker of the Marxist world view. Sartre still holds that men define themselves in terms of their projects, that is man is a purposeful being who seeks to transform his existence into a future possibility. Man is above all an historical agent who struggles to overcome the practico-inert. The category of the practico-inert encompasses nature and the reified structures of man's own work. (The second aspect of the practico-inert echoes Marx's depiction of capital as 'man's inorganic body'. However, the concept of practico-inert seems to have a more general significance in that it represents natural as well as social barriers to human freedom).

Sartre claims that a Marxist anthropology conceives of man as 'the product of his own product'. Historical conditioning and historical agency are reciprocally connected. Sartre embraces Marx's argument that the foundation of social structure and historical change is the mode of production. However, his particular interpretation of Marx is coloured by the concept of scarcity, the general material limits to human possibilities. Reified structures of the practico-inert are generated through the economic exploitation of one class by another; the producer is denied his product. In agreement with Marx, Sartre holds that men make history, but not within conditions of their own choosing. The whole problem turns for Sartre on the possibilities of *dépassement*, that is the transcendence of alienation. According to Sartre, a heuristic Marxism must attempt within any given period to determine 'the field of possibilities, the field of instruments etc.' (Sartre 1968b: 33).

In this context it is impossible to provide more detail about the premises of existential phenomenology or latterday Sartrean Marxism. One can only hope that the general questions are illuminated by my discussion of Sartre's contribution to the sociology of literature.

Literature Engagée

In a series of articles published in *Les Temps Modernes* in 1947 and later collected in the volume *What is Literature?* Sartre applied his early theory of freedom to the literary enterprise. Because man is free, according to Sartre, he must choose his mode of existence. Like Kant, Sartre links moral choice with the individual's responsibility to the human community. Sartre confronts the writer with freedom and points to his moral and political responsibility. Writing is a social act, an exigence to communicate with others. This is why Sartre is more interested in prose than poetry. The modern crisis of language in which the sign is cast adrift from the signified, observes Sartre, is a problem for the poet rather than the prose writer. Poetry becomes a self-signifying discourse whereas prose retains an anchorage in external reality. Thus, there is a sense in which the word when used in prose has a greater materiality than it has in poetry. For Sartre, prose is a practical political instrument and he exhorts writers to regard it as such.

Sartre's argument at first glance appears to be a rather myopic piece of political prognostication. Yet on closer examination an interesting sociological kernel is revealed by the following statement, 'reading is a pact of generosity between author and reader' (Sartre 1967: 39), which contains a theory of literary meaning, initially phenomenological, moving towards an historical explanation. Literary meaning is an interpersonal accomplishment. The text has no immutable truth. The origin of the text in an intentional consciousness does not legislate for its meaning. Reading is an act, an imaginative reconstruction of the text. In 1959 Sartre was to say 'reading is a sort of re-writing' (Sartre 1974: 30). A reader has the option of withholding or offering his generosity. Writer and reader are free beings drawn together by the words on the page. Sartre sums up his point 'To write is thus both to disclose the world and to offer it as a task to the reader' (Sartre 1967: 43).

As he does in *Nausea*, Sartre here regards language as a medium through which men modify and change the world. Writing may be secondary to the class struggle, yet nevertheless it is a social and political act of considerable importance. Sartre argues this through with a discussion of the role of literature in history. He examines the relationship of writing to class ideology. Writers have traditionally performed an ideological function for the ruling-class, but during periods of political instability writers take up an interesting position on the margins of class conflict. For instance, in the eighteenth century, writers like Voltaire rejected the ideology of the ruling-class. In such a context a writer becomes a political agent. The breakdown of ruling-class power and ideological domination is reflected in the declassed position of the writer who acquires the opportunity to use his pen as a political instrument. But in the case of an eighteenth century writer, as Sartre observes, 'by demanding for himself and as a writer freedom of thinking and expressing his thought, the author necessarily serves the interests of the bourgeois class' (Sartre 1967: 79). In this situation the writer's role became historically progressive.

Sartre thought, at the time, that the situation of writers in 1947 paralleled that of the eighteenth century *philosophes*. His doctrine of *extreme situations* derives from this assumption. Sartre argued that historically significant writing has always had a public of a class character and an ideologically formed myth of literature. He also held the view, not uncommon among Marxists at the time, that writers should try to communicate with the working-class. The doctrine of extreme situations was supposed to provide a myth and as such a rationale for writing. The Second World War and its aftermath generated an extreme situation for everyone, including writers, particularly those who had lived through the occupation of France. According to Sartre, the experience of resistance 'made us feel what a literature of the concrete universal might be' (Sartre 1967: 170). (I will be returning to this notion of the 'concrete universal' in my discussion of Sartre's later concept of the 'singular universal'). Those who had written articles for the underground press addressed themselves to a coherent community, the unity of which derived from the opposition to a common enemy. Sartre tries to show what relevance this experience and the contemporary social situation might have for a politically engaged aesthetic. The following passage outlines the doctrine of extreme situations.

> Since we were situated, the only novels we could dream of were novels of situation, without internal narrators or all-knowing witnesses. In short, if we wished to give an account of courage, we had to make the technique of the novel shift from Newtonian mechanics to generalised relativity; we had to people our books with minds that were half lucid

and half overcast, some of which we might consider with more
sympathy than others, but none of which would have a privileged
point of view either upon the event or upon itself. We had to present
creatures whose reality would be the tangled and contradictory tissue
of each one's evaluations of all the other characters – himself included
and the evaluation by all the others of himself, and who could never
decide from within whether the changes of their destinies came from
their own efforts, from their own faults or from the course of the
universe.

Finally, we had to leave doubts, expectations, and the unachieved
throughout our works, leaving it to the reader to conjecture for himself
by giving him the feeling, without giving him or letting him guess our
feeling, that his view of the plot and the characters was merely one
amongst many (Sartre 1967: 166).

Sartre's sketch for a political aesthetic, although formed by
existentialism, is not unlike Brecht's theory of epic theatre, art for a
revolutionary situation. It is fairly easy to identify the limitations of
both Sartre's and Brecht's excessive optimism about the political
potential of art. However, more interesting is the profound sense of the
historicity of aesthetic form which enabled them to link social analysis
and literary practice.

In summary, the doctrine of extreme situations contains three
important dimensions: an embryonic sociological analysis of writing, a
theory of the historicity of form, as well as the distinctive emphasis on
the writer's reflexivity. All three go beyond what is often regarded as a
vulgar political prescription for literary practice.

The Singular Universal

Sartre's thought is often criticised for excessive voluntarism. For
Sartre, historical totalisation is ultimately traceable back to the praxis
of individuals and groups, as federations of individuals. The principal
weakness of this sort of theorising is that it undervalues the determinate
role of extra-individual structures, particularly class relationships and
language, too easily dismissed by Sartre as elements of the practico-
inert. However, Sartre's stress on human agency is an important
rejoinder to the excesses of certain structuralist positions.

Even in his later Marxist work Sartre remains intrigued by the
creative moment of choice. He is fascinated by the personality of
writers, most notably Baudelaire, Flaubert and Genet. In an interview
with *New Left Review* in 1969 Sartre explained why he decided to analyse
his own desire to write in the short autobiography *Words*. 'The reason
why I produced *Les Mots* is the reason why I have studied Genet or

Flaubert: how does a man become someone who writes, who wants to speak of the imaginary' (Sartre 1974: 63). He goes on to say 'it is the birth of the decision to write that is of interest'. This statement brings us to Sartre's concept of the 'original choice'. Sartre has always maintained that very early in childhood an individual makes a choice which will more or less colour his whole life. According to Sartre, an important moment in understanding the meaning of an imaginative artist's work is the discovery of the fundamental project which originates with this choice made during childhood.

The practical application of the concept of original choice is demonstrated very clearly in Sartre's study of the life and work of Jean Genet, *Saint Genet: Comedian and Martyr* (1952). Genet's novels and plays are characterised by the inversion of basic bourgeois values concerning crime and sexuality. Sartre attempts to show that Genet's mode of life and artistic work are shaped by a creative response to a crisis brought about by a violent experience suffered as a child. The crisis was concentrated into an incident which occurred when the illegitimate Genet was the adopted child of a peasant family in the village of Morran. While playing in the kitchen one day Genet, aged ten, put his hand in a drawer. He became aware that someone had entered the room and was watching him from behind. The voice of the other announced to him his identity 'You are a thief'. Soon the whole village community knew that the young Genet was a thief. What began as an insignificant action of a subject turned into an objective thing, a theft. Suddenly Genet's 'eternal essence' was revealed and rapidly transmitted to the village community of Morran (Sartre 1968a: 380). Shocked that they had an apprentice thief in their midst the villagers projected their narrow-minded fears and darkest impulses into the wretched child. The adult Genet's constant predisposition to steal was the negation of the right behaviour of the good people of Morran. In a sense, Genet was turned inside out. This involved embracing the negative moment of his existence concentrated in the incident which occurred when he was ten. He came to see the world in reverse. Sartre contends that this is the basis of his homosexuality. Genet's choice was conditioned by the ignorance and prejudice of the village community. Firstly, Genet had been rejected by his mother and then he found himself rejected by his adoptive family. As Laing and Cooper say, 'Genet felt himself to be undesirable in his very being, not the son of this woman but her excrement' (Laing & Cooper 1971: 69). Finding himself abandoned, Genet chose to retain his outsider status rather than attempt to obtain conventional acceptance. Having a powerful imagination he decided to replace his absent mother with God, and he became himself a saint. Genet was plunged into a situation of potential despair. Refusing to give in, he responded by making every action an element of permanent revolution. His negation of bourgeois morality is the secret of his creativity. Genet's art is thus the product of his socially situated experience.

Sartre's emphasis on understanding the experience of the writer is associated with the refusal of deterministic forms of sociology. A text is not simply the product of a social structure, but is mediated by the lived experience of the writer. In his later work Sartre seeks to locate particular consciousnesses in their social context, rather than, as in *Being and Nothingness*, analysing the structure of consciousness as such. The relevance of this for the sociology of literature is the stress on a kind of *Verstehen* analysis of lived experience demanding considerable powers of imagination. This does not deny the possibility of making judgments about the ideological formation of a writer's work, for instance in the case of Zola, 'a particularisation of bourgeois idealism and individualism' (Sartre 1974: 274). Sartre uses the notion of particularity to categorise the mode of an individual's insertion into the world. This brings us to the concept of the 'singular universal': the dialectical relationship between the particular experience and the social totality. Sartre says of himself

> The apparition which is constituted in a world that produces me by assigning me through the banal singularity of my birth to a *unique adventure*, while at the same time conferring on me by my situation (the son of a man, of a petty bourgeois intellectual, of such and such a family) a *general destiny* (a class destiny, a family destiny, an historical destiny), is none other than what I call *being-in-the-world* or the *singular universal* (ibid 274).

Sartre goes on to discuss the dialectic of interiorisation/exteriorisation. An individual interiorises the social totality in a particular manner through, for instance, the mediations of family and class membership. His actions cannot be explained by a stimulus-response model. The moment of individual choice must be grasped. The individual creatively expresses the unity of his experience, that is he is a totalising agent. He actively transcends his particularity towards the universal. This rather abstract argument about social psychological processes is homologous with Sartre's earlier position on morality. In choosing, the individual universalises a value. Sartre observes, 'The writer is not a special case: he too cannot escape his insertion in the world, and his writings are the very type of the singular universal' (Sartre 1974: 275).

The Progressive-Regressive Method

In the fifties Sartre criticised contemporary Marxism on the grounds that it had degenerated into an abstract system which no longer had any methodological efficacy. Sartre attempts to justify a critical attitude to contemporary Marxism by claiming to return in his own researches to the fundamental methodology of Marx. Marx had developed his theoretical approach dialectically through concrete analyses of social processes giving, especially in *The Eighteenth Brumaire*, adequate consideration to conscious human agency.

> The original thought of Marx, as we find it in *The Eighteenth Brumaire of Louis Napoleon Bonaparte*, attempts a difficult synthesis of intention and result, the contemporary use of that thought is superficial and dishonest (Sartre (1968b: 45).

According to Sartre, Marxists formed in the Stalinist era operate with a fixed set of categories which they mechanically impose on reality. Evidence is sought only to illustrate a deterministic theory of the laws of social change. Marxism has thus been reduced to a 'paranoiac dream'. Sartre suggests that existentialism might resuscitate Marxism, by offering a moment of concrete description. For instance, if one wants to understand literary production, its historical context and function, existentialism can provide insights about the lived experience of the writer and thus illuminate how a particular insertion into the world colours the meaning of a text. Writers are members of classes and as such articulate class viewpoints. But it is a mistake to reduce writing to class ideology. The relationship between the class and the text is mediated by the writer. As Sartre says, 'Valéry is a petit bourgeois intellectual, no doubt about it. But not every petit bourgeois intellectual is Valéry' (Sartre 1968: 56). Sartre proceeds:

> Marxism lacks any hierarchy of mediations which would permit it to grasp the process which produces the person and his product inside a class and within a given society at a given historical moment.

Sartre commends Henri Lefebvre's synthesis of Marxism with the mediating concepts of modern sociology, particularly the dimension of community in the relationship between class and culture. Inspired by Lefebvre, Sartre proposes the idea of a hierarchy of mediations linking the social totality to individual projects, like writing. For instance, family, community and work relations are important mediations. This idea of specific mediating levels is informed by existentialism's emphasis on lived experience, which Sartre says:

> intends without being unfaithful to Marxist principles, to find
> mediations which allow the concrete individual – the particular life,
> the real and dated conflict, the person – to emerge from the
> background of the general contradictions of productive forces and
> relations of production (Sartre 1968b: 57).

Existentialism, like humanist versions of Marxism, stresses the role of human agency. Sartre suggests that the notion of project is consistent with the Marxist concept of praxis. An individual's project is related in a highly mediated way to class praxis. Existential psychoanalysis, according to Sartre, is a valuable instrument for understanding the particular forms the expression of a class viewpoint takes in the work of individual writers. The contradictions of a class-structured society shape the project of the child, albeit mediated by family tensions which add a specific hue. In *Search for a Method* Sartre illustrates a child's negotiation of family experience with a brief discussion of Flaubert's relationships with his parents and elder brother (Sartre 1968b: 106). During recent years Sartre has extended the preliminary outline into a full scale study of the life and work of Flaubert, *L'Idiot de la Famille*.

According to Sartre, a heuristic Marxism requires a dialectical method oscillating between the regressive moment investigating experience and a progressive historical totalisation, that is working in a two-way movement through the mediating levels. The emphasis on experience is a rejoinder to orthodox Marxists who insist on totalising too quickly, who see only large scale historical transformations and never human actions. Sartre argues that it is necessary to work back through the mediations to the individual project in order to grasp 'the profundity of the lived'. This is associated with Sartre's firm conviction that 'It is the work or the act of the individual which reveals to us his conditioning' (Sartre 1968b: 152). Human agency is very clearly revealed in the work of a writer. Signification is the product of human praxis and literature is an especially sophisticated form of signification. As we have seen in the case of Genet, biographical understanding may illuminate the structure of an artistic response. Following from this, a totalising analytical moment is required to locate the meaning of the individual work historically. The method necessitates continual cross-reference between particular experiences and historical forces in concrete situations.

Sartre Today

During the last decade or so Sartre has found himself in theoretical dispute with the structuralist movement. In an interview in 1971 he stated his basic disagreements with structuralism. Sartre is specifically concerned with the way structuralists appear to deny history, which he believes constitutes a denial of Marxism. He maintains that the structuralist conception of diachrony, the movement from one structure to another, does not account for praxis. Foucault's work is criticised in this connection. Sartre claims that Foucault 'replaces cinema with a magic lantern' (Sartre 1971: 110). He is interested only in macro-historical transformations and ignores human choice and action. In Sartre's view, history cannot be studied apart from the human struggle for material survival, that is the mode of production and the associated social relations. Although, as Sartre points out, superstructural forms have a relative autonomy, the fundamental Marxist axioms concerning class exploitation cannot be ignored. This raises the whole question of class praxis. The problem for Sartre turns on the way the relationship between structure and praxis is conceptualised.

Sartre regards structuralism as an interesting methodological option as long as the limitations of its theoretical cornerstone, the linguistic model, are kept in mind. For Sartre, structuralism exaggerates the determination of thought by linguistic structure. Structuralists over-react to the traditional idea of language as the instrument of thought and emphasise thought as the instrument of language. In another interview, the one given to *New Left Review* in 1969, Sartre was pressed very hard by a tenacious interviewer to clarify his position on language. The interviewer pointed out that language cannot simply be regarded as the totalisation of speech acts and went on to observe acutely, 'The subject who speaks never totalises linguistic laws by his words. Language has its own intelligibility as a system which appears heterogeneous to the subject' (Sartre 1974: 51). Sartre's response was the rather lame assertion that language is the product of human totalisation. In the later interview (1971) he provided a more satisfactory answer by arguing that language has two levels. Firstly, language is the totalisation of multiple speech acts over time and secondly language like all human praxis ossifies into a practico-inert structure. Thus, at this second level language appears as an autonomous system. Structuralists concentrate on language at the level of the practico-inert and ignore the human practices in which it originates, an essentially dehistoricising operation. Sartre says, 'to understand how a structure is made, it is necessary to introduce praxis as that totalising process. Structural analysis must pass over to a dialectical comprehension' (Sartre 1971: 111).

At the heart of structuralist thought, notably the work of Levi-Strauss, Foucault, Lacan and even the Marxist Althusser, Sartre claims to identify an attitude of resignation, a denial of the possibility of *dépassement*. Presumably this is characterised by a refusal to relate theory to practice. In fact, such an indictment is rather curious when Sartre's own activities during the late sixties and early seventies are taken into account, the gulf between his long and complex study of Flaubert and his political adherence to the voluntarism of the French Maoists. However, I think Sartre's criticisms, particularly of Foucault, are important. Structuralism applied to history can only account for macro-historical transformations, a valid enough enterprise in itself, but the specific mediations at the level of experience are left begging. Sartre's notion of hierarchy of mediations and the progressive-regressive method provide a way of studying the social context and meaning of individual writing projects.

Sartre's whole philosophical orientation is towards what he calls *dépassement*, the human transcendence of alienation, whether, in the early work, the denial of freedom by strategies of bad faith or the later Marxist notion of class exploitation. Literature retains an important role for Sartre in promoting freedom although it is secondary to class struggle. Sartre emphasises a writer's use of language as a moment of cultural negation. Language is a structure of the practico-inert, a barrier to freedom. The dead weight of tradition lies on the minds of the living. As Sartre says in *Search for a Method* an individual is 'inside' culture and language. However, language is both limiting and liberating, limiting because it is a totalisation which has become a system functioning over and above human will, yet liberating because words are so rich with connotations. Culture runs deep with latent and potential meaning. The multi-dimensionality of words presents the writer with a chink in the armoury of the practico-inert. He can exploit the ambiguity of words to press meaning to its limits. Thus, there is the possibility of pointing towards the silence, that which has not yet been articulated.

Barthes' distinction between *ecrivants* and *ecrivains* is employed by Sartre. *Ecrivants* are literal writers who transmit information; that is, they directly signify the world for others. On the other hand, *ecrivains* produce autonomous verbal objects, which do not have direct significations. This type of writing is in a sense 'misinformation'. Sartre comments, 'if to write is to communicate, the literary object appears as a form of communication beyond language – a form of communication that rests on the non-signifying silence enclosed by the words (though also produced by them)' (Sartre 1974: 272). A writer can evoke what has not been said by pointing to the mysteries of interior experience of the social world.

As God to his subject matter a writer is a totaliser. But he is not a God. What appears to be a 'birds eye view' is in fact a point of view. Out of his particularity a writer universalises. He offers his work as a 'counterfeit' totality. This universalising particularity is revealed in the writer's style. Barthes says of style 'Its frame of reference is biological or biographical, not historical: it is the writer's "thing", his glory and his prison, it is his solitude' (Barthes 1970: 17). Quite clearly, style is what marks out an individual writer from others. Barthes provides a rather deterministic Freudian basis to style. Sartre, although now more sympathetic to Freudian theory than in his youth, would still resist its inherent reductionism. As we have seen, Sartre places great stress on the original choice of a project during childhood. However, he would probably agree with Barthes that when an individual comes to write, his style emerges from the very depths of experience and may not be understood on the level of intention. Style, according to Barthes, is a vertical dimension which cuts through the horizon of speech. He says, 'The language functions negatively, on the initial limits of the possible. Style is a Necessity which binds the writer's humour to his form of expression' (Barthes 1970: 19). This seems to accord with Sartre's view that writing is a transcendental enterprise, a way of breaking from the present in pointing to the future concealed by the silence. As Sartre has said, the *écrivants/écrivains* distinction must be superseded (Sartre 1973: 84). The task of writing is to disclose both the particular and the universal and their mutual interpenetration. Sartre's argument cannot be reduced to legislation for a specific form of literary production. There is a variety of techniques which may be used. A writer is condemned to choose:

> The relation between the singular and the universal can equally be captured in a hundred other ways (Robbe-Grillet, Butor, Pinget etc.). None of these forms has any precedence over the others – their choice depends on the enterprise in question. To claim the contrary is to lapse *both* into formalism (the universalisation of a form that can only exist as *one* expression of a *singular* universal: for example, the *vous* in *La Modification* is valid only in its context – but there it is perfectly valid) and into reism (the conversion of a form into a *thing*, an etiquette, a ritual, whereas it is simply the inner unity of a content) Sartre 1974: 283).

Jim McGuigan

However, Sartre does offer some guidance for literary evaluation:

> On the other hand no work is valid unless it accounts, in the mode of non-knowledge, or lived experience, for *everything:* that is to say, the social past and the historical conjuncture, insofar as they are *lived* without being *known.*

Sartre retains faith in literature's capacity to articulate the relationship between experience and history. Also, the enduring emphasis on the freedom of the writer returns us full circle to *literature engagée.*

> The commitment of the writer is to communicate the incommunicable (being-in-the-world as lived experience) by exploiting the misinformation contained in ordinary language, and maintaining the tension between the whole and the parts, totality and totalisation, the world and being-in-the-world, as the *significance* of his work (Sartre 1974: 284).

University of Leeds

REFERENCES CITED

Barnes, Hazel (1974), *Sartre*, Quartet, London.

Barthes, Roland (1970), *Writing degree zero*, Jonathan Cape, London.

Jameson, Fredric (1974), *Marxism and form*, Princeton University Press.

Laing, R. D. and Cooper, D. G. (1971), *Reason and violence*, 2nd ed., Tavistock, London.

Meszaros, Istvan (1975), 'Jean-Paul Sartre: A critical tribute' *The Socialist Register*, Merlin, London.

Sartre, J-P (1948), *Existentialism and humanism*, Methuen, London.

Sartre, J-P (1967), *What is literature?*, Methuen, London.

Sartre, J-P (1968a), *Saint Genet: Comedian and martyr*, in Cumming, R. D. (ed), *The Philosophy of Jean-Paul Sartre*, Methuen, London.

Sartre, J-P (1968b), *Search for a method*, Vintage, New York.

Sartre, J-P (1970), *Nausea*, Penguin, Harmondsworth.

Sartre, J-P (1971), 'Replies to structuralism: an interview', *Telos* 9, Fall.

Sartre, J-P (1972a), *Being and nothingness*, Methuen, London.

Sartre, J-P (1972b), *The transcendence of the ego*, Octagon, New York.

Sartre, J-P (1973), 'The writer and his language', *Politics and literature*, Calder and Boyars, London.

Sartre, J-P (1974), *Between existentialism and Marxism*, New Left Books, London.